The Existentialist Critique of Freud

THE
EXISTENTIALIST
CRITIQUE
OF FREUD

THE CRISIS OF AUTONOMY

BY GERALD N. IZENBERG

1976

PRINCETON UNIVERSITY PRESS

PRINCETON, NEW JERSEY

Library of Congress Cataloging in Publication Data will
be found on the last printed page of this book

Publication of this book has been aided by
The Andrew W. Mellon Foundation

This book has been composed in Linotype Baskerville

Printed in the United States of America
by Princeton University Press, Princeton, New Jersey

To My Mother and Father

Preface

I FIRST became interested in the subject of this book for two apparently unrelated reasons. Though psychoanalysis offered profound insights into the meaning and origins of inner conflict and suffering, it seemed to me to be couched in a theoretical language that was abstract, mechanical, and remote from the living, feeling human being with whom it dealt. My attention was therefore drawn to the existential critique of the natural scientific foundations of Freud's metapsychology and to an examination of the existential alternative. At the same time, I was strongly impressed with descriptions of psychic states and emotions in the literature of existentialism that captured crucial concerns of contemporary life and that could not be found in Freud's writings.

As I got into the topic, I found that my two interests were related, and that the key to the significance of the relationship between Freud and existentialism was historical. The conceptual issues in psychoanalytic theory were important and, while the existentialists were far from solving the problems of metapsychology, they raised questions and made suggestions that are of continuing interest. However, I soon felt that it was not a matter of choosing between psychoanalysis and existentialism, but rather of understanding the meaning of their different approaches and concerns as embodiments of different aspects of European intellectual history, and particularly of progressive stages in the crisis of confidence in human autonomy and rationality that has characterized modern thought.

Much happens between the conception and execution of a work. When I first began the dissertation on which this book is based, my familiarity with psychoanalysis was limited to Freud's writings. Since the existentialists addressed themselves almost exclusively to Freud in their critique, I confined my study to an analysis of their work in relation to his. It was only after I was well into the revision of my original manuscript that I became familiar with the large body of post-Freudian psychoanalysis and discovered that certain characteristic concerns of existential psychology had been incorporated within the Freudian framework through its extension into the pre-oedipal period of development and into the psychopathological manifestations of the developmental disturbances of this period that are found in borderline and narcissistic illness.

A sharp opposition between existentialism and contemporary psychoanalysis on this score is therefore not warranted. Nevertheless, the perspective of the book is still valid. The psychoanalytic interest in the existential themes of pre-oedipal pathology is itself a historical development, which was antedated by their description in existentialism. And just because psychoanalysts came upon the same problems within the framework of psychoanalytic theory, they did not see how the sorts of issues raised by pre-oedipal pathology challenged some of the core assumptions of the theory itself. It is to such issues that this book is addressed.

I wish to thank H. Stuart Hughes, who directed the dissertation from which the book originated and who introduced me to many of the concerns of modern intellectual history that have become my own. Medard Boss discussed his work with me, allowed me to tape our conversations and to examine the notes of some of his discussions with Martin Heidegger. Alasdair MacIntyre and Rudolph Binion read chapters of the manuscript with sharp and discerning eyes. I have learned far more from them, and from Fritz Ringer, about the study of ideas than is reflected in this work. Paul de Man's penetrating and sensitive understanding of existentialism helped me clarify my ideas on the subject. Marshall Berman's thinking about authenticity has been a constant source of stimulation and I have worked out some of my ideas about it in internal dialogue with him. I am grateful to the graduate students in the History of Ideas at Brandeis, who listened to and helped further my interpretation of Heidegger, and to my seminar colleagues and teachers at the Boston Psychoanalytic Institute, who broadened enormously my knowledge of contemporary psychoanalysis and thus complicated my task. A Foreign Area Foundation Fellowship from the Social Science Research Council and the American Council of Learned Societies enabled me to spend a year in study and research for the original dissertation, and a grant from the Canada Council supported me while I was writing it. Finally, I wish to thank my wife Ziva, whose support, patience, and critical intelligence sustained and aided me through many rough spots.

Table of Contents

The Existentialist Critique of Freud

"*An evolving clinical science of the mind is colored . . . by ideological trends even as it inadvertently influences the intellectual and literary climate. . . . Maybe, then, a clinical science of the human mind will eventually demand a special historical self-awareness on the part of the clinical worker and scholar.*"   Erik Erikson, *Young Man Luther*

"*Freedom exists and the will also exists; but freedom of the will does not exist, for a will that is directed towards its own freedom thrusts into emptiness.*"

Thomas Mann, *Mario and the Magician*

The Crisis of Autonomy

THIS book is a study of the critique of Freud's theories advanced by a number of existential philosophers and psychiatrists. On one level, it is necessarily concerned with philosophical psychology, for the existentialists saw themselves in relation to Freud primarily as opponents of what they regarded as the humanistically inappropriate and conceptually unsound structure of explanation in psychoanalytic theory. On another level, however, it is the history of a stage in the crisis of the European rationalist tradition. Behind the methodological issues raised by the existentialists was a conception of the self that ran counter to the one that had dominated progressive European thought since the Enlightenment and that still informed Freud's theoretical categories.

There is a double irony in the view of the crisis presented in this study. Freud openly proclaimed the revolutionary and unsettling nature of his conclusions from the perspective of human autonomy. In demonstrating that the ego was not master in its own house,[1] psychoanalysis seemed to have struck the ultimate blow against rationalist optimism about the prospects of human freedom. Yet at the heart of Freud's interpretation of irrationality there were theoretical assumptions about the basic nature of human motivation and ideation which preserved in a priori form the idea of man's freedom and rationality, and thus created crucial gaps and inconsistencies in his explanations of clinical phenomena. Conversely, the existentialists were self-professedly militant proponents

[1] S. Freud, *The Standard Edition of the Complete Psychological Works of Sigmund Freud*, ed. J. Strachey, London, 1953-1966. (Hereafter cited as *S.E.*) Vol. XVII, p. 143.

3

of the goal of authenticity in human life, of man's potential to be himself, to assume responsibility for his own possibilities and choices, and to live in accordance with this freedom rather than in subservience to the dictates of predetermined norms and roles. But the existential concept of authenticity had no positive content. The real substantive content of existentialism was a motivational theory of human unfreedom that was more appropriate to the major clinical discoveries of Freud than some of his own metapsychological concepts and could be said to furnish their implicit theoretical underpinnings.

The best approach to the understanding of these apparent anomalies is historical. Psychoanalysis and existentialism represented successive stages in the contemporary European loss of self-confidence in human rationality and autonomy. In this progression, existentialism can be seen as having done two things. First, it grasped in its basic concepts the meaning of the clinical content of psychoanalysis denied by psychoanalytic metapsychology. Secondly, as a result of this, it went beyond Freud's characterization of conflict to present a more radical version of the problem of selfhood than the psychoanalytic picture of an opposition between instinct and reason, pleasure and reality, and the asocial and social self.

The point of departure for the existentialist critique was the attack against "positivism" in the human sciences launched by a number of European thinkers in the last decades of the nineteenth century. Rarely explicitly defined or elaborated, positivism, in the minds of its critics, denominated the tendencies prevalent in many currents of European thought to give materialist, mechanistic, or biological explanations for social and individual belief and behavior. Such explanations were held by critics to be illegitimately reductionist because they claimed to furnish the necessary and sufficient conditions of behavior and belief without reference to their subjective intention or meaning. In psychology the attack was aimed particularly at the then dominant tendencies of experimental, physiological, and association psychology. Its purpose was to establish a logically distinct psychology of the person that would take account of human subjectivity and freedom by insisting on the primacy, if not indeed the exclusive validity, of "subjective meaning," i.e., intentions, motives, and beliefs, in the explanation of behavior.

The effect of psychoanalysis was also to undermine one kind of positivism in psychology and especially psychiatry. After Freud, it was impossible to ignore the meaning of the psychic manifestations of mental illness and to restrict the search for its causes to physical pathology. But psychoanalysis did not originate in the anti-positivist movement; on the contrary, by training and temperament Freud was a committed positivist and his characteristic modes of explanation were those of nineteenth-century mechanistic materialism and biology. Moreover, his continual reaffirmations of allegiance to physicalistic explanation after he dropped much of its terminology were not simply the pious utterances of someone who felt guilty over his apostasy[2] or who hoped that psychology would ultimately return to its proper physical foundations. The permanent basic categories of psychoanalytic explanation, and equally significantly, as we shall see, the psychoanalytic psychological concepts of motivation and meaning, such as the concept of unconcious phantasy, are unintelligible without an understanding of their derivation from mechanistic and biological theory.

It is only relatively recently that the significance of these facts has been appreciated by English-speaking philosophers and even "orthodox" Freudian analysts,[3] in an effort either to undermine or to establish better foundations for psychoanalysis. One of Freud's earliest followers, however, the German Swiss psychiatrist Ludwig Binswanger, concerned by the

[2] It is, however, true that Freud was most insistent on the mechanistic and materialistic foundations of psychoanalysis when he got furthest away from them, as in his speculations on the occult. Cf. *S.E.*, Vol. XVIII, p. 179.

[3] See, for example, the work of R. S. Peters and R. K. Shope in philosophy and of G. Klein and R. Schafer in psychoanalysis.

positivist elements in what otherwise appeared to be a radical, descriptive approach to psychology in terms of meaning, tried in the early decades of the century to mediate between Freud's new psychiatry clothed in the old positivist dress, and the new philosophical attempts to found a truly humanistic psychology. His initial efforts were based on the work of the Neo-Kantians, Dilthey, Husserl, and Scheler. Even in his own estimation, however, they failed to give psychiatry a conceptually clear and clinically fruitful theoretical foundation. They failed partly because they were too abstractly methodological, not inspired by concrete clinical problems, and partly because, though they raised valid philosophical issues, they were too obviously permeated by the ideological aspects of neo-idealism. When Binswanger criticized Freud for slighting distinctive human intentions and meanings in favor of instinctual categories, he meant specifically the ideal values of Neo-Kantian moral philosophy. Thus, in its concern to defend the autonomy of *Geist* or absolute spiritual values against Freud's apparent undermining not only of religious but of moral beliefs, Binswanger's early work could be seen as part of the "mandarin" ideology defined by F. K. Ringer: the neo-idealism developed after the 1880's to defend the conception of a culture of absolute values and pure learning that had served as the traditional justification for the status of the educated elite in German society.[4]

It was Martin Heidegger who gave fresh impetus to Binswanger's efforts. His book *Being and Time*, published in 1927, furnished both a new approach to the explanation of meaning and what was in effect, though not in intent, a new theory of motivation. In its insistence on the role of the self in structuring a unified world of meaning by disclosing different aspects of reality through the realization of its various purposes and possibilities, *Being and Time* represented in one of its dimensions the climax of the pre-war critique of positivist determinism. However, Heidegger rejected the idealist

[4] F. K. Ringer, *The Decline of the German Mandarins: The German Academic Community, 1890-1933*, Cambridge, Mass., 1969.

claim that the norms and concepts comprising the world of meaning were objective, timeless entities that were the necessary constituents of experience independent of human choice, decision, and history. Such claims, in fact, contradicted the idealist defense of subjectivity and freedom against determinism. In reality, the ideal of pure objectivity, of universal, atemporal meanings, was an illusion produced by man in the course of his "quest for Being," his attempt to create a fixed and permanent identity for himself. Man tried to escape his temporal condition by absolutizing the historical circumstances into which he had been thrown, by seeing them as unchangeable givens, as his destiny. In this way he could avoid the truth that there was nothing metaphysically necessary about his existence and that concepts, self-definitions, norms, and values continued to exist for him only to the extent that he actively sustained them as binding on himself.

Heidegger claimed that his work was not a psychological enterprise but an analysis of the fundamental structures of human existence and therefore the necessary foundation for the human sciences. Ludwig Binswanger, and later Jean-Paul Sartre and Medard Boss, developed Heidegger's philosophical framework into a general attack on Freudian metapsychology. They argued that Heidegger's characterization of the self as a historical, purposive, meaning-giving, and meaning-disclosing subject was more appropriate as a starting point for psychology than Freud's concept of man as a biological organism powered by a few basic drives, or his notion of a psyche reified into a mental apparatus with spatial divisions, containing ideational representations of a fixed external reality and operated by energy displacements. They claimed that the concept of causality Freud derived from his model of mental functioning was inappropriate for explaining behavior and ideation because it confused description and explanation, conflated present meaning with past cause, and provided an inadequate account of symbolic processes. Using Heidegger's concept of man as "being-in-the-world," they tried to give alternative accounts of the unconscious and of the relationship between mind and body, subject and object, past and present, which were the foundations of the psychoanalytic explanation of dreams, symptoms, and defenses. They also reinterpreted the basis of psychoanalytic therapy, using Heidegger's notion of man's essential social relatedness.

The existentialists, however, did not realize that the issue between Freud and themselves went deeper than philosophical differences about the proper theoretical foundations of psychology and psychiatry. They were not aware that inherent in Freud's positivism there was a set of assumptions that embodied the rationalist view of human nature and freedom; they were only partly aware that inherent in Heidegger's work and in their own methodological approach there was a view that contradicted it. For Freud's psychology, as heir to the rationalist tradition of the eighteenth and nineteenth centuries, represented the most important of the intellectual syntheses in the period between 1880 and 1914 that tried to come to grips with the increasing awareness of human irrationality by way of previous rationalist assumptions and conceptions. It can be demonstrated, though the wider argument is beyond the scope of this book, that the assimilation and understanding of irrationalism was for the most part incomplete, inconsistent, and ambivalent in the period before the war, and that it was in fact only afterwards, partly because of the political and social upheavals of the First World War and the post-war years, that the implications for thought, art, and action of the earlier discoveries about irrationalism were fully realized. In the specific case of Freud this meant, for example, that his initial explanation of the clinical discoveries of self-alienation, or passivity in all its aspects—the need to be loved, idealization and the over-valuation of the love-object, masochism, the internalization of authority, the persistence of infantile dependency—was constructed in such a way as to conceal or deny the existence of a will to unfreedom or self-abnegation. It was only in the post-war period that Freud's theory of the death instinct, with all its ramifications, attempted to do partial justice to what he had long since known clinically. Even then the inconsistencies caused by the dubious nature of the concept and the failure to integrate fully the earlier and the later frameworks left him with admittedly unsolved basic problems in the explanation of infantile fixation.

Existential philosophy and psychology supplied the elements missing in psychoanalytic metapsychology—a theory of motivation that could render intelligible the rejection of authenticity inherent in such psychoanalytic concepts as the formation of ego-ideals, masochism, internalization and identification, and the power of the past over the present. To take just one example of this dimension of the significance of existential analysis: the real historical point of the existentialist attack on the psychoanalytic category of instinct was not the unsuitability of a biological concept for dealing with specifically human intentions and purposes. It was rather that, for Freud, instinct on the theoretical level meant a desire for gratification, and therefore an expression of self-assertion and autonomy, while existential-phenomenological description of so-called "instinctual activities" revealed them to be exactly the opposite.

The existentialists, however, were not, at least at first, clearly aware of the purely negative implications of their analysis of human nature, and especially of the difficulty of giving any substantive meaning to their call for authenticity and being oneself. This created a serious problem for an existentialist ethic and in psychiatry for a viable existential concept of mental health. Freud had no such problem because the purpose of life was embodied for him in instinct and the pleasure principle, and in the concomitant need to orient belief and action to reality in order to achieve genuine gratification. The existentialists, however, had no such recourse to biological norms of health, and each took a different path out of their common dilemma. Heidegger defined authenticity in such a way as to permit and indeed demand commitment to historical activism in the form of nationalist renewal; when, in the guise of Nazism, this proved to be bankrupt, he turned toward a mystical form of idealist absolutism that betrayed his original concept of authenticity. Sartre, under the impress of extra-existential moral commitments and political events—the near-triumph of Fascism, the continuing post-war class struggle at home, and the fight against colonialism abroad—attempted to convert existentialism into a social philosophy by fusing it with the older rationalist tradition and reinterpreting many of its original concepts to provide an external causal instead of an internal and individual explanation of inauthenticity. The psychiatrists, in different ways—one by supplementing Heidegger, the other by adopting the perspective of his later work—also tried to develop a therapeutic ethic that would embody both the ultimate freedom of the patient and the existential belief that the vehicle of psychotherapeutic liberation was a social relationship resting on the authority of the analyst—in other words, both the negative idea of authenticity and a sense of a positive direction for life supplied from the outside.

All of these efforts represented attempts to rescue contemporary thought from the impasse to which its own discoveries had brought it. We may judge them to be largely unsuccessful, for they appear to have come back full circle to familiar positions in European intellectual history—Marxism, the technological critique of modernity, secularized faith. Yet even the familiar positions were couched in new ways and addressed to different problems. On the way to them, the existentialists produced many interesting suggestions; perhaps more importantly, they posed some of the basic questions that modern social theory must answer and showed the inadequacy of many of the old answers that rested on too comfortable assumptions about human nature.

A few words are necessary about the structure of the book. Its organization presented certain problems because I wanted to do two things: to explicate and discuss the specific issues in the foundations of psychoanalytic theory and practice raised by the existentialists, and to interpret the significance for intellectual history of the existential critique as a whole. This seemed to require a two-part approach. However, a clearcut distinction between philosophical and historical analysis was not possible. On the one hand, the existential criticism of Freud, even in its own terms as philosophical psychology, was part of a historically self-conscious movement of revolt against positivism in the moral sciences; this movement had its own development, which Binswanger, for one, was keenly aware of being part of, and which had to be traced insofar as it illuminated the intellectual background of the problems raised by the existentialists. On the other hand, the historical interpretation I propose rests on a reinterpretation of the conceptual issues in philosophical psychology from a social-theoretical and historical perspective not available to our figures, and indeed at odds in important respects with their own self-understanding.

As a result, there is a certain overlap in approach between the two parts of the book. Chapter Three, the culmination of the first part, is a point-by-point conceptual analysis of the main elements of the existential critique of Freud, on which the existentialists were largely in agreement. These elements are therefore extracted from their work without regard to chronology and without an assessment of the full range and internal development of their work or of the important differences between them. However, the framework of the first part of the book is historical in the way it leads up to the existential critique. The development of Freud's basic concepts up to 1914 is traced historically in order to bring out the way in which the positivist framework of his thought shaped his clinical evidence; the result, I believe, casts new light on our understanding of the origins of psychoanalysis. Similarly, a historical and biographical approach was necessary to understand the motives and sources of Binswanger's pre-existential dissatisfaction with aspects of psychoanalytic theory and its connection with his adoption of Heidegger's work as a

11

more adequate starting point for founding a humanistic depth-psychology than he found in neo-idealism, *verstehende* psychology, and phenomenology.

In the second part of the book, the conceptual issues dealt with earlier are shown to have a different dimension. Freud's positivism is seen to be not only an approach to explanation in the moral or human sciences but a vehicle for the preservation of rationalist assumptions about motivation and ideation at a point in European history when these assumptions were being challenged, not least by Freud's own findings. Similarly, the existential critique emerges in the context of a crisis of the rationalist tradition of freedom as formulating a different, more radical view of the problem of selfhood than that delineated by Freud. It is in this context that it becomes necessary, for two reasons, to treat the work of each of the existentialists separately. First, while their criticisms of Freud were similar or parallel, their ideas on the problem of selfhood were elaborated in different ways as parts of their own individual enterprises. Second, the existentialists diverged sharply in their efforts to cope with the dilemma posed by existentialist conclusions for a positive ethic and norm of health. Understanding this divergence and the different solutions they arrived at involved assessing the interaction of personal, socio-historical, and conceptual factors for each of the figures. The result is a cross-section of ideological positions on the problem of modernity in contemporary European intellectual history.

CHAPTER ONE

The Positivist Foundations of Freud's Theory of Meaning

THAT the existentialist critique of psychoanalysis originated in Freud's positivism can appear puzzling in the light of the generally accepted version of his achievement. It was Freud after all who definitively broke with the conventional approach of nineteenth-century psychiatry, which viewed the psychic manifestations of mental illness as meaningless and looked exclusively for physical pathology as the necessary and sufficient cause of irrational behavior. By discovering hidden intentions, emotions, and beliefs in neurotic behavior and ideation, Freud called into question, for many if not all cases, the nineteenth-century "medical model" of mental illness.

This interpretation, of course, is today considered to be somewhat oversimplified even by those who take it to be substantially true. Historians, philosophers, and analysts recognize that Freud's enduring ideal of explanation was physicalistic[1] and that his theories, derived from an outdated mechanistic brain physiology, "remained couched in positivist terms of a rather crude order."[2] But whether it is held that "the question of the origin of the terminology and fundamental assumptions of psychoanalysis is . . . of only historical interest [and] has nothing to do with the question of [their] value . . . for psychoanalysis as a science";[3] or whether it is

[1] S. Bernfeld, "Freud's Earliest Theories and the School of Helmholtz," *Psychoanalytic Quarterly*, Vol. 13, 1944, p. 361.

[2] H. S. Hughes, *Consciousness and Society*, New York, 1961, p. 135.

[3] Ernst Kris, in the Editor's Introduction to S. Freud, *The Origins of Psychoanalysis: Letters to Wilhelm Fliess*, trans. E. Mosbacher and J. Strachey, New York, 1954, p. 47.

argued that Freud's theory of the mental apparatus was "the ghost of the nervous system sitting crowned on the grave thereof"[4] and of no explanatory value, there is general agreement that Freud redescribed human behavior and found meaning where it had been thought that none existed.

It is, therefore, a conceptual puzzle of critical significance that Freud arrived at his theory of meaning not only without the aid of but against the direction of the contemporary philosophical upheaval that was shaking the foundations of the human sciences in Europe. Thinkers such as Brentano, the Neo-Kantians, Bergson, Dilthey, Simmel, Weber, Husserl, and Scheler were arguing that contemporary psychology ignored intention and meaning in favor of causal explanations in terms of antecedent physical or environmental conditions, and were calling for new methodological approaches to the explanation of behavior and belief.

There were certainly similarities between Freud's defense of the investigation of mental life independently from organic changes, and the efforts of Brentano and the Neo-Kantians to distinguish between mental and physical phenomena. There were perhaps even more pregnant similarities between Freud's insistence on the purposiveness of psychic processes in dreams and neurotic symptoms and the insistence of "act-" and phenomenological psychology on the fundamentally intentional, meaningful character of psychic life.[5] Almost simultaneously, Dilthey and Freud were emphasizing the need for a genetic and historical approach to psychology, and Dilthey's claim that a hermeneutic method was the only one appropriate to a study of the historical individual found a parallel in Freud's conception of interpretation.

Yet, with the exception of Brentano,[6] Freud was not direct-

4 A. MacIntyre, *The Unconscious, A Conceptual Analysis*, London, 1958.

5 P. Ricoeur, *De L'Interpretation, essai sur Freud*, Paris, 1965, pp. 366-380.

6 The case of Brentano is somewhat complex. Freud took a number of philosophy courses with Brentano as an undergraduate, and it was during this period that the latter's *Psychologie vom empirischen Standpunkt* was published (1874). There is no evidence that Freud read it, however,

14

ly acquainted with much, if any, of the work of the major figures in the attack on natural scientific psychology, and was
hostile to whatever he learned about it at second hand. When
he encountered it in the writings of such critics of psychoanalysis as Kronfeld, he rejected it without consideration,[7]
but he was not much more sympathetic to the efforts of Binswanger, a friend and a practicing (though theoretically increasingly heterodox) psychoanalyst, to analyze the new philosophical trends and relate psychoanalysis to them.[8] When
Freud did turn to academic and philosophical psychology,
either to discover more about it as his own work led him into
psychological theorizing, or for actual theoretical assistance,
it was to the very men whose assumptions were the objects
of the new philosophical criticism, among them Taine, Lipps
and Fechner. It was not Freud but the psychiatrist Karl Jaspers who explicitly introduced to psychiatry the ideas of descriptive phenomenology and of a *verstehende Psychologie,* a
psychology of meaningful connections, claiming in this venture to be extending the work of Dilthey, Simmel, and Weber
into a new sphere.[9] In his early work, Jaspers attempted to

---

and the philosophy courses were not specifically concerned with psy-
chology. (See in this connection P. Merlan, "Brentano and Freud,"
Journal of the History of Ideas, 6, 1945, pp. 375-377 and Merlan, "Bren-
tano and Freud—A Sequel," *JHI,* 10, 1949, p. 451.) Nevertheless some of
Freud's attacks on philosophy seem to be aimed directly at Brentano.
See p. 17. Barclay's contention of the direct influence of Brentano on
Freud, based on a similarity of intentional approaches, ignores the radi-
cally different way Freud arrived at a theory of meaning. (J. R. Barclay,
"Franz Brentano and Sigmund Freud," *Journal of Existentialism,* Vol. v,
No. 17, Summer 1964, pp. 1-36.)

[7] See, for example, A. Kronfeld, "Über die psychologischen Theorien
Freuds und verwandte Anschauungen," *Archiv für die gesamte Psychologie,* Dec. 1911, Vol. XXII, pp. 130-248.

[8] L. Binswanger, *Erinnerungen an Sigmund Freud,* Bern, 1956, pp.
76-77.

[9] K. Jaspers, "Kausale und 'verständliche' Zusammenhänge zwischen
Schicksal und Psychose bei der Dementia praecox," *Zeitschrift für die
gesamte Neurologie und Psychiatrie,* Vol. 14, 1912, p. 158; also *Allgemeine
Psychopathologie,* Berlin, 1913.

bring order into what he considered to be the chaotic and fragmented state of contemporary psychiatric theorizing by distinguishing between the logically different spheres of descriptive understanding and causal explanation in the analysis of psychiatric symptoms, and by attempting to work out criteria for the appropriate application of each.

Freud's aloofness from these developments is not difficult to explain, even discounting such factors as his professed hostility to academic philosophy or his preoccupation with the concrete clinical problems of the neuroses. (Neither of these, as has been suggested, prevented him from looking into the current literature of philosophical psychology when he felt the need for it.) The case of Brentano is the most obvious. In distinguishing psychic from physical phenomena, Brentano had equated the psychic with consciousness. He did not specifically mean by consciousness reflective self-awareness articulated verbally. His primary concern had been to sort out the confusion between physiology and psychology, and he did this by arguing that psychic phenomena differed from physical ones in their character as acts, in their always being directed at a specific content or having reference to an object. They were, therefore, not amenable to measurement as physiological responses were. Contemporary quantitative experimental psychology was thus misconceived; it was not psychology but physiology. Part of Brentano's argument held that, as acts of a self, psychic phenomena were necessarily accessible in principle to direct knowledge by the self. On these grounds he rejected the idea of unconscious psychological phenomena as self-contradictory and fictitious.[10] Here again the object of his attack was the kind of psychology that confusedly referred to the physiological processes underlying mental life as unconscious mental processes. But for Freud, who defined consciousness in terms of awareness and verbalization, and whose clinical observations of the unavowed and unverbalized meanings in behavior demanded some notion

[10] F. Brentano, *Psychologie vom empirischen Standpunkt*, Leipzig, 1874, Bk. II, ch. 2.

of unconscious mental processes, Brentano's equation of the psychic with consciousness seemed to be an insuperable obstacle to any fruitful encounter with the idea of intentionality and hence later with phenomenology. Freud's critical comment on contemporary philosophical psychology in the *Interpretation of Dreams* thus seems to have been aimed directly at Brentano:

"So long as psychology dealt with this problem (i.e., the unconscious) by a verbal explanation to the effect that 'psychical' *meant* 'conscious' and that to speak of 'unconscious psychical processes' was palpable nonsense, any psychological evaluation of the observations made by physicians upon abnormal mental states was out of the question. The physician and philosopher can only come together if they both recognize that the term 'unconscious psychical processes' is the appropriate and justified expression of a solidly established fact."[11]

As far as contact with *verstehende* psychology is concerned, the important documents in its development were for the most part either coterminous with the development of Freud's own ideas, or appeared after his basic theories were already formulated and under attack.[12] This chronological argument does not, of course, explain why Freud did not later evince any interest in a methodological approach that, it could plausibly be contended, might have at least furnished some support for his own insistence on the meaningfulness of all mental phenomena. Here too conceptual issues are important in understanding why this was not and could not be the case.

Freud was not philosophically prepared to recognize the distinction between *Geisteswissenschaft* and *Naturwissenschaft*, out of which the concept *Verstehen* and its contrast with causal explanation had developed. Accepting fully the

[11] Freud, *S.E.*, Vol. v, p. 611.

[12] Dilthey's *Einleitung in die Geisteswissenschaften* appeared in 1883; the other relevant works of Simmel, Windelband, Rickert, and Dilthey appeared in the 1890's and the first decade of the twentieth century.

explanatory model of mid-nineteenth-century natural science, he arrived at his very conception of meaningfulness through a priori assumptions about the mechanical functioning of the nervous system. As we shall see, even the clinical, ostensibly purely descriptive, language of psychoanalysis combined description and theoretical causal analysis. Freud's definition of interpretation indicated how divergent was his conception of the meaningfulness of psychic phenomena from that contained in the idea of *Verstehen*: " '[I]nterpreting' a dream implies assigning a 'meaning' to it—that is, *replacing it* by something which fits into the chain of our mental acts as a link having a validity and importance equal to the rest."[13] The element to be interpreted was not to have its meaning drawn out of itself in terms of manifest contextual significance, but was to be replaced by another element, itself meaningful, whose relationship to the first was a causal one, and in fact mechanically causal. Whatever the variations in the concepts of *Verstehen* advanced by Dilthey, Simmel, Weber, and Jaspers, they all rested on the idea of meaning as immanent in, not causally related to, the expression to be interpreted. The Freudian theory of meaning was a unique synthesis on the boundary of two conceptual worlds.

Further analysis of the two conceptions of meaningfulness suggests the important underlying ground for the differences between them—indeed for their incompatibility. Freud's theory of meaning grew out of his clinical judgment of the symptomatic, that is to say irrational, character of neurotic behavior. Thus it was initially predicated upon a specific conception of rationality. Just what this conception involved has to be examined in some detail—it included norms and values as well as principles of logic and empirical reasoning—but it was an exclusionary criterion that divided behavior into one class that, as rational, required no further explanation and one that did. Insofar as Freud held the latter class of behavior to be "meaningful," it was, and could only be so to the extent that it conformed to the original criteria of rationality. Para-

13 Freud, *S.E.*, Vol. IV, p. 96. Italics added.

doxical as this statement appears, it is just what Freud meant in the passage quoted from the *Interpretation of Dreams*, in which he spoke of replacing the irrational by something that fit into the chain of our mental acts as a link "having a validity and importance equal to the rest." Freud's positivistically grounded theory of meaning functioned to preserve a concept of rationality in its very demonstration that irrationality was meaningful.

The concept of *Verstehen* developed in a very different context—in a sense, the opposite context. The purpose of its advocates was to defend the rationality of certain beliefs and goals against the kind of reductive analysis that stripped them of their autonomy and made them nothing but disguises for other beliefs and goals or mere effects of antecedent causes. In its origins, *Verstehen* was associated with the Romantic and conservative tradition in German historiography, which interpreted individual behavior and creative production as manifesting the "spirit" of a larger historical whole; the individual was definable only as an embodiment of the "organic" cultural and spiritual norms that governed his behavior. To understand the individual was to enter into the objective spirit of the whole. This position was aimed at the atomistic individualism and universalist rationalism of the Enlightenment, which in the view of the Romantics ignored history, the social nature of the individual, and his emotional and religious needs; it was used to defend existing hierarchical, social, and political institutions and religious beliefs.

Dilthey had demystified the concept of "objective spirit" by making it nothing but the sum total of those cultural artifacts and institutions embodying the shared norms of a society. Weber had gone even further, to insist that the individual was the basic unit of action, the sole carrier of meaningful conduct, and that *Verstehen* was the method for interpreting individual intentions and beliefs. Nevertheless, Weber's concept of *Verstehen* still preserved the emphasis on making intelligible, and hence "rational," those absolute values—moral and religious beliefs and needs—that were under attack from positivism, Darwinism, and economic determinism. He had argued in *The Protestant Ethic and the Spirit of Capitalism* that "A thing is never irrational in itself, but only from a particular rational point of view,"[14] that is, that rationality was not predicated of individual ends in themselves but only of the relationship among ends. On these grounds Weber had introduced the category of *Wertrationalität*—activity oriented to the attainment of absolute moral and religious goals, and had insisted on accepting such goals in the interpretation of historical action as irreducible givens.

Applied to psychology, this general attitude meant viewing all modes of human behavior as, in the Rankean phrase actually used by Binswanger, "immediate to God."[15] In other words, no judgmental attitude was to be taken towards them from a privileged position of rationality; behavior was simply to be described in its own terms, as seen from the perspective of the agent and using his own criteria.

This permissiveness towards experience as given in the consciousness of the subject was also the main thrust of Husserl's phenomenology, which from a somewhat different point of view was concerned with the defense of ideal values and timeless concepts. The primary purpose of his early *Logical Investigations* was to attack psychologism, the doctrine that the concepts of logic were reducible to empirical generalizations about mental operations, and so to defend the autonomy of logic. This approach was later extended to concepts or universals in general. These, Husserl argued, were given in experience as "essences," fixed unities that were hypostatizations of all possible temporal and spatial perspectives on an object. Concepts were not experienced as the products of such mental operations as abstraction and generalization from particulars, or as the syntheses of historical experiences in the life of the individual or society always in principle subject to

14 M. Weber, *The Protestant Ethic and the Spirit of Capitalism*, trans. T. Parsons, London, 1948, p. 194.

15 L. Binswanger, *Being-in-the-World*, ed. and with a critical introduction by J. Needleman, New York, 1963, p. 170.

change. The phenomenological emphasis on the theoretically unprejudiced examination of the immediate givens of consciousness in search of such essences culminated in the concept of the phenomenological "reduction," the philosophical operation that "bracketed" or suspended the question of the existence in reality of the data of consciousness in favor of a purely descriptive analysis of their contents.

Aside from his repugnance for the ideological ambience of the idealist revival, which stemmed both from its sharp separation between *Geist* and body, and from his opposition to religion, Freud's clinical orientation alone precluded the *verstehende* or phenomenological neutrality toward behavior and belief, neither of which allowed for or was concerned with judgments of irrationality or pathology. But the issue went deeper than the clinician's need for normative concepts of health. Freud's concept of rationality included a theoretical presupposition about human autonomy, a presupposition that flew in the face of his clinical discoveries about human unfreedom. Conversely, the neo-idealist defense of subjectivity and freedom, as manifested in belief in ideal values and universal concepts, undermined the idea of authenticity insofar as it subjected the self to norms and concepts held to be objectively valid, necessary and binding, or emotionally compelling. Weber was one of the few figures in this tradition who realized this. He showed his discomfort at the equation of true human spontaneity with adherence to absolute values and charismatic leadership when he contradicted his own insistence that rationality was not logically attributable to ends in themselves by classifying ends in a hierarchy of rationality defined by the criterion of autonomy. According to this classification, affectively determined behavior, and behavior governed by absolute values, were less rational than the self-interest behavior of the utilitarian model.

The difference in attitude to autonomy was as yet only implicit in the differences between psychoanalysis and idealism. It suggests, however, why it was that Freud's theory of meaning had to emerge from a different source than *Verstehen* or phenomenology. We must examine this source before we can understand the basis of the existentialist critique; but this examination will also be the basis for going beyond that critique to place existentialism in perspective as well.

PSYCHOANALYSIS AND MEDICINE

Psychoanalysis grew out of the theory and practice of nineteenth-century medicine. In later years, in a polemical mood, Freud was to insist that the fact that psychoanalysis was discovered by a physician in the course of efforts to assist his patients was irrelevant to its scope and import; he even observed contemptuously that few people were less fitted by training and attitude to be analysts than were doctors.[16] Nevertheless, the medical origins of psychoanalysis established the context within which its distinctive theory of meaning, including such key concepts as unconscious phantasy and primary process, developed.

The theoretical structure of medicine is based on a value judgment and an imperative to action; "sick" designates something harmful, inferior in character, and unwanted. The positive values corresponding to such negative judgments were largely taken for granted and left unanalyzed in the nineteenth century; health meant "life, long life, ability to procreate, physical capacity, strength, little fatigability, absence of pain, a lasting state in which the body, apart from pleasurable feelings, is disregarded as much as possible."[17] Embodied within this unsystematic list was a more or less unitary conception. The enumerated criteria were essentially biological: they related to man as an "organism." The basic perspective was not the subjectivity of the person but the objective needs of "life": self-preservation and the perpetuation of the species.

The organism, the object of medical concern, was con-

[16] Freud, *S.E.*, Vol. XX, pp. 230-232, 250.

[17] K. Jaspers, *General Psychopathology*, 7th ed., trans. J. Hoenig and M. W. Hamilton, Manchester, 1963, p. 781.

ceived of theoretically as a complex of structures and processes, increasingly viewed through the nineteenth century as mechanical and chemical in nature, each of which individually and in coordination with others had a necessary, empirically ascertainable, function in the sustenance of life. Specifically, medicine was concerned with pathological anatomical and physiological manifestations and their cure. Within this framework, the first problem was the clinical-nosological one of classifying diseases—regularly appearing series and sequences of clinically detectable pathological manifestations—but the ultimate purpose of this classification was to discover causes. The effort of the early nineteenth-century clinical school was to correlate the diagnostic results of clinical examination with the anatomical lesions discovered through autopsy. With the advance of the basic sciences through the century, this approach was supplemented by the attempt to study disease as a function of pathological physiology, that is, as a process rather than as a static entity. The real justification for the classificatory enterprise, however, was established only with Pasteur's work in bacteriology; for the first time in history the causal agents of diseases became known, and the pathological syndromes determined on the basis of contiguity and succession were seen to have connections with specific bacterial agents.[18] In this whole process of defining diseases and determining causes, physical events were of primary importance; emotions, thoughts, and behavior were considered merely as epiphenomenal functions of organic processes, and disturbances of these functions were regarded as symptoms, signs of an objective disease entity. Since the underlying assumption of such a purely biologized medicine was one of physical pathology and causation, the "person" as a logically distinct entity did not have to be taken into account. Such a conception, it has been noted, was not without certain social implications: "In a medical science governed by such a spirit there was certainly a very great dan-

[18] E. H. Ackerknecht, *A Short History of Medicine*, New York, 1955, pp. 164-165.

ger that doctors would be concerned only with the quick restoration of that degree of health necessary for the most efficient possible functioning of the organism, or at least only with striving for as low a degree of pain as possible at any price, for pain could only disturb the management and profit-ableness of human labor power."[19]

By the last third of the nineteenth century, psychiatry had been almost completely assimilated to the medical outlook just described. The mentally and emotionally disturbed had come to be seen as "sick," and the cause of the sickness was looked for exclusively in organic pathology. This develop-ment was promoted by the discovery of pathological lesions in the brains of psychotic individuals suffering from general paresis and in the speech centers of the brains of some aphasics. But, despite their substantiality, these were relative-ly modest advances in the face of the enormous range of men-tal disturbances for which no physical pathology could be demonstrated, and the subsumption of insanity and neurosis under the category of sickness concealed a crucial conceptual problem.[20] In the absence of physical pathology, what justi-fication could there be for considering affective and cognitive problems as illnesses? In one sense the standard medical cri-teria could be legitimately invoked because behavior and in-telligence could be considered as necessary life functions, disturbances of which imperiled survival. In fact, however, the designation "pathological" concealed a judgment from another conceptual realm, a judgment about the logic of the ideas, emotions, and behavior involved; from the observer's point of view (and often from the subject's as well) they

[19] M. Boss, *Einführung in die psychosomatische Medizin*, Bern, 1954, p. 28. It is interesting to note in this connection an early remark of Freud's that "hysteria in men, since it has the greater significance of being an occupational interruption, is of greater practical importance than hys-teria in women." (*S.E.*, Vol. I, p. 52.)

[20] The definition of madness as illness predated these discoveries. On the conceptualization of madness as a theoretical and historical problem see T. Szasz, *The Myth of Mental Illness*, New York, 1961, and M. Fou-cault, *Histoire de la folie*, Paris, 1961.

seemed to be in the general class of meaningful phenomena, but were things that could not be understood by the ordinary criteria of meaningfulness. "In hysterics . . . excessively intense ideas strike us by their oddity. They are ideas which produce no effects in other people and whose effects we cannot appreciate. They appear to us as intruders and usurpers and accordingly as ridiculous. Thus hysterical compulsion is (1) incomprehensible, (2) incapable of being cleared up by any process of thought, and (3) incongruous in its structure."[21]

The central issue was really one of intelligibility and rationality. It was because of the "incomprehensible" and "incongruous" nature of these psychic manifestations that nineteenth-century psychiatry could not accord them status as meaningful behavior and so felt it necessary to explain them —reintegrate them into an ordered, lawful structure. Since, by definition, such a structure was ruled out of the realm of meaning, they could apparently be causally explained only by presumed changes in the physical substratum of the psyche. Thus the *leitmotiv* of late nineteenth-century psychiatry was furnished by Wilhelm Griesinger's famous dictum: "*Geisteskrankheiten sind Gehirnkrankheiten*"—mental illnesses are diseases of the brain.

It was from this general medical and psychiatric background that Freud came to the study of the neuroses. The best example of his effort to preserve the theoretical framework of contemporary medicine intact can be found in his early handling of the so-called "anxiety neuroses." The ostensibly free-floating or immoderate character of the anxiety in these disturbances facilitated Freud's regarding it not as intentional, a meaningful human attitude towards something, but as a toxic substance. Believing that he had found some form of sexual frustration in every case of anxiety, he hypothesized that sexual excitation, also conceived of as a physical substance, was changed into anxiety whenever it could not be adequately discharged through coitus (as in coitus

[21] Freud, *Origins of Psychoanalysis*, pp. 405-406.

interruptus). This was an explanation in straightforwardly chemical terms.[22] The causal factor in this transformation was the disturbance of a biological function rather than an organic lesion. Though Freud had received most of his early formal training in psychiatry from Theodor Meynert, a strong believer in the anatomical localization theory of mental illness, he was also able to employ current advanced medical thinking, which stressed a dynamic, physiological approach.

The implications for therapy of the organic approach to mental illness were that cure depended on some sort of physical intervention. It was on this issue that Freud first broke with psychiatric orthodoxy. From Josef Breuer's report of his treatment of Anna O., Freud learned that hysterical symptoms could be cured through interpersonal communication— having the patient relate the history of their occurrence under hypnosis. In his studies with Charcot a few years later, he learned that such symptoms could also be induced through interpersonal communication, by hypnotic suggestion. But Freud did not conclude from these startling discoveries of psychic influence that hysterical symptomatology consisted of meaningful behavior. In fact, from his point of view, Charcot's great merit was to have demonstrated medical "law and order" in hysteria by proving that it had a regular symptomatology, thereby elevating it from mere malingering to the rank of a genuine illness.[23] This formalized the judgment that hysterical behavior was pathological in the biological sense, and confirmed its essential absurdity and irrationality. Freud *did* conclude from the work of Breuer and Charcot that hysteria

[22] In 1920, Freud added the following footnote to the *Three Essays on the Theory of Sexuality*: ". . . neurotic anxiety arises out of libido . . . it is the product of a transformation of it . . . it is thus related to it in the same kind of way as vinegar is to wine." The parallel with Taine's classically positivist analysis of character—"Vice and virtue are products, like vitriol and sugar"—may not be accidental. Freud had read and been impressed by at least one of Taine's works, *De l'intelligence*. Freud abandoned this conception of anxiety in 1926, advancing a new one in *Inhibitions, Symptoms and Anxiety*.

[23] Freud, *S.E.*, Vol. I, p. 12.

had a psychic *cause*,[24] but precisely what this meant in view of his concept of psychology is a serious problem.

As has already been suggested, it did not mean the introduction into psychiatry of a psychology that would describe and explain behavior in terms of desires, purposes, and intentions; in Karl Jaspers' terms, a psychology of meaningful connections. There are two basic reasons for this. The first has to do with Freud's conceptualization of irrationality. Leaving aside the somewhat different issue of hysterical paralysis, we can distinguish three different types of behavior that Freud labeled irrational and symptomatic. The first was "alienated" behavior, behavior the subject himself was consciously aware of but that was unintelligible to him and often felt foreign to his real self. The second was marked by what Freud called "false connections." One of its forms involved a subject's explanation of his behavior by antecedent conditions that an observer knew had not existed. Neither of the two cases just described ruled out explanation in terms of motives and intentions, and in fact Freud used just such explanations where he could discover them.[25]

The second form of behavior manifesting "false connections" was both more problematic and theoretically more significant for the evolution of psychoanalysis. It was what has come to be called "inappropriate behavior." Inappropriate behavior meant emotions and actions that did not seem to suit the circumstances in which they were expressed: as Freud put it, they were "abnormal exaggerated reactions to psychic stimuli." The idea that an agent's response is inappropriate, and that therefore his citing the antecedent conditions as an explanation of his action is inadequate, is empirically justified only if the action is in fact inappropriate according to the

24 Freud, *S.E.*, Vol. I, p. 41. See also O. Andersson, *Studies in the Prehistory of Psychoanalysis*, Stockholm, 1962, pp. 34-40, 48-58.

25 See Freud's discussion of the "counter-will" in "A Case of Successful Treatment by Hypnotism," *S.E.*, Vol. I, pp. 115-130, and his analysis of "false connections" in the case of "Emmy von N.," in *Studies on Hysteria*, *S.E.*, Vol. II, pp. 66-67.

agent's own criteria. In these circumstances the agent is contradicting himself by offering as an explanation what he would not generally accept as valid for himself and others. Where such contradiction does not exist, however, the designation "inappropriate" has no empirical force, or rather its force is simply to show the difference between the agent's norms and those of the judging observer. The reason Freud was generally right and not merely ideological in attributing inappropriateness to his patients' behavior was that they shared his sense of social norms and conventions. But he was not aware of the social, and hence conventional, nature of the relevant norms. Because of this he was not initially aware of the possibility of a discrepancy between social and private norms, motives, and descriptions of situations.[26] Given the theoretical presuppositions derived from contemporary biology and the positivistic world view upon which it was based, Freud assumed that situations had a fixed, determinate, and objective character, and that there was only one set of natural responses to them.[27] Deviant responses were irrational in the

[26] Just such a discrepancy, of course, was what was assumed and explained by the fully developed theory of psychoanalysis. The point of this section is to show that the notion of such a discrepancy was arrived at in a different way.

[27] A particularly good example of normative reasoning from biological theory can be found in the "Dora" analysis. Freud was commenting on Dora's reaction of disgust when she was, at the age of fourteen, suddenly seized and kissed by "Herr K.": "This was surely just the situation to call up a distinct feeling of sexual excitement in a girl of fourteen who had never before been approached . . . in this scene . . . the behavior of this child of fourteen was already entirely and completely hysterical. I should without question consider a person hysterical in whom an occasion for sexual excitement elicited feelings that were preponderantly or exclusively unpleasurable; and I should do so whether or not the person were capable of producing somatic symptoms." (*S.E.*, Vol. vii, p. 28.) The assumption here is that there is such a thing as an objective "occasion for sexual excitement" independent of education, social custom, and context, and that any reaction other than the natural one is a sign of illness even when there is no sign of inner conflict.

The possible ideological bearing of this approach can be seen in a passage of a review that Freud wrote in 1889 of Forel's book on hypnotism.

28

FREUD'S THEORY OF MEANING

sense of not being behavior at all, not being intentional or motivated. Failure to act in the correct way was a biological aberrancy—in other words, an illness—that had to be explained in biological terms. This theoretical outlook permitted conventional social criteria of intelligible—i.e., acceptable and expectable—behavior to be incorporated into medical concepts of health; deviant behavior was interpreted as symptoms or disease effects to which a medical aetiological schema of hereditary predisposition, specific cause and releasing cause could be applied.[28]

Given this framework, it was not surprising that Freud initially defined hysteria in physiological terms: "Hysteria is based wholly and entirely on physiological modifications of the nervous system and its essence should be expressed in a formula which took account of the conditions of excitability in the different parts of the nervous system. A physio-pathological formula of this kind has not yet, however, been discovered."[29] Yet in the very same article he recommended treatment of hysteria by hypnotic suggestion, which he explained and justified in the following terms: "Direct treatment consists in the removal of the psychical sources of stimulus for the hysterical symptoms, and is understandable *if we look for the causes of hysteria in unconscious ideational life.*"[30]

In the review Freud defended the therapeutic use of hypnotism against criticism that it involved the suppression of the patient's free personality by the physician: "The suppression of a patient's independence by hypnotic suggestion is always only a partial one . . . it is aimed at the symptoms of an illness . . . the entire social upbringing of human beings is based on a suppression of unserviceable ideas and motives and their replacement by better ones." (*S.E.*, Vol. I, p. 94.) The equation of mental illness with socially unserviceable ideas and motives in this passage was almost explicit.

[28] Examples of this kind of reasoning can be seen in such statements by Freud as "The normal, expected decease of an aged father is not an experience which usually causes illness in a healthy adult"; "a healthy mother usually reacts only with normal grief to the loss of a child." *S.E.*, Vol. III, p. 105.

[29] Freud, *S.E.*, Vol. I, p. 41.   [30] *Ibid.*, p. 56. Italics added.

Freud also suggested the use of Breuer's therapeutic technique of leading the patient under hypnosis back to the psychic prehistory of the ailment and compelling him to acknowledge the occasion on which the hysterical symptom originated. This technique, he claimed, was the most appropriate therapy because "it precisely imitates the mechanism of the origin and passing of these hysterical disorders."[31]

The juxtaposition of a quest for a "physio-pathological formula" for hysteria and a reference to its causes in "unconscious ideational life" in the same article brings us to the second reason that psychic causation did not mean for Freud a psychology of meaningful connections. There was at this time for him no real distinction between psychic and physiological explanation. In fact, Freud argued against the concept of a totally independent psychic cause for hysteria. During the 1880's there was a controversy between Charcot and the French psychiatrist Bernheim as to the nature of the processes at work in hypnosis. Bernheim argued that all hypnotic phenomena were purely psychological, the effects of suggestion from one person to another; Charcot insisted that the manifestations of hypnotism were based upon physiological changes in the nervous system, brought about through auto-suggestion triggered by a physical stimulus or by the physical situation of the subject's body (as when raising the subject's arm or stroking it caused paralysis). In this debate, Freud sided essentially with Charcot. While not denying the psychic nature of auto-suggestion, he pointed out that it could equally well be described as physiological because it worked, as did suggestion in general, on the basis of the laws of association, whose linkages lay "in the nature of the nervous system and not in any arbitrary action by the physician."[32] Hence Freud rejected the idea of an antithesis between the psychic and physiological phenomena of hypnosis:

"There was a meaning in this antithesis so long as by suggestion was understood a directly psychical influence exer-

<hr>

[31] *Ibid.*

[32] Freud, *S.E.*, Vol. I, p. 83.

cised by the physician which forced any symptomatology it liked upon the hypnotized subject. But this meaning disappears as soon as it is realized that even suggestion only releases sets of manifestations which are based upon the functional peculiarities of the hypnotized nervous system. . . . *We possess no criterion which enables us to distinguish exactly between a psychical process and a physiological one, between an act occurring in the cerebral cortex and one occurring in the subcortical substance*: for 'consciousness,' whatever that may be, is not attached to every activity of the cerebral cortex, nor is it always attached in an equal degree to any one of its activities. . . ."[33]

Evidently then, according to Freud, psychic processes differed from other physiological processes not in nature but in physical location. The terminology of intention and meaning was a way of transcribing into ordinary language the underlying material processes of the nervous system.[34] Because of the purely empirical, clinical context of Breuer's first breakthrough into the riddle of hysteria, Freud talked about the triggering event of the neurosis in ordinary psychological terms, but its real scientific description as well as explanation could only be physiological.

There was thus necessarily an uneasy shuttling back and forth between two different conceptual sets in Freud's early

---

[33] *Ibid.*, p. 85. Italics added. Thus, before he had any concept of defense or repression, Freud considered a good deal of psychic functioning to be "unconscious."

[34] This epiphenomenal conceptualization of psychology was made explicit in an article on the brain written by Freud at the same time as the one on hysteria. In this article he spoke of the processes of the nervous system as "a causal nexus of mechanical events" that were only occasionally accompanied by such phenomena of consciousness as attention, perception, feelings, and intentions. The presence or absence of conscious phenomena did not imply that any part of the sequence of material events had to occur in a different way in either case; i.e., in both cases, reflex mechanisms were at work. (See Andersson, *Studies*, pp. 65-67.) In the next section we will be concerned with the model Freud used in this article.

31

work. Even where psychological language was used, however, it could only be to describe the antecedent conditions of the neurosis and not the symptoms themselves, which were conceptualized as unmeaningful. The resulting confusion was reflected in the summary of the 1888 article on hysteria, in which Freud defined hysteria as "an anomaly of the nervous system which is based on a different distribution of excitations, probably accompanied by a surplus of stimuli in the organ of the mind," and then went on to hypothesize that "this surplus is distributed by means of conscious or unconscious ideas."[35]

Two factors, then—Freud's medical interpretation of abnormal psychology, and his theoretical conception of normal psychology in general—led him to his quest for a "physiopathological formula" for hysteria. In his initial usage of Breuer's cathartic technique, however, he did not yet have such a formula. The technique was justified partly on the grounds that it reversed the sequence of events assumed in Charcot's hypothesis that hysteria was caused by auto-suggestion,[36] and partly by purely pragmatic considerations. It was only with the development of the abreaction theory that the cathartic procedure received independent theoretical grounding. This development represented a penetration into the more fundamental levels of neuro-physiological theorizing that had been only hinted at in Freud's earliest psychological works.

MECHANICAL EXPLANATION

The problematic nature of the relationship between psychological and physiological conceptions in Freud's thought

[35] Freud, S.E., Vol. I, p. 57.

[36] For more details on this point, see Andersson, Studies, pp. 58, 78. Andersson's discussion of Freud's earliest therapeutic procedures and the relationship of suggestion to Breuer's technique is much clearer than that of Jones.

was evident in the various formulations of the abreaction theory. In psychological terms Freud described a hysterical attack as "the hallucinatory reliving of a scene which is significant for the onset of the illness."[37] The original scene had been emotionally very upsetting, but the patient had not been able to react to it for one of a number of reasons, the most important one being that "it was a question of things which the patient wished to forget, and therefore *intentionally repressed* from his conscious thought."[38] Despite this description, however, no motive, no psychological reason was given for the reliving of the traumatic scene.[39] In a subsequently famous line from the *Preliminary Communication* Breuer and Freud spoke of hysterics as "suffering from reminiscences," but suffering from reminiscences was not engaging in behavior. These terms, in fact, represented transcriptions and approximations in psychological language of hypotheses drawn from a totally different conceptual realm.

A first, cryptic hint of this realm was contained in one of the unpublished drafts for the *Preliminary Communication,* which briefly adumbrated an energic model of the nervous system: "The nervous system endeavours to keep constant something in its functional relations that we may describe as the 'sum of excitation.' It puts this precondition of health into effect by disposing associatively of every sensible accretion of excitation or by discharging it by an appropriate motor reaction. . . . the psychical experiences forming the content of hysterical attacks . . . are all the impressions which have failed to find adequate discharge . . . any impression which the nervous system has difficulty in disposing of by means of

[37] Freud, *S.E.,* Vol. I, p. 137.

[38] J. Breuer and S. Freud, *Studies on Hysteria, S.E.,* Vol. II, p. 10. Italics added.

[39] In a lecture to the Vienna Medical Club, Freud tried to give a plausible psychological analogy for this reliving by comparing it with the mortification aroused by the memory of an unanswered insult, but the analogy accounted neither for the persistence of the memory nor for the symptoms.

associative thinking or of motor reaction becomes a psychical trauma."[40]

The assumptions underlying this kind of thinking were not apparent in the passage itself, but the mechanistic terms were obvious. The nervous system operated as a self-regulating mechanism to maintain a certain energy equilibrium; for some reason it occasionally failed in its task of discharge or abreaction. Seen in this framework, traumas were not meaningful events but *"accretion[s] of excitation* in the nervous system, *which the latter has been unable to dispose of adequately by motor reaction,"* while hysterical attacks were attempts of the mechanism "to complete the reaction to the trauma."[41] The passivity of the pseudo-psychological language "suffering from reminiscences" was appropriate because hysterical symptoms were not acts but mechanical products, "the effects and residues of excitations which have acted upon the nervous system as traumas."[42]

The pattern Freud established in advancing the abreaction theory was repeated throughout the intensified and increasingly exciting research of the next few years that led to the discovery of the psychoanalytic theory of meaning. The impetus for each new step was a clinical observation phrased in psychological terms (e.g., emotional trauma). Immediately, however, Freud tried to redescribe and explain the observation in mechanical language (e.g., accretion of excitation). Certain conclusions would be drawn from assumptions about the mechanical functioning of the nervous system; the results would then be retranscribed or paraphrased in psychological language (e.g., "suffering from reminiscences"). It was out of this complex and often confusing process that the unique psychoanalytic concepts of unconscious phantasy and primary process functioning were born.

One major problem raised by the abreaction theory was the relationship of the symptomatic material to the traumatic

---

40 Freud, *S.E.,* Vol. II, pp. 153-154. Italics omitted.
41 Freud, *S.E.,* Vol. I, p. 137.
42 Breuer and Freud, *S.E.,* Vol. II, p. 86.

event that had caused the outbreak of hysteria. In the *Preliminary Communication* to the *Studies on Hysteria*, Breuer and Freud put forward the notion that the alienated ideas and physical symptoms were the products of "hypnoid states," peculiar mental states of unknown origin in which intense ideas were cut off from associative connection with the other contents of consciousness. Freud, however, was dissatisfied with this idea. The hypothesis of hypnoid states seemed unnecessary in view of the earlier suggestion in the same article that what made the causal situation traumatic was the unacceptability of the events or ideas. In one of the seminal works of psychoanalytic theory, "The Neuro-Psychoses of Defence," Freud suggested instead that symptoms be viewed as the result of a defensive effort of the self against ideas it found incompatible with its sense of morality or self-esteem.

On one level the concept of defense was a straightforwardly psychological concept. "The splitting of the content of consciousness," Freud wrote, "is the result of an act of will on the part of the patient; that is to say, it is initiated by an effort of will whose motive can be specified."[43] By this he meant that the patient had consciously tried to suppress an unbearable idea at the time of its occurrence. But the account of the formation of the symptom as a result of the defensive effort was not psychological at all; the concepts of conversion and displacement, according to which a sum of energy corresponding to an emotion was stripped from an idea and "converted" into somatic manifestations or "displaced" onto another idea, were, as Freud explicitly acknowledged, the products of mechanistic speculation:

"Between the patient's effort of will, which succeeds in repressing the unacceptable sexual idea, and the emergence of the obsessional idea, which, though having little intensity in itself, is now supplied with an incomprehensibly strong affect, yawns the gap which the theory here developed seeks to fill. The separation of the sexual idea from its affect and the attachment of the latter to another, suitable but not incompatible idea—these are processes which occur without

[43] Freud, *S.E.*, Vol. III, p. 46.

consciousness. Their existence can only be presumed but cannot be proved by any clinico-psychological analysis. *Perhaps it would be more correct to say that these processes are not of a psychical nature at all, that they are physical processes whose psychical consequences present themselves as if what is expressed by the terms 'separation of the idea from its affect' and 'false connection' of the latter had really taken place.*"[44]

Having indicated that the real meaning of the concept of defense lay in physical processes, Freud's next step was to attempt to describe them in some detail, to give the concept more concrete content. This was the central purpose of the so-called *Project for a Scientific Psychology*, a neurological account of psychological processes that Freud drafted and sent to Wilhelm Fliess in 1895. It was in this outline that he made explicit for the first time the assumptions that underlay his idea of scientific explanation in general and of the nature of psychological processes in particular, assumptions he had alluded to before without adequate clarification.

We now know a good deal about the historical background of the key ideas in the *Project*. In sum, the scheme of nervous functioning outlined in it was a restatement and modification of that of Freud's teachers Brücke, Exner, and above all Meynert, itself based on a materialist-mechanist view of science associated with the so-called "Helmholtzian school."[45]

[44] *Ibid.,* p. 53. Italics added.

[45] The literature on this subject is extensive and growing. The best work to date on the influence of contemporary neurological theory on Freud is P. Amacher, *Freud's Neurological Education and its Influence on Psychoanalytic Theory, Psychological Issues,* Vol. 14, No. 4, New York, 1965. See also Andersson, *Studies in the Prehistory of Psychoanalysis;* W. A. Stewart, *Psychoanalysis, The First Ten Years: 1888-1898,* New York, 1967; Ernst Kris's introduction to the English edition of the Fliess correspondence; the articles by S. Bernfeld that first linked Freud to the Helmholtz school, "Freud's Earliest Theories and the School of Helmholtz," *op.cit.,* "Freud's Scientific Beginnings," *The American Imago,* Vol. VI, Sept. 1949, pp. 162-196; H. F. Ellenberger, "Fechner and Freud," *Bul-*

The compelling force of Meynert's neurological psychology for Freud was its apparent fulfillment of the contemporary criteria for truly scientific explanation. These had been laid down for the sciences of man by one of the founders of the movement that came to be known as the Helmholtz school of medicine, the physiologist du Bois-Reymond, in a letter of 1842 to his colleague Carl Ludwig:

"Brücke and I pledged a solemn oath to put into effect this truth: No other forces than the common physical-chemical ones are active within the organism. In those cases which cannot at the time be explained by these forces one has either to find the specific ways or forms of their action by means of the physical-mathematical method or to assume new forces equal in dignity to the chemical-physical forces inherent in matter, reducible to the forces of attraction and repulsion."[46]

This was the ideal that underlay Freud's *Project*. His declaration of purpose in the introduction stated: "The intention of the project is to furnish us with a psychology which shall be a natural science; its aim, that is, is to represent psychical processes as quantitatively determined states of specifiable material particles and so make them plain and void of contradictions."[47] For Freud, natural science was the only model of science, and contemporary natural science meant description and explanation in terms of matter and motion. Psychology could have no other foundation than this; and it is important to remember, when attempts are made to distinguish between Freud's psychology and metapsychology, that he had no logically independent conceptual framework for

---

letin of the Menninger Clinic, Vol. 20, No. 4, 1956, pp. 20ff.; M. Dorer, *Historische Grundlagen der Psychoanalyse*, Leipzig, 1932; L. Binswanger, "Freud and the Magna Carta of Clinical Psychiatry," in *Being-in-the-World*. A long footnote in Andersson's book gives a useful summary of the published investigations into the early scientific and cultural influences on Freud to that date and suggests some other interesting lines of research (pp. 6-9).

[46] Quoted by Bernfeld, "Freud's Earliest Theories," p. 348.

[47] Freud, *Origins of Psychoanalysis*, p. 355.

psychology as a science.[48] It is not enough, then, to say that the *Project* contains the origins of much of Freud's metapsychology, or to recognize that his continuing use of its terminology indicated that his enduring ideal of explanation was physicalistic. Psychoanalytic psychology itself grew directly out of the theoretical structure of the *Project*.

The fundamental mechanical principle of Freud's psychology, the "principle of constancy," entered nineteenth-century psychiatry from two sources. Gustav Fechner, to whose work Meynert referred for psychological theory, first introduced the idea of an independent, mobile mental energy and a so-called "tendency to stability" into psychology. The necessary material base for these ideas was furnished by contemporary neurological theory. One part of this base had been laid by Freud's professor of physiology, Ernst Brücke, with his particular variant of the conception of the human organism as a reflex mechanism. Starting from the work of du Bois-Reymond and Helmholtz, who had detected and measured variations in the electrical current in nerves and the velocities of nerve impulses, Brücke assumed that all nervous functioning involved a sum of excitation or energy that originated at the endings of the afferent nerves and was transmitted through the nervous centers to the efferent nerves like fluid through a pipe and then discharged. The excitation originated in the ends of the afferent nerves when they were stimulated either by external forces or by the non-nervous parts of the organism. The whole process was fully automatic; the mechanism operated so as to remain in a state of zero-energy equilibrium.

The extension of the scheme of reflex function to all of human activity, including the sphere of ostensibly voluntary acts of will, was made possible only by the incorporation of

[48] Freud's embarrassment at using descriptions in ordinary language in connection with neurotic illness was recorded in his celebrated comment in *Studies on Hysteria:*, "It still strikes me myself as strange that the case histories I write should read like short stories and that, as one might say, they lack the serious stamp of science." *S.E.*, Vol. II, p. 160.

association psychology into neurology. Previous thinkers had not reduced all nervous functioning to reflexes because they thought that at least some kinds of behavior could be explained only on the assumption that mind played an active role in their initiation and control.[49] Association psychology eliminated mind in this sense by making it a merely passive spectator to the reception and combination of sense perceptions. The atomistic, reified nature of these perceptions made it easy to translate them into localizable material elements such as brain cells or "association fibre-bundles," and the psychic functioning of association could be conceptualized as the flow of energy among the material elements.[50]

The work of Theodore Meynert was an attempt to account for the learning of meaning and of logical processes and hence also for irrational behavior and ideation. In his version of neuropsychology,[51] the objects of sense perception were sources of energy that impinged on the afferent nerves, thus disturbing the equilibrium of the system and necessitating discharge. Discharge was accomplished by motor acts whose purpose was to put an end to the influx of energy: incoming energy was thus transmitted as motor impulses to the muscles via subcerebral pathways innately determined. (This model was intended to explain such reflex actions as withdrawing the hand from a hot stove.) At the same time, energy also flowed to the cerebral cortex, producing a memory image in its cells. If different parts of the cortex received excitation simultaneously from two different sensory pathways, the association-bundles joining the two points of impingement became connective pathways for the transfer of excitation from one image to another. Then, after a given pathway had been laid down by the conjunction of two external stimuli, the appearance of one of them would cause the impinging energy to flow automatically to the associated image through the as-

[49] Amacher, *Freud's Neurological Education*, p. 26.
[50] The reification and passivity involved in association psychology were the counterparts of the biological idea of "natural responses."
[51] Amacher, *Freud's Neurological Education*, pp. 21-41.

sociation-bundle, calling up the memory of the associated stimulus. The same model could be used to explain ostensibly voluntary acts. Meynert assumed that a motor act that was originally an innate reflex acted like any sensation in producing an image in the cortex. In the example of the hot stove, the withdrawal of the hand produced an image in the cortex linked by association-bundles with the sight and feel of the stove. If on another occasion the person's hand came close to the stove, the impinging energy would flow from the image of the object to the image of the withdrawal of the hand, from there to the motor nucleus of the muscles that effected the withdrawal, and then to the appropriate muscles. The hand would be withdrawn without actually coming in contact with the stove.

This elementary learning model was extremely important to Meynert's theory because it covered a class of events for which reflex theory could not account. Energy came into the organism not only from without, but from within, from the basic organic needs, such as hunger and sex. In the case of these endogenous sources of energy, innate reflex mechanisms of avoidance or flight could not put an end to the influx of energy. Only a specific action, such as the procuring of food, could accomplish this. The infant, however, was incapable of carrying out the necessary specific action; instead it discharged the energy of hunger in reflex acts such as crying and aimless movements that did not stop the impingement of excitation. Only intervention from the outside, such as presentation of the mother's breast, could trigger the correct reflex—sucking—which would put an end to the release of energy. This intervention introduced into the cortical pathways of discharge images of the external agent that had made the successful reflex possible (the breast), of the reflex movement itself, and of the relief attained by it (the ending of the impinging excitation). These became associated with the sensation of hunger and in subsequent occasions the child would learn to look for the breast and begin sucking.

Through the repetition of many such sequences, patterns

of learned behavior were established that, taken together, Meynert called the "primary ego," the nucleus of personality. Learning a pattern, however, was not an immediate process; initially, the associative paths would include many images incidental to the main sequence of events granting relief. Only after repeated experiences would one set of cortical connections acquire greater intensity and the child thus learn to discriminate the central from the merely peripheral associations. From this circumstance Meynert felt able to deduce certain consequences that could explain the strange psychological processes of dreams and mental illness. If the main goal ideas in the ego no longer controlled the flow of energy in the cortex (as regularly happened in sleep) or if there were any physical damage to the association-bundles, the discharging energy would be transferred at random among the peripheral associations, producing disorder and illogical associations.

The fundamental conception of Freud's *Project For a Scientific Psychology* followed Meynert's ideas closely.[52] In particular, Meynert's theory was the nucleus of Freud's crucial distinction between primary and secondary processes. In outlining these processes, however, Freud pursued more rigorously than Meynert the mechanistic principles of the model and was thus led to a new position beyond that of his teacher.

In Freud's scheme, an experience of the satisfaction of a need, such as hunger, led to an associative connection among the set of neurones representing the memory images of the various parts of the process: the accumulation of energy from the internal source, the external object that satisfied the need, and the reflex movement that had made satisfactory discharge possible. When hunger recurred and energy accumulated in the appropriate neurones, it would, according to mechanical principles, naturally tend to "cathect" or charge

[52] The discovery of the neuron in the interim made it possible for Freud to speak with more precision about the material elements involved in nervous functioning and postulated as the substratum of psychic processes. For the contributions of other figures, see Amacher, *Freud's Neurological Education.*

41

the other two memory images and activate them, producing "something similar to a perception—namely a hallucination."[53] This assumption was based on purely quantitative considerations that ignored the phenomenological distinctions between memory and perception and conceptualized the difference between them as one of intensity of energy charge. A hallucination was a memory so highly charged that it was taken for a perception. Full-strength cathexis of the memory images would thus trigger the reflex action without bringing satisfaction. If the state of excitation were equivalent in psychological terms to a desire for gratification, then the activation of the memory image of the desired object, and the action resulting from this, corresponded to a hallucinatory wish-fulfillment.

This, then, was Freud's original version of the primary process. Hallucination, in the sense of mistaking "inner" for "outer" perception, was the primordial tendency of the neurological mechanism because of the principle of immediate discharge or constancy. Only if the flow of energy were somehow inhibited and prevented from cathecting memory images with its full force was it possible to use sensory reports ("indications of quality") as a criterion for distinguishing between a perception and a memory. The ego did gradually learn to "bind" energy in this way because of the failure of primary process functioning to stop the inflow of energy, which was experienced qualitatively as pain. (Freud was not able to give a satisfactory mechanical account of the process of binding and was forced to explain it as the product of "biological experience"—learning through pain.) If for any reason the ego did not perform its inhibiting function, the natural tendency of the mechanism to immediate discharge and hallucination automatically took over.

All of these processes had been elaborated as part of Freud's description of normal psychological functioning. They were a necessary preliminary to attacking the problems of psychopathology. The great discovery they occasioned was

[53] Freud, *Origins of Psychoanalysis*, p. 381.

something in the nature of an unintended byproduct. For the model first furnished the key not to the problem of neurotic symptomatology but to the riddle of dreams. Primary process functioning in the early stages of development was purely conjectural, a deduction from the a priori assumptions about the mechanical functioning of the brain. In dreams, however, there were in phenomenological fact concrete images of a hallucinatory nature, that is, images that "awaken consciousness and meet with belief."[54] Applying the theoretical deductions to those images, Freud came to the momentous conclusion that "Dreams are *the fulfillments of wishes*— that is, primary processes following an experience of satisfaction. . . ."[55] The form of the conclusion showed clearly once again that the psychological language was a transcription of hypothesized underlying mechanical processes rather than a description. Freud granted that "We shall not find . . . a wish that is conscious and afterwards its fulfillment hallucinated; but the latter only will be conscious and the intermediate link will have to be inferred. It has quite certainly occurred, but without being able to give itself a qualitative shape."[56] The great significance of this psychological language, however, was that for the first time a hitherto unintelligible "mental" phenomenon was apparently re-integrated into the sphere of meaningful human behavior as a human act embodying an intention.

The *Project* was less fruitful in coming to grips with the problem that had first inspired it, the problem of defense and neurotic symptomatology. In his discussion of dreams, Freud described a phenomenon similar to one hypothesized for obsessional neurosis, that of displacement. In dreams this meant the appearance in the dream-imagery of ideas that seemed only peripherally related to the wish-fulfillment reconstructed after the dream by association, but that had appeared instead of other ideas central to the dream content.[57] Freud's expla-

[54] *Ibid.*, p. 401.　　[55] *Ibid.*, p. 402.　　[56] *Ibid.*, p. 404.
[57] In the *Project*, Freud gave no account of his actual method of dream interpretation, though it seems safe to assume that the technique was

nation was that the relaxation of the daytime cognitive and inhibitory activity of the ego during sleep allowed energy to move freely among the elements of association, producing senseless and illogical phenomena. This was essentially Meynert's original idea, and it was not yet integrated with Freud's own discovery of purposefulness in dreams; but it did mean at least an important extension of the idea of primary process.

In connection with the neuroses, however, Freud already knew more than this about displacement, since there it was clearly a defensive measure. Instead of clarifying this link, however, the *Project* seemed only to raise more problems. In the course of his description of normal psychic processes, Freud had given an account of normal procedures of defense against painful memories. These defenses, he noted, never succeeded in expunging such memories so thoroughly that fresh perceptions could not arouse them again. Yet supposedly this total suppression was exactly what happened with the traumatic memories that caused neurosis. The problem was to explain such total exclusion, or repression.

Here, two clinical observations appeared to be of some help. Clinical investigation showed that only sexual ideas were subject to defense that caused neurosis. Perhaps there was something unique about them that led to pathological defense. On this point the other observation proved useful. As Freud probed the memories of his patients to identify the traumatic scene whose residue seemed to be active in their neuroses, it appeared increasingly necessary to go back all the way to events in early childhood, since these came up repeatedly during therapy.[58] Yet the neuroses themselves had set

___

substantially that of free association, as described in connection with the dream of "Irma's injection" in *The Interpretation of Dreams*, the same dream used as illustration in the *Project*.

[58] It is not known when Freud first came to this conclusion. The case of "Katharina" in *Studies on Hysteria*, the last case to be written up for the book, was the first to follow memories back to pre-pubertal experiences. It may well be that though Freud had not found it necessary to

in only years later. One possible explanation was that the early scenes developed traumatic force only some time *after* the actual event. This could be made intelligible on the conventional assumption of the asexual nature of childhood. Events of sexual significance would have no impact on the child before the onset of his own sexuality at puberty; he would not even understand them. Revived in memory after puberty, however, they could then have a traumatic effect.

The success of normal defense depended upon the ego's efforts at the time of the original painful experiences to ward it off by diverting its own attention to other things, or, in the conceptual language of the *Project*, diverting the influx of energy into cathexes of neutral perceptual or memory images. Thereafter, whenever the ego was faced with a perception that recalled the painful experience, it tried to reproduce this situation by sending the energy along the associative paths set up in the initial experience. If, however, an experience was not initially painful but became so only in retrospect, the ego would not have prepared defenses, nor would it be directing preventive attention at incoming perceptions. This, according to Freud, was what happened in hysteria. The memory of a sexual assault that had not originally had an impact was aroused by some occurrence with sexual overtones after puberty; the memory, now experienced as painful, released a large quantity of sexual affect that caught the ego by surprise. Since the ego was unable to channel the energy influx, a primary process resulted—hallucinatory cathexis of the memory image as if it were a current perception, and displacement of cathexis in erratic patterns among associations.

Despite its neatness, this solution was at best only partly satisfactory, even from Freud's own point of view. It gave a more or less mechanically adequate account of displacement in neurosis as he then understood it, but it failed to explain why the traumatic event, supposedly available to memory up

do this thus far in all his cases, the theoretical considerations discussed here made him see the significance of this procedure.

to puberty, should be repressed. Nevertheless it was the base from which Freud worked from now on, modifying it in the light of new clinical information as well as resolutions of the theoretical problems still existing in the explanation.

Moreover, the discussion of pathology in the *Project* made at least one crucial and lasting contribution to the development of the psychoanalytic theory of meaning. Up until now there had been no mention of the relationship between the memory-residue of the traumatic event and the ongoing life of the patient in his current social interactions, since in the first simple aetiological scheme there was only one traumatic scene, or a series closely linked in time, immediately preceding the appearance of the symptom and obviously furnishing its content. In the example of hysteria Freud used in the *Project*, however, the memory of the sexual assault that came up in therapy preceded the traumatic event that actually precipitated the outbreak of the hysterical symptom by a number of years. Freud was thus forced to relate past and present events and came to the conclusion that "disturbance of the normal psychical process depends on . . . the sexual release being attached to a memory instead of to an experience."[59] This conclusion, which totally separated memory and present experience and declared the latter irrelevant to the meaning of the symptom, was possible only within the framework of Freud's neurological psychology. That framework allowed the past to coexist literally with the present as a separate event and then to replace it, because the past had material status and because sexual emotion, as a free-flowing quantity of energy, could be generated in a contemporary situation but "really" belong to the past if it flowed to the appropriate neurones. This spatialization of temporal and meaningful processes remained a key constituent of psychoanalytic theory and created great problems when, as happened shortly, psychoanalysis became a theory of action.

[59] Freud, *Origins of Psychoanalysis*, p. 414.

The very day that Freud sent the *Project* off to Fliess, the first revisions were made in it. In an accompanying letter he wrote that his most recent clinical observation showed that the primary pre-pubertal sexual experience causing hysteria was accompanied by revulsion and fright, while the one causing obsessional neurosis was accompanied by pleasure.[60] These observations seemed to throw the mechanical explanation of displacement out of the window, since it depended on the neutral quality of the early sexual experiences and the consequent lack of defensive preparations by the ego that allowed the ego to be overwhelmed by a primary process after puberty. Freud tried to rescue the explanation with the assumption that the peculiarity of unpleasurable pre-pubertal sexual memories was that, if remembered after puberty, they were able to produce large quantities of "fresh unpleasure" beyond the merely remembered unpleasure of other bad memories, because of the access of sexual energy accompanying puberty.[61]

But the new information also raised intriguing new issues. On the one hand, Freud was puzzled by the unpleasure caused by premature sexual stimulation and felt that its explanation required a comprehensive theory of the sexual process, since normally sexual stimulation should be accompanied by pleasure. On the other hand, the fact that the sexual assaults *were* unpleasurable suggested that the reason they were not recalled until therapy was that they had been repressed in childhood, and not later at the time of the triggering event. This represented an important development in Freud's thought. When he had first introduced the concept of defense, he meant by it the conscious effort of the adult ego to rid itself of uncongenial ideas. The notion of repressed infantile experiences shifted the focus to a much earlier stage, with de-

---

[60] *Ibid.*, p. 126. (Letter of Oct. 8, 1895.) Even in the case of the girl discussed in the *Project*, it was clear that the assault had hardly been a neutral experience. See *Origins*, p. 411.

[61] *Ibid.*, p. 176.

fense relegated to a later, secondary stage of symptom formation.[62] The result was the relative eclipse of the psychological
idea of defense and its replacement by a hypothetical, non-
descriptive concept of primal repression.[63]

This was the position Freud had reached at the beginning
of 1896. Though he had not been successful in explaining repression in mechanistic terms, he was sure he had found the
clinical-theoretical solution of the neuroses. Neurosis represented the return of repressed memories of early sexual assaults in the form of disconnected ideas and emotions produced by only partially successful defenses against the
traumatic memories. Yet even as he strove to find more tales
of infantile seduction to corroborate this structure, other
observations were gathering force to undermine it and to
bring the problem of the neuroses into connection with another but hitherto unrelated discovery of Freud's—the meaning of dreams.

The new developments seem to have been triggered by
Freud's increasing awareness of the element of pleasure, both
in the original supposedly traumatic event itself and in the
patient's recounting of it in therapy. This had perhaps been
implicit in Freud's understanding of the nature of even the
frightening assault that caused hysteria,[64] and was certainly
explicit in the account of the attack that caused obsessional
neurosis. In any case both Freud's interest in and observations of the scope of this pleasurable element increased. In
a long letter to Fliess at the end of 1896, a number of these

[62] *Ibid.*, p. 148.

[63] It was not until the reconstruction of psychoanalysis in the 1920's
that the concept of the defense of the ego was reintroduced to become
the center of psychoanalytic ego-psychology.

[64] Cf. once again the account of the assault on the girl in the *Project.*
The eight-year-old girl returned to the scene of the attack and afterwards,
Freud noted, "reproached herself for having gone the second time, as
though she had wanted to provoke the assault" (p. 411). See also the
letter of August 12, 1895, where Freud writes of the root of hysteria lying
in a conflict between sexual pleasure and unpleasure.

observations were brought together. "Not all sexual experiences release unpleasure," he wrote, "most of them release pleasure. Thus the reproduction of most of them is accompanied by uninhibitable pleasure."[65] He also noted that this pleasure was of a decidedly perverse nature, relating to what were ordinarily considered non-sexual parts of the body; the stimulation of what he called erotogenic zones, normally abandoned in adulthood, must have been the result of perversion on the part of the child's adult seducer. The defenses of the neurotic were thus directed not against sexuality but against perversion.[66] Then in one bold, climactic statement he drew the conclusion that was in fact implicit in all of this information about the evident sexual pleasure displayed by the adult neurotic: "A hysterical attack is not a discharge but an *action*; and it retains the original character of every action —of being a means to reproducing pleasure."[67]

It is impossible to overstate the importance of this sentence. It was this conclusion that transformed psychoanalysis in the direction of a dynamic theory, a theory of action. But the transformation was very far from complete. Though he was not explicitly aware of it, Freud now had two theories on his hands, and their relationship to each other was not at all clear. On the one hand, neurotic symptoms represented actions whose purpose was the attainment of pleasure of a sexually perverse kind; on the other hand, they represented memories of early assaults, the "return of the repressed," which was a mechanical rather than an action concept. Somehow it was necessary to reconcile the two.

Just a few months later Freud hit on the key to such a reconciliation. "The missing piece in the hysteria puzzle which I could not find," he wrote to Fliess on April 6, 1897, "has turned up in the form of a new source from which an element in unconscious production flows. I refer to the hysterical phantasies which, I now see, invariably go back to things heard in early infancy and only subsequently understood."[68]

---

[65] Freud, *Origins of Psychoanalysis*, p. 176. Letter of Dec. 6, 1896.
[66] *Ibid.*, p. 180.   [67] *Ibid.*   [68] *Ibid.*, p. 193.

Freud did not indicate just how he distinguished phantasy from memory, but it would appear that "phantasies" referred to experiences he knew the patients who recounted them could not have had, though they may well have observed or heard about them. These phantasies were, Freud informed Fliess a month later, "defensive structures . . . psychical outworks constructed in order to bar the way to . . . memories."[69] But phantasies were also something else. According to the theory outlined in the *Project*, phantasies that were not known *as* phantasies were, like dreams, "images which inspired belief," or hallucinations; hence they must be hallucinatory wish-fulfillments. They were not just defensive bulwarks against memory, then; they were a way of "hark[ing] back to the primal scenes."[70] It followed that hysterical symptoms were not merely passively returning memories but motivated structures, returned *impulses*. "The psychical structures which in hysteria are subjected to repression are not properly speaking memories," Freud wrote in the same letter, "because no one sets his memory working without good cause, but impulses deriving from the primal scenes."[71] Finally, in a letter at the end of the same month, he summarized his new conclusion briefly and explicitly: "Remembering is never a motive but only a method—a mode. The first motive force, chronologically, for the formation of symptoms is libido. Thus symptoms are *fulfillments of wishes*, just as dreams are."[72]

When Freud wrote this, he still held to the seduction theory. But whether or not he realized it consciously, the wish-fulfillment theory had already rendered the seduction hypothesis untenable. The latter was based on the assumptions of the fundamental sexual passivity of the child and the essentially unpleasurable nature of the seduction experience. Hallucinatory wish-fulfillment, however, depended upon previous experiences of gratification, which must have been preceded

[69] *Ibid.*, pp. 196-197. Letter of May 2, 1897.
[70] *Ibid.*, p. 197.   [71] *Ibid.*, p. 196.
[72] *Ibid.*, p. 200. Letter of May 31, 1896.

by desires. From the patient's wish-fulfillment phantasies of early childhood sexual experiences it followed theoretically that as an infant he had had sexual impulses. Such a conclusion made necessary a theory of universal infantile sexuality.

It was at this point that Freud embarked on his self-analysis. From the account up to now it is clear that theoretical considerations played a fundamental role in initiating this venture. Essentially Freud turned to self-analysis to test a hypothesis that could only have been worked out on other, theoretical, grounds.[73]

That Freud already had an alternative theory at hand seems to be borne out by the equanimity with which a few months later, in September 1897, he reported to Fliess that he no longer believed his patients' tales of seduction. Though his great aetiological achievement—the discovery of the cause of neurosis in infantile seduction—seemed to be in ruins, he was able to tell Fliess cheerfully, "between ourselves I have a feeling more of triumph than of defeat (which cannot be right)."[74] But it was. For a brief moment, Freud did toy with the possibility that later (adult) traumatic experiences were causative and gave rise to phantasies that "throw back on childhood."[75] It was true that the original rationale for placing the basic causal event in childhood—the need to give a theoretical account of pathological defense—was no longer very compelling if the clinical evidence for the occurrence of any such event could not be trusted. Nevertheless, the theoretical demands of the concept of hallucinatory wish-fulfill-

[73] The reference is to the theoretical concept of unconscious infantile phantasy, which will be analyzed in more detail below. But this was true even for the purely clinical parts of the theory. As Freud wrote to Fliess at a point when his self-analysis had reached one of its numerous temporary blocks: "I can only analyse myself with objectively acquired knowledge (as if I were a stranger); self-analysis is really impossible." (*Origins*, Letter of Nov. 14, 1897, p. 234.) It should also be noted that Freud apparently discovered the Oedipus complex first in his patients and only later in himself. *Origins*, pp. 207, 223.

[74] *Ibid.*, p. 217. Letter of Sept. 21, 1897.

[75] *Ibid.*, p. 216.

ment could not be gainsaid. Phantasies with infantile content appeared to demand infantile gratifications. Less than two months later, on November 14, Freud sent to Fliess with mock fanfare the first outline of his theory of infantile sexuality and symptom formation, complete with the concepts of abandoned oral and anal erotogenic zones, regression, and reaction formation.[76]

Though there was much filling in of detail left to be done, the psychoanalytic theory of the meaning of neurotic symptomatology had in essence been completed. A few months later, Freud was to drop his self-analysis and start work on his theory of dreams, the full explication of which had only now become possible. The time has come, therefore, to examine the nature of the new theory more closely.

(1) The concept of neurotic symptoms as wish-fulfillments of infantile wishes involved a reconciliation between the recognition that what was defended against in neurotic behavior was an impulse rather than a memory, and the conclusion, based on the material of free association, that the ideational content related to the symptom derived from traumatic events of the past that had been repressed. The theory of hallucinatory wish-fulfillment made such a reconciliation possible by locating the wish that was being fulfilled in the patient's current life literally *in his past*; this idea was in turn made possible by the physical model of the *Project*, which reified time and allowed the past to co-exist as a thing in the present. The wish was infantile, not in a metaphorical or normative, but in a literal, sense.

It has been suggested that an essential aspect of Freud's concept of unconscious motivation was his redescription of abnormal behavior in terms of (unconscious) purpose. According to this analysis, the concept of unconscious motive compressed into one notion both the cause *behind* the neurotic symptom, in terms of childhood events, and the purpose

[76] *Ibid.*, pp. 229-234.

in the symptom, in terms of present behavior. It is possible, therefore, to unpack the term "unconscious motive" and distinguish between present purposes and intentions, on the one hand, and infantile causes, on the other.[77] This is certainly one way in which logical sense could be made of the concept. Nevertheless, this account ignores the nature of the wish that is being fulfilled. The concept of phantasy wish-fulfillment was a peculiar hybrid that blurred the distinction between description and explanation because it was based on an initial denial of the meaningful, intentional nature of neurotic behavior in a current context. In its classical form, the theory held that neurotic behavior had no reference, whatever the appearances, to the current environment, to the people or objects to which it seemed addressed, or for that matter to the adult subject himself in interaction with his contemporaneous world.[78] The meaninglessness of behavior in terms of current rationality or purposiveness was summarized in the concept of primary process functioning.

It is in a sense unfortunate that Freud first worked out his theory systematically in the case of dreams, which in the very nature of things dealt with phenomena isolated from social intercourse. Nevertheless, the issue of the relationship of past to present was an important one in dream interpretation because material from the daily life of the dreamer provided

[77] MacIntyre, *The Unconscious*, pp. 61-62.

[78] An exceptionally clear statement of this can be found in the explanations Freud gave to his patient in the "Rat Man" case. "The unconscious, I explained, *was* the infantile; it was that part of the self which had become separated off from it in infancy, which had not shared the later stages of its development, and which had in consequence become *repressed*. In the further course of our conversation I pointed out to him that he ought logically to consider himself as in no way responsible for any of these traits in his character; for all of these reprehensible impulses originated from his infancy, and were only derivative of his infantile character surviving in his unconscious; and he must know that moral responsibility could not be supplied to children." (*S.E.*, Vol. x, pp. 177, 185.) The obvious importance of this kind of theoretical attitude for therapy will be discussed later.

much of the manifest content for most dreams. Despite the appearance of wishes from the contemporary life of the subject in his dreams, Freud insisted that "*a wish* which is represented in a dream must be an infantile one."[79] In one of the key formulations of *The Interpretation of Dreams* Freud defined a dream as "*a substitute for an infantile scene modified by being transferred on to a recent experience.*"[80] The repressed infantile wish could gain access to consciousness only by transferring its energy to recent ideas already in the preconscious; these latter were essentially nothing but covers for the repressed wish.[81] Once they had been cathected by energy from unconscious wishes, however, even preconscious ideas, which were originally perfectly coherent and rational, "of no less validity than normal thinking,"[82] could not gain access to consciousness until they underwent severe distortion. This distortion stripped the ideas of any vestige of rationality: they were abandoned by the secondary process and discharged their energy in a primary process resulting in the "irrational" ideational forms of displacement and condensation. The key point about primary process discharge was that it was an unmotivated, mechanical, and hence random process in which such associative connections as did appear were in the form of chance similarities of words, sounds, or images. The real meaning of the dream, however, was not even in the rationally reconstructed dream thoughts but in the unconscious infantile wish that had "attached" itself to them.[83]

How this interpretive structure worked in the case of neurotic behavior can be seen in Freud's explanation of impotence.[84] The neurotic was unable to feel sexual desire for the women he loved and unable to love women for whom he

---

[79] Freud, *S.E.*, Vol. v, p. 553.   [80] *Ibid.*, p. 546.

[81] *Ibid.*, p. 662.   [82] *Ibid.*, p. 597.

[83] Freud, *S.E.*, Vol. xi, pp. 179-190.

[84] It should be noted that Freud's practice did not coincide with his theory. In *The Interpretation of Dreams*, the concealed wishes elucidated from Freud's dreams were usually wishes from his adult life. This discrepancy between theory and practice makes a systematic analysis (and critique) of psychoanalytic theory extremely difficult and is rarely appreciated by philosophical critics of psychoanalysis.

felt sexual desire. According to the theory of unconscious phantasy, the impulses directed at women represented hallucinatory attempted fulfillments of sexual wishes toward the man's mother. To prevent his acting upon them, he suppressed all sexual feelings unless he could degrade the woman as unworthy. This explanation precluded any description of the man's desire for or experience of the woman as a current reality (as distinct from a causal explanation of how he came to experience her in a particular way) or of the current meaning of his wishes (as distinct from an explanation of how these wishes came to be valued by the man). That the woman attracted him because she had certain *general* characteristics valued by the man (characteristics that he might indeed have come to value *because* they originally belonged to his mother); that the honorific definition of a woman—a woman worthy of love—precluded her being a sexual creature; these considerations were elided by the concept of unconscious phantasy.

Freud did point out that anyone suffering from psychic impotence "regards the sexual act basically as something degrading, which defiles and pollutes not only the body,"[85] but the role of general concepts and values was not integrated by Freud into a theory of how past and present, inner and outer, experience were connected. The notion of unconscious phantasy expressed all this by saying that the tabooed sexual desire for the mother was equivalent to or expressed in impotence toward another love object. But if the *general structure* was similar in both cases, it was not correct to say that the inhibited sexual desire for a woman *was* the expression of a desire for the mother according to any ordinary notion of the ways of fulfilling or expressing a desire, including any ordinary way of understanding the notion of a substitute fulfillment.[86]

(2) Nevertheless, psychoanalytic theory held that the desire for the woman was identical with the desire for the

[85] *Ibid.*, p. 186.

[86] On this point see R. K. Shope, "The Psychoanalytic Theories of Wish-Fulfillment and Meaning," *Inquiry*, Vol. x, 1967, pp. 421-438.

mother. This did not mean, however, that the impulse was connected with its expression through such psychological processes as belief and rational calculation. That is to say, it was not the case, according to strict psychoanalytic theory, that the neurotic unconsciously believed that the woman *was* his mother and therefore directed his impulses towards her, or that he rationally defended himself against these impulses by becoming impotent. As we have seen in the discussion of *The Interpretation of Dreams*, Freud held that these processes were not directed by a guiding intelligence but were the results of the primary process functioning of the mental apparatus:

"The irrational processes which occur in the psychic apparatus . . . appear wherever ideas are abandoned by the preconscious cathexis, are left to themselves and can become charged with the uninhibited energy from the unconscious which is striving to find an outlet. . . . these processes which are described as irrational are not in fact falsifications of normal processes—intellectual errors—but are modes of activity of the psychical apparatus that have been freed from an inhibition."[87]

It was not, therefore, a meaningful but a causal connection, transferred from a physiological theory, that was invoked to explain the connection between an impulse or wish and its expression, and between an impulse and the defense mounted against it.[88]

BIOLOGICAL EXPLANATION

The mechanistic framework out of which the psychoanalytic theory of meaning developed had been constructed with

[87] Freud, *S.E.*, Vol. v, p. 605.

[88] R. S. Peters, *The Concept of Motivation*, London, 1958, pp. 62-70, 87-94. It should be pointed out that on this issue, too, Freud's practice was inconsistent with his theory. He frequently spoke as if just such unconscious beliefs as the theory denied were in fact held by neurotics. Contrary to Shope, it is not at all rare for analysts to talk about such beliefs on the part of their patients.

the purpose of explaining man as a biological organism: the endogenous sources of the energy whose impingement initiated reflex discharge were the biological needs, hunger and sex. In his original energy model, however, Meynert had denied the need for a separate category of instinct in the explanation of behavior, and, while the genetic viewpoint was central to his explanation of learning and regression, he did not develop it separately from his mechanical account of cortical functioning. Two related developments now caused Freud to turn explicitly to a more purely biological conceptual framework. The discovery of the varieties of sexual experience in neurosis created the need to introduce some sort of qualitative differentiation into the previously exclusively quantitative conception of sexual energy, and the integrally related concept of infantile sexuality demanded a developmental schema to relate it to adult sexuality. The language of instincts, genetic development, and evolution was joined to the mechanistic terminology in the conceptual structure of psychoanalytic theory.

As with mechanical explanation, the question must be raised of what Freud was trying to explain in resorting to such biological categories as instinct and what kind of explanation it was. It might be supposed that once psychoanalysis had become, even in the special sense discussed in the last section, a theory of meaning, there would be no reason to borrow a conceptual framework from another specialized discipline. The ordinary language concepts of desire, intention, and wish, it would seem, would have been totally adequate to account for at least normal infantile and adult behavior, while the concept of unconscious phantasy called for a different mode of the same categories and not a different order of category. Yet though Freud expressed his full awareness of the external, abstract, and conventional nature of such theoretical organizing categories as instinct,[89] and even spoke deprecatingly of his instinct theory as a "mythology,"[90] he had no

89 Freud, S.E., Vol. xiv, pp. 117-118.
90 Freud, S.E., Vol. xxii, p. 95.

sense of going outside the legitimate logical limits of one discipline to borrow from another. In the first place, it was perfectly natural for him as a doctor of the late nineteenth century to think of man as an organism, for which meaningful activity was synonymous with fulfillment of objective life-needs. But, beyond this, the all-pervasive influence of Darwinism, which had captured much of German thinking just before Freud's formative years, had elevated the biological viewpoint into a comprehensive world-view.

It is impossible to discuss here in any detail why and how Darwinism came to exercise a cultural influence in late nineteenth-century Europe far beyond its legitimate scope as a scientific hypothesis.[91] Like all systems that so succeed, it performed the functions of giving an ultimate account of human origins and destiny while justifying the values and interests of different social and national groups, without appearing to do so, by rooting them in a trans-human scheme of necessity. Specifically, by assimilating man to the animal, Darwinism offered a unified total conception of human behavior, grounded not in supernatural religion or in a mythical state of nature but in the imperatives of eternal Nature: survival and preservation of the species.

The content of the phantasies, emotions, and impulses of Freud's patients presented him with material that was an irruption into the contemporary moral universe. It was common in the medical science of the day to regard sexual aberrations as symptoms of nervous degeneracy. In the first of his *Three Essays on Sexuality*, however, Freud suggested that the sexual instinct might not be a simple thing but that it was put together from components that had separated in the so-called sexual perversions.[92] What he did by biologizing sexual deviations as "component instincts" was somewhat analogous to the neurologists' reduction of mental illness to organic disease, but in reverse. The categorization of deviations as in-

[91] For a dimension of this influence that is crucial for the thesis of this work, see chapter four, pp. 181-184.

[92] Freud, *S.E.*, Vol. VII, p. 162.

stincts integrated socially unacceptable and unintelligible behavior, now, however, shown by Freud's own work to be purposive, into intelligible categories bearing the authoritative imprimatur of science. Because the range of the permissible is an important determinant of the range of the thinkable, this was an important step. Labeling deviant behavior as instinctual exorcised the stigma of the judgment of abnormality, with its connotations of the unhuman and unknown, and gave men a handle on it, by subsuming it under familiar categories. The first of the *Three Essays* was essentially an essay in persuasive definition, an attempt to expand the definition of normal sexuality in the honorific sense, with the argument that common sexual practice was marked by omnipresent deviations from the rigid norm of heterosexual genital union. The rejection, therefore, of certain forms of sexual conduct as perversions was purely conventional, determined not by empirical observation of statistical norms or "laws of nature" but by feelings of loathing. Freud was fighting a battle on two fronts: on the one hand, he wanted to shock his contemporaries into recognizing themselves; on the other hand, he wished to assuage them by having them recognize Nature. The ambivalence of this position was summarized by Freud himself on another occasion: "we are not as rational as we thought we were but we are not as unnatural as our irrationality makes us seem."

Freud's instinct theory was an attempt to integrate biological, physiological, and psychological perspectives. Like the concept of primary process derived from the theory of reflex functioning, the concept of instinct was not intended to be one of essentially human meaning or motivation; it belonged to an independent systematic construct. Its ultimate reference was not to the purposes of the individual but to those of Nature; instinctual behavior was seen from the point of view of its biological function, an external perspective not logically congruent with the purposes of an individual.[93] Instincts,

[93] For an extended discussion of this point see C. Taylor, *The Explanation of Behavior*, New York, 1964, pp. 221-223.

59

however, had to be grounded organically, in keeping with Freud's view of the nature of the forces at work within the organism; thus he defined an instinct as "the psychical representative of an endosomatic, continuously flowing source of stimulation"[94] and as "a concept on the frontier between the mental and the somatic."[95] This meant that instincts had subjective correlatives in "body feelings"; they were thus translatable into motivational terms as a striving for "organ pleasure," or an avoidance of physical pain.

The concept of instinct circumscribed any analysis of the nature and content of human motivation. In his use of ordinary language Freud recognized the widest range of emotions and desires; when he wished to explain them, however, the preconceptions of this theoretical framework forced him to reduce them to, or define them in terms of, the teleologically oriented biological drives or the subjective quest for organ pleasure. Whatever the phenomenological significance, it made no theoretical difference when Freud insisted that the psychoanalytic concept of sexuality should not be interpreted narrowly but must be understood to include everything generally included in the term love; so far as basic theory was concerned, love had to be defined as aim-inhibited sexuality. In a similar manner, other forms of behavior were squeezed into the straight-jacket of the instinctual categories. Idealization of the lover was seen as an extension of sexual attraction; the desire to subjugate was explained in terms of its biological significance as an expression of the need to overcome the resistance of the sexual object by means other than the process of wooing.[96] Finally, terms such as sublimation were required to designate "instinctual" behavior which wasn't instinctual.

The designation of repressed material as meaningful and natural raised the question of the criteria by which perverse

94 Freud, S.E., Vol. VII, p. 168.
95 Freud, S.E., Vol. XIV, p. 122.
96 Freud, S.E., Vol. VII, pp. 157-158.

behavior could be judged pathological. In the *Three Essays* Freud introduced the concepts of exclusiveness and fixation as indices of pathology. These concepts contained the seeds of a conception of health based, not on biological considerations, but on a notion of freedom and openness that emphasized not the content but the mode of the activity. Nevertheless, the full implications of the new criteria were avoided. They would have stigmatized any fixed, repetitive form of behavior—even a predominantly genital sexuality—as pathological and would have opened the gates for polymorphous perversity. Another criterion, however, was operative simultaneously to forestall such a possibility: the behavior in question was seen not only as fixated but as regressive.

The concept of unconscious phantasy had already placed the impulses at the heart of neurosis in the past. A developmental scheme functioned to keep them there. The concept of regression both kept psychoanalysis within a biological framework and maintained the value judgments whose basis in nature might have been undercut with the redefinition of normality in the first of the *Three Essays*. The two functions were in fact integrally connected. One way of grounding the condemnation of the repressed impulses in something more solid than loathing, once they had been admitted as natural, was to allocate them to an early and passing stage of development. Thus the ontogenetic approach not only preserved human dignity by legitimizing "unnatural" and unsocial impulses but preserved specific values by characterizing these impulses as stages to be naturally outgrown.

The model for this scheme was the unfolding of plant and animal organisms to their predetermined maturity. With the end state taken as the norm, the ontogenetic model of explanation involved locating a particular configuration as a stage in the total developmental process, i.e., its relation to its end state. This mode of thinking was second nature to anyone trained in the biological sciences. Its application to psychology and psychopathology was the work of the British neurologist J. H. Jackson, who transferred the notion of development from organs to "functions"—meaningful human behavior viewed from the perspective of biological utility. Jackson's doctrine of psychophysical parallelism, which defined the psychic as a "dependent concomitant" of the physical, permitted the transference of concepts appropriate to material organs and organic development to the reified human activities they subtended. In attempting to explain speech disorders, Jackson had introduced Herbert Spencer's principles of cosmic evolution, integration and disintegration, or involution and disinvolution, as Jackson called them, into his theory of mental functioning. As the nervous system matured, the various mental functions such as the "speech apparatus" became more complex and hence delicate. When the nervous system was damaged, the speech apparatus returned to a primitive mode of functioning, the latest developing and most complex functions being the first to suffer. Thus, the types of aphasia were interpreted as cases of varying degrees of the functional disinvolution, or retrogression, of a highly organized function to levels that corresponded to earlier stages of its development.

Freud had used Jackson's ideas in his own book *On Aphasia* (1891) to attack brain localization theories of speech disorders. In *The Interpretation of Dreams* the concept of regression was introduced to describe the hallucinatory character of dreams as a return to the biologically prior mode of functioning of the mental apparatus. In the *Three Essays* it became the basis for his account of sexual aberrations in adulthood. Despite his statement that "the limits of disgust are . . . often purely conventional,"[97] which seemed to imply that traditional normal sexual practice was a social form, Freud re-biologized it by defining normal genital sexuality as the natural culmination of an organic development whose earlier stages were what in the adult were called the sexual aberrations. This involved a subtle confusion between the biological ripening of a specific organic capacity and the

[97] *Ibid.*, p. 158.

valuation of one physically possible mode of behavior as the only proper one. The socialization of sexuality was evaded by the teleological biological judgment that the sexual instinct after puberty "becomes subordinated to the reproductive function,"[98] and even more explicitly by the assertion that the obstacles to perverse sexuality were organically determined, fixed by heredity, and capable of occurring without any help from education.[99] It was thus possible to characterize deviant forms of sexuality as regressions of the sexual function to an earlier mode of functioning or, if the individual had never engaged in genital sexuality, as inhibitions of full development and fixations at early stages.

Freud's statement that "We are thus led to regard any established aberration from normal sexuality as an instance of developmental inhibition and infantilism" was not an explanation but a programmatic announcement, a normative judgment. When, in fact, he tried to explain why adults engaged in regressive behavior, he fell back on tautologies such as the constitutional strength of the component instincts compared with genital sexuality, or on mechanical metaphors deriving from the original neurological theory. According to these, libido that was prevented from normal discharge because of external frustration or because of repression acted like water in a stream whose main bed had become blocked. It flowed into "collateral channels," paths of discharge laid down in the past but up to now empty.[100] So far as the ultimate explanation of fixation was concerned, this was not a psychological problem at all: "the work of psychoanalysis," Freud wrote, "comes to a stop; it leaves that problem to biological research."[101]

In the *Three Essays on Sexuality*, Freud had interpreted the contents of the repressed in instinctual terms. Though he had spoken of the repressing forces as innate, biologically rather than socially determined, he had not explicitly attrib-

[98] *Ibid.*, p. 207.
[99] *Ibid.*, pp. 137-138.
[100] *Ibid.*, p. 170.
[101] Freud, *S.E.*, Vol. xii, p. 318.

63

uted a biological function to them. The repressing forces were still described in exclusively phenomenological terms as shame, disgust, and morality. This gap in the theory was made up in a short article on psychogenic disturbance of vision published in 1910.[102] There, psychic conflict was described as conflict between the sexual instincts, which aim at the attainment of sexual pleasure, and the ego-instincts, which aim at the self-preservation of the individual. In saying this, Freud was not saying that human beings consciously intended to promote their own welfare in exercising moral restraints or that the effects of their moral intentions were such as to accomplish this result. The theoretical point of view was biological and teleological, not motivational, but the effect was reductive because he made no distinction between the two: shame, disgust, and morality were interpreted in utilitarian terms as instruments for survival.

Freud did not advance any arguments in the essay to support this position. The one point he did make—that suppression of the component instinct made possible the dominance of genital sexuality—was on behalf of the propagation of the species, not the survival of the individual. The suppression of phantasy in the interests of reality-testing was certainly necessary for survival, as Freud was to point out a few years later in defining the reality principle,[103] but phantasy was not the object of shame, disgust, and morality that he usually had in mind. What he did have in mind was indicated by the reiteration of the opposition between the needs of sexuality and the needs of civilization, which he had explored in detail in the essay "Civilized Sexual Morality and Modern Nervous Illness." In citing the needs of civilization as expressions of the ego-instincts, Freud reasserted the ambivalence of his concerns. The defense of society was a defense of the individual on two counts: the surrender of aggression by all made existence safer for each, and the incest taboo was a device to promote wider social units against family introversion and

---

102 Freud, *S.E.*, Vol. IX, p. 209.   103 Freud, *S.E.*, Vol. XII, p. 213.

thus facilitate the social cooperation necessary for self-preservation. Yet, in defending society, Freud was defending the achievements of culture and civilization against the individual, the sacrifice of personal gratification for higher values. Biologizing repression thus reified the values of nineteenth-century liberalism, which included a characteristic ambivalence between individual autonomy, on the one hand, and social harmony and higher values, on the other.

The pseudo-motivational category of ego-instinct was not sufficient in itself to account for the content or the form of the repressive forces. Freud explicitly rejected the idea of an innate aversion to incestuous intercourse;[104] the horror of incest was not instinctual. This created one problem. Morality was imposed by parents and accepted by children prior to any experience in which its utility could have been learned. Since it was not instinctual, its origin required explanation. A second problem was created by the fact that morality was imposed and accepted without any knowledge of its real point, its biological utility. Phenomenologically, moral commands and prohibitions were generally expressed, not in terms of the exigencies of life, but in universal and prescriptive maxims, the violation of which led to a sense of guilt. Within the framework of instinct theory there was no place either for the categorical form of morality or for the accompanying phenomenon of guilt that transcended the natural consequences of failure to obey the demands of reality.

Evolutionary theory suggested a solution to the first problem by direct analogy and to the second one by an illegitimate extension of evolutionary thinking. Though *Totem and Taboo*, Freud's first and most important anthropological venture, was not intended as a contribution to psychoanalytic theory but as an example of how the theory could illuminate problems in other fields, his anthropology and his Lamarckianism were not accidental excrescences on psychoanalysis.

[104] Freud, *S.E.*, Vol. XIV, pp. 123-124.

He was driven to them by the logic of his biological assumptions and his mode of questioning. If men displayed a response that was not instinctual but that had not been learned in an appropriate situation either, it seemed necessary to assume that at some point in his evolution man had developed that response in a real situation and that it was then transmitted by heredity. The response would thus have no intrinsic meaning to later generations and could not be described in terms of their own motivations and intentions. Phylogenetic interpretation proceeded at a level completely independent of the concrete psychology of the subject.

The specific form of explanation Freud used in *Totem and Taboo* was familiar to him from his pre-psychoanalytic work in biology and physiology. Under the aegis of Carl Gegenbaur, one of the earliest and most influential Darwinians in Germany, much of the study of biology in the middle and later decades of the nineteenth century was concerned with the problem of origins, the discovery of so-called "primal types" out of which the anatomical forms of higher species had developed. The ultimate purpose of this quest was to determine the mutual relationship of the different life-forms and thus to affirm the unity and continuity of all life. The principal branch of investigation in the enterprise was comparative anatomy; Gegenbaur and his school sought to discover homologies of structure between the organs of different species and then postulated the existence of certain primal forms as the origins of these developments. The primal forms were either speculative reconstructions of no longer existing forms which were the ancestors of present ones, or anatomical forms of existing lower species, such as the shark's cranium, elevated into an archetype from which the same part in all higher vertebrates must have been derived. A structure in some species was considered to be explained if it could be inserted into the evolutionary chain between archetype and present or higher form. Freud's work on the Petromyzon in Brücke's Physiological Laboratory, in which he interpreted the mysterious Reissner cells in the spinal cord of the primitive fish as primitive forms of the spinal ganglion cells in higher vertebrates, was carried out essentially along these lines.

In *Totem and Taboo*, Freud did more than reason by analogy from the behavior of children and neurotics to the behavior of primitive man. He assumed a developmental sequence from primitives, taken as chronologically older, to civilized men, in which certain basic behavior patterns underwent modifications through time in the direction of greater rationality. A core pattern remained, however, and instances of its older forms consistently reappeared in modern man. In children this reappearance could be understood as a psychological variant of the principle of ontogeny recapitulating phylogeny. This concept had been put forward by Gegenbaur's pupil Ernst Haeckel; the idea that each individual organism recapitulated the entire life history of the species in its own development was an extension of the primal type notion. Thus children, in their phobic fears of animals, which represented displacements of feelings toward their fathers, reproduced primitive totemism. Though Freud used the Oedipus complex to explain the origins of totemism, he used the child's "primitive" closeness to nature as well as the historical emergence and transmission of totemism to account for the child's use of animals as displacement objects; hence the title of the fourth essay in *Totem and Taboo*, "The Return of Totemism in Childhood." In the case of adult neurotics, Freud considered the reappearance of older patterns a psycho-biological throwback. Neurotics, who, like primitive peoples, suffered from heightened ambivalence toward dead relatives and were forced to produce taboos in their struggle against their own hostile impulses, could "be said to have inherited an archaic constitution as an atavistic vestige."[105] Both explanations ignored the level of subjective meaningfulness and motivation, and gave instead an evolutionary explanation of irrationality—strange beliefs identifying humans with animals, and violently ambivalent emotions.

[105] Freud, *S.E.*, Vol. XIII, p. 66.

The major contribution of *Totem and Taboo* to psycho-analytic theory came in the fourth essay, with the idea of the primal crime, the murder of the father of the primal horde. It was crucial for Freud that the act he hypothesized be historically true; only in this way could he supply a rationale for the irrational, the prohibitions of incest taboo specifically and morality generally. Given the motives of the brothers for slaying the father and the situation resulting from his death, a taboo on incest made perfect sense as a measure to preserve society from anarchy and destruction. Freud also postulated that with the primal crime, "A sense of guilt made its appearance."[106] This explanation of the origins of guilt, however, was far more problematic than that of the incest taboo; the two were not symmetrical.

As a prudential measure, a taboo on incest was intelligible under the circumstances. But given the initial emotions and considerations of the brothers, a sense of guilt was not. Out of love, need, the remorse for loss and the anger at self generated by these emotions, it was impossible to derive a sense of guilt experienced as the transgression of transcendent norms; the sense of guilt *presupposed* such non-utilitarian norms. One possible explanation of Freud's error here is that he confused the problem of explaining guilt feelings for acts actually committed with that of explaining guilt feelings for mere thoughts and wishes. The existence of guilt for mere wishes was one of the empirical findings of psychoanalysis and it flew in the face of the normal social expectation about guilt with which Freud had begun his work. By postulating an actual historical act of murder against the father at the dawn of history, he lent substance to the guilt feelings involved in the adult Oedipus complex: "In the beginning was the Deed."[107] Conflating this explanation with that of guilt it-

[106] *Ibid.*, p. 143.

[107] Corroboration for this can be seen in Freud's insistence that even contemporary neurotics are not defending themselves only against physical reality but that "historical reality has a share in the matter." *S.E.*, Vol. XIII, p. 161.

self, Freud could perhaps feel that by finding an original deed he had explained the origin of guilt.

One problem in his explanation that Freud was aware of was that of the transmission of an emotional disposition to guilt to generations that had not committed the act that had given rise to it. Here Freud was forced to assume a version of Lamarckianism, a doctrine that had been resuscitated and popularized by Haeckel. The explanation for the persistence of the original guilt and the morality and religion they had created could only be "the inheritance of psychic dispositions."[108] Thus yet again, on the phylogenetic level Freud's explanations omitted a consideration of meaningful phenomena in terms of individual intentionality and motivation.

[108] *Ibid.*, p. 158.

CHAPTER TWO

The Background of the Existential Critique

THE historical background of the existential critique of psychoanalysis was the attack against positivism mounted toward the end of the nineteenth century. The link is to be found in the early writings of Ludwig Binswanger, the Swiss psychiatrist who introduced the idea of existential analysis. The works of his pre-existentialist period were concerned with the theoretical and methodological issues involved in the debate about the nature of the human sciences that preoccupied continental philosophy in the decades before the First World War. Indeed, Binswanger is an interesting figure in twentieth-century intellectual history not only for his own contributions but because his work faithfully reflected so many of the different facets and stages of the subjectivist trend in European philosophy and psychology. To a certain extent this represented the eclecticism of the auto-didact, but it also showed both the basic continuity and the underlying meaning of the subjectivist current of thought.

Binswanger's intellectual aim throughout his life was the conceptual clarification of the theoretical structure of psychiatry. Behind it lay the more fundamental goal of humanizing psychiatry by giving it an autonomous foundation in a unified psychology of the person. Contemporary psychiatry, he felt, largely ignored the level of meaning, the beliefs and intentions, of the mentally ill, in favor of physiological explanations that presupposed the meaninglessness of their utterances and behavior. To look for the physical causes of psychic disturbances, however, was to go about things in a

70

backwards manner: ". . . the question is whether, on the contrary, the investigation of the person is not the first and most pressing goal of psychiatry and whether, starting from this point, the other still more or less indispensable methods of research [i.e., the physical] cannot be arranged in a sensible order of precedence."[1]

Though these concerns were not articulated until after he met Freud, they help to explain why Binswanger, committed by family background and education to academic psychiatry,[2] was attracted to psychoanalysis during the very period it came under violent public attacks from psychiatric orthodoxy. Binswanger became acquainted with Freud's work through Jung, under whom he was serving in 1906 as a volunteer physician in the Burghölzli clinic in Zurich; he accompanied Jung on the latter's first visit to Freud in February 1907. Strongly impressed by the man and his work, Binswanger began analyzing patients; he published his first case study in the opening volume of the first psychoanalytic periodical, the *Jahrbuch für Psychoanalyse*.[3] (The analysis was carried out in the clinic at Jena whose director was Ludwig's uncle, Otto Binswanger, an eminent psychiatrist and author of a prestigious monograph on hysteria. It was the first analysis done in a German psychiatric clinic.) In an evaluation written a few years later Binswanger based his claim for Freud's importance on the grounds that Freud was the first psychiatrist to take psychology seriously and to systematically shift the basis of psychiatry from physical causality to "pure" or subjective psychology. The great achievement of psychoanalysis was to have proved with its concrete results that

---

[1] L. Binswanger, "Welche Aufgaben ergeben sich für die Psychiatrie aus den Fortschritten der neueren Psychologie?" (1924), *Ausgewählte Vorträge und Aufsätze*, Bd. II, Bern, 1955, p. 139.

[2] Binswanger's family had for some generations run a private sanitarium at Kreuzlingen; Ludwig took over its direction when his father died.

[3] L. Binswanger, "Versuch einer Hysterieanalyse," *Jahrbuch für Psychoanalyse*, 1909.

"Psychiatrists have been far too ready . . . to abandon their belief in the connectedness of psychical processes."[4]

In these early years Binswanger even took up the cudgels on behalf of psychoanalysis against its opponents. The occasion was particularly ironic. In his articles of 1910–1913 and in his *Allgemeine Psychopathologie*, Karl Jaspers had introduced into medical psychology the notion of *Verstehen*, the understanding and interpretation of action in terms of subjective meaningfulness. He specifically contrasted it with the causal explanation of unintelligible behavior in terms of antecedent physiological conditions: motives were internal to actions, whereas causes were separate from them.[5] Understanding and causal explanation were thus two completely different methods of knowing, deployed according to the meaningfulness or lack of it of the psychic manifestations in question. The task of a psychology of meaningful connections, in Jaspers' opinion, was twofold: to extend our understanding to such unusual, remote, and ostensibly incomprehensible phenomena as sexual perversions and instinctual cruelty, and to recognize the universal and in themselves intelligible connections in those psychic states, such as hysterical reaction, determined by abnormal mechanisms.[6] It might seem that this approach would have made Jaspers an admirer of psychoanalysis and Binswanger an eager philosophical ally of Jaspers. In fact, however, despite a certain admiration for Freud, Jaspers saw little that was original in his work and thought his therapy a secular version of religious confession, his insights a vulgarized edition of the profounder *verstehende* psychology of Nietzsche. Moreover, he felt that Freud had overstepped the limitations of the method of *Verstehen*. *Verstehen* was based on empathy, our ability to understand the behavioral manifestations of others

---

[4] L. Binswanger, "Psychologische Tagesfragen innerhalb der klinischen Psychiatrie," *Zeitschrift für die Gesamte Neurologie und Psychologie*, Bd. 26, 1914, p. 574.

[5] K. Jaspers, *Allgemeine Psychopathologie*, Berlin, 1913, p. 146.

[6] *Ibid.*, p. 152.

because of their similarity with our own; whole ranges of the mental life of the mentally ill were therefore necessarily shut off from the comprehension of the normal man.[7]

In his first theoretical articles, Binswanger took issue with Jaspers on two points. Jaspers' conception of causality, he argued, was much too narrow. Psychological events could also have psychological causes—to have discovered such causes was precisely Freud's great contribution to psycholgy—and only by including them was a *science* of psychology, a body of laws about psychic events, at all possible. Second, Jaspers was wrong in closing off human experience a priori from any possibility of understanding. Psychoanalysis had shown that there was no absolute barrier between normality and illness, and had broadened human understanding of the psychic life of neurotics in precisely an empathic sense.[8]

Even in the days of his most enthusiastic apprenticeship, however, Binswanger's allegiance to psychoanalysis was never total. The reasons for this were both personal and theoretical. Binswanger's father and uncle represented establishment psychiatry; his uncle in particular was an opponent of psychoanalysis. Ludwig himself had received a solid academic training in preparation for taking over the medical directorship at Kreuzlingen (which he did on his father's death in 1910). Under the circumstances of the establishment's hostility to Freud, Binswanger's involvement with psychoanalysis was unusual enough (his announcement upon assuming the directorship that psychoanalysis would be included among the therapeutic methods employed at Bellevue created a furor), and it is hardly surprising that he tempered it by downgrading psychoanalysis to the dimensions of a "branch of psychiatry."

[7] *Ibid.*, pp. 153, 323.

[8] L. Binswanger, "Bemerkungen zu der Arbeit Jaspers' 'Kausale und verständliche Zusmamenhänge zwischen Schicksal und Psychose bei der Dementia praecox,'" *Internationale Zeitschrift für Ärztliche Psychoanalyse*, 1913, I, p. 387.

Binswanger's identification with orthodox psychiatry was a major source both of Freud's interest in him and his constant irritation with him. Freud saw Binswanger as a "link to academic psychiatry,"[9] an entering wedge into the world of university clinics and sanatoria, a means by which psychoanalysis might be made more respectable there. But he was often annoyed at what he regarded as Binswanger's tendency to "tread too softly" in the promotion and defense of psychoanalysis. At one point he accused Binswanger of a public attitude to psychoanalysis similar to that of someone from respectable society apologizing to his equals for mentioning his relations with an inferior whom he finds useful for various reasons.[10] Binswanger repudiated the social analogy, but there was more to it than a figure of speech. The staid, conservative, Protestant Swiss adherents of Freud always looked down on the informal, erratic, and excitable Jews of the Vienna Society, and the discomfort of the former with Freud's emphasis on the "lower" functions was to show up as much in Binswanger's later emphasis on the autonomy of *Geist* as in Jung's desexualization of the libido and his interest in religion.

These considerations, however, do not diminish the significance of Binswanger's theoretical reservations about psychoanalysis. Despite his high estimation of psychoanalysis as a therapeutic tool, he felt uneasy about its philosophical grounding, the nature of its conceptual structure and its presuppositions. It was obvious that Freud had not abandoned the notion of a "psychophysical apparatus" and that the central theoretical concept of psychoanalysis—instinct—was biological rather than psychological. Binswanger could not, therefore, hold up psychoanalysis to academic psychiatry as an unproblematic model of a person-centered psychology. When he embarked on his project of acquiring the scientific and philosophical background he felt he lacked for the task of assessing the relationship between psychiatry and psycho-

[9] L. Binswanger, *Erinnerungen an Sigmund Freud*, Bern, 1956, p. 48.
[10] *Ibid.*, p. 32.

analysis,[11] he was thus faced with two problems: the first was to work out a set of categories and methodological concepts adequate to a science of persons, a *Personenwissenschaft*, as a distinct and rigorous discipline; the second was to undertake a critique of the foundations of psychoanalysis on the basis of the new concepts.

The work went slowly; a book dealing with the first problem did appear in 1922, but the second volume, which was to have dealt with psychoanalysis, was never published because Binswanger, on encountering Heidegger's work, came to feel that his initial positions were inadequate. Nevertheless, they are worth examining both because they deal with live issues in the explanation of behavior—indeed, they anticipate much contemporary discussion of the subject—and because they show the continuity with his later work.

Binswanger's *Introduction to the Problems of General Psychology* was essentially a critical survey of recent work in philosophical psychology, with a view to extracting from it a core that might serve as the basis for a humanistic psychology. His philosophical starting point was the Neo-Kantian analysis of concept-formation in the sciences. Rickert had argued that the subject-matter, or object, of a science was not simply copied from nature but was rather a complex mental construct. The formulation of this construct was closely related to the kinds of questions raised and the kinds of explanations looked for by the investigator; these were in turn related to some specific purpose.

Binswanger applied this analysis to psychology. He began with what he called the natural-scientific presentation of psychic phenomena exemplified by the "founders of modern psychology"—Lotze, Fechner, Helmholtz, Wundt, and Bleuler—but also by their predecessors Herbart in Germany, Taine in France, and Hobbes, Hume, and the associationists in Britain. Their approach was to attempt to explain psychic

[11] Binswanger had no formal training in psychology or philosophy.

events as the product of certain assumed, more basic elements and the laws of their appearance and succession. More generally their aim was to establish causal generalizations about the antecedent conditions of psychic events. Considering psychic events as nothing but the effects of antecedent causes necessarily meant, according to Binswanger, no longer treating them as they were given in "immediate experience" but as reified entities, as composites of hypothetical "sensations" or "representations."[12] Binswanger then reviewed the charges brought against this conception of psychology in the preceding decades by Dilthey, Rickert, Bergson, James, Brentano, Natorp, and others: the reification of the psyche ignored the unity, uniqueness, and concrete individuality of psychic life, its free, creative character, its nature as a temporal flow, its unquantifiability, and its essential open-endedness. "All objections against a psychology structured along natural-scientific lines," he wrote, "culminate in the demand to come to grips with the eternal basic problem of psychology—the problem of 'subjectivity as such.' . . . [C]onsciousness . . . the immediate experience [*unmittelbare Erleben*] of the agent must be recognized as something distinctive, totally different from the concept of objectivity and appreciated in its independence at least as a problem."[13]

Binswanger's analysis suffered from both the survey approach and its own conceptual fuzziness. He never clearly defined what he meant by "subjectivity as such," nor did he differentiate amongst the types of "psychic events" with which psychology dealt. His argument appeared to be that to give a causal explanation of a psychic phenomenon was necessarily to distort it by denuding it of precisely those characteristics which made it the phenomenon it was. In this form his argument was untenable—he himself had earlier argued the case for law-like generalizations and causal laws against Jaspers. The point he was trying to make, however, was an

12 L. Binswanger, *Einführung in die Probleme der allgemeinen Psychologie*, Berlin, 1922, p. 24.
13 *Ibid.*, pp. 102-103.

important and valid one. It was that to give a causal explanation of a psychic phenomenon was reductive when that
explanation purported to give the necessary and sufficient
conditions of the phenomenon in terms that excluded the
descriptive concepts of meaning, intention, and belief necessary to characterize what was being explained in the first
place. Contemporary psychology eliminated the subject in at
least two ways: it either reduced the psychic to physical
movement or physiological states, or it made the self a merely passive recipient of atomistic external impressions.

In the "act psychology" of Brentano, Husserl, and Natorp,
Binswanger found a conceptual base he thought could make
psychology adequate to the nature of its true object, human
subjectivity. The key was Brentano's concept of the intentional directedness of consciousness, expanded upon in Husserl's phenomenology as the concept of intentionality. According to this concept, consciousness was characterized by
directedness at a content; it was always consciousness of
something—knowledge of something, anger about something,
and so on. The definition of consciousness as intentionally
directed involved two important points. In the first place, a
psychic act or event was not fully specifiable without the description of its intentional object; reference to an internal
physical state or to physical movement was insufficient. Secondly, the intentional object was in part constituted by the
intention directed at it. The force of this second point in relation to perception and cognition was that it precluded the notion of data of perception independent of a consciousness that
bestowed meaning on them through specific orientations to
them or through organizing concepts. The self thus had a role
in shaping its knowledge of the world; the world was always
given to consciousness in terms of meaning, never in terms
of purely "objective" stimuli.[14] Just as the same sensory data
could be grasped differently so that they produced different

[14] Binswanger was careful to retain the distinctions made by Husserl
between pure and empirical phenomenology; these distinctions, important
for the understanding of phenomenology, do not concern us here.

perceptual objects, just as, in other words, the same set of events could be characterized under many different descriptions, so also the same object could be perceived through different sets of sensory data. For example, different perspectives on an object yielding different sensory data could still produce the impression of the "same" object.[15]

In Binswanger's view, Husserl's phenomenology gave psychology an object, a task, and a method. The object was the ego constituted as the unified sequence and syntheses of intentional acts. This concept of the self was far broader than the concept of consciousness employed up to then in psychology because it did not limit consciousness to reflective self-consciousness or attention: intentional acts were not necessarily themselves the objects of consciousness. The task of psychology was to work out "the kinds and forms of intentional experiences from the kinds and forms of intentional objects,"[16] in other words, to understand subjective meaningfulness through close phenomenological description of the intentional objects of consciousness. The psychologist was not primarily interested in the intentional object itself, the

[15] Binswanger, *Einführung*, pp. 145-147. The preceding summary has stressed the subjective aspect of Husserl's notion of the constitution of meaning, but the meaning that Husserl was most concerned with in the *Logical Investigations* was objectivity; the problem he was grappling with was the relationship between the subjectivity of knowing and the objectivity of the content of knowledge. How was it that through the constantly changing stream of experiences, marked by temporal flow and different spatial orientations, I perceived the "same" object? For Husserl the answer was the "objectivating act," the intentional act that served as the basis for all others, such as acts of evaluation and emotion. The constitution of objectivity lay, in part but crucially, in the imposition of a criterion of identity, which enabled sensory contents seen at different times and from different angles and under different aspects to be interpreted as the same object. There was thus an important distinction between the meaning as an "ideal unity" and the experiencing of that meaning as an individual, subjective act. On this subject see R. Sokolowski, *The Formation of Husserl's Concept of Constitution*, The Hague, 1964, pp. 37-73.

[16] Binswanger, *Einführung*, p. 164.

meanings in terms of which the world was experienced, but in the meaning-bestowing acts that made the world what it was for the subject; however, it was only insofar as the latter "objectified" themselves that they were knowable.[17]

This conceptualization of psychology raised a fundamental problem of other minds. If access to the objects of consciousness through phenomenological description was the way to psychological knowledge, it appeared that we could have such knowledge only of ourselves. Indeed, traditional theories about the sources of our knowledge of other minds—the association, analogy, and empathy theories—all assumed, Binswanger asserted, that we can perceive directly only our own consciousness and the other's body: the other was constituted as a subject or agent having emotions and intentions only through some form of transference or projection from our experience of ourselves. In principle, then, the other as subject could never be really known; his existence could be assumed and emotions and intentions might plausibly be assigned to him, but they could never be directly observed.

Existing critiques, however, had already shown this view to be internally inconsistent. Against it Binswanger adopted the phenomenological position of Max Scheler.[18] Scheler had challenged the two main assumptions of traditional theories on phenomenological grounds. He argued that we perceive others initially not as bodies animated by minds or psyches whose presence was merely hypothesized or deduced but as unified body-subjects engaged in meaningful activity. He also attacked the assumption that we know our own mental life immediately but that of others only indirectly. Quite the contrary, we could think the thoughts, feel the emotions, and

[17] The interest of the psychiatrist can be seen in this formulation. From the point of view of "normal" experience, the concepts, perceptions, and experiences of the mentally ill were strange. The point of the phenomenological approach was to try to understand the needs and interests that made them what they were.

[18] M. Scheler, *Zur Phänomenologie und Theorie der Sympathiegefühle und von Liebe und Hass. Mit einem Anhang über den Grund zur Annahme der Existenz des fremden Ich*, Halle, 1913.

have the aims of others just as much as we could our own. Indeed, children did this as a matter of course. Initially they were completely absorbed in the conceptual life of the family milieu; only gradually did individual personality emerge from the influence of the thoughts and feelings of the environment, and the process could never be complete. This was because we learned the very meaning of our own behavior from others. Not only did we learn what were appropriate norms, beliefs, and emotions from them; the very conceptualization of our behavior was possible only through language, which was a social process.

Self-knowledge thus presupposed an initial intentional directedness toward others as agents. Scheler referred to this intentional act (somewhat unhappily) as "inner perception" (*innere Wahrnehmung*), by which was to be understood neither introspection nor some mysterious form of intuition, but the interpretation of behavior in terms of meaning, purposes, and intentions rather than of physical movements. So understood, inner perception could be either of others or of oneself. In principle there was no difference between the two, because one depended on the observation of bodily movements neither more nor less than the other. On the one hand, behavior did not have to be grasped first as physical movement or physiological event before it was grasped as meaningful action. The interpretation of something as action was not simply an addition to its description as physical movement, but something conceptually quite different. On the other hand, even with oneself, it was impossible to interpret something as an action unless it had some effect on the condition of the body, i.e., until it was manifested in some form. In this sense, bodily events were necessary, though never sufficient, conditions of the perception of action.

In Scheler's concept of inner perception Binswanger saw the foundation of an autonomous science of psychology independent of the natural sciences, especially biology and physiology. "The point of departure of this psychology," he wrote, "is now no longer the body and physical movements which are 'interpreted' or 'empathized with' one way or another but rather a world of primary mental data accessible to direct observation [*Anschauung*]."[19]

Only later, and even then only in part, did Binswanger become aware of the problematic nature of the concept of "direct knowledge" of the meaning of others' behavior. For it seemed to suggest that one could not be mistaken in interpreting the emotions and intentions of other people. Yet in the next section of his book Binswanger went on to analyze different types of *Verstehen*, pointing out, for example, that there was an important difference between logical and psychological understanding, between understanding the meaning of an utterance and its point for the individual who expressed it. Knowing the first did not automatically mean knowing the second. Moreover, Binswanger also argued that, though at times an observer was better able to understand the point of an agent's behavior than was the agent himself, an agent could in principle always conceal his motives and intentions from an observer, thus making *Verstehen* impossible. This obviously suggested that self-knowledge and knowledge of others were not congruent, and that an agent ultimately had special authority over the knowledge of his own actions. Therefore, direct observation of the meaning of another's action was impossible.

Binswanger also criticized Jaspers' conception of *Verstehen* in such a way as to cast doubt on the notion of an infallible knowledge of others. Jaspers had claimed that a meaningful connection of psychic events, such as that discovered by Nietzsche linking weakness, the will to power, and morality (i.e., *ressentiment* as the meaning of morality), was established on the basis of a self-evident intuition that carried immediate conviction as a "necessity of thought." To Binswanger this was not only wrong but dangerous because it smacked of mysticism and foreclosed all rational argument. Connections such as that demonstrated by Nietzsche were matters of contingent fact discoverable only by observation

---

[19] Binswanger, *Einführung*, p. 242.

81

and comparison. If in a particular case it was asserted that moral principles were held out of *ressentiment*, there had to be behavioral evidence for the claim. It could not be held to be true a priori of moral beliefs in general.

Nevertheless, without a concept of direct inner perception, it appeared that psychology would be thrust back on some form of behaviorism. So, for example, Binswanger also criticized Jaspers' concept of phenomenology or "static understanding," according to which a psychic state, such as anger, could be adequately described without reference to the object or point of the anger, leaving it to genetic understanding, or *Verstehen* proper, to establish the relationship to preceding events. Here Binswanger's argument was that an emotion was not separable from its intentional object; for in order to know that a certain piece of behavior was an expression of anger it had to be grasped as, for example, the reaction to an insult, that is, in its historical context.

In a later article,[20] Binswanger tried to clear up some of the problems left by the confusions and inconsistencies of his *Introduction*, particularly on the issues of causal explanation versus *Verstehen*, and the roles of induction and interpretation in establishing meaning. He now accepted a distinction between *Nacherleben*, the ascertaining of empirical connections among experiences, and *Verstehen*, the disclosure of the meaningful interconnections of the observed sequences of behavior. The essence of scientific *explanation* lay in the inductive establishment of lawful relationships among events; there was no reason why actions could not be generalized about and explained by other events or experiences with which they were seen to be regularly connected. But to establish such regularities about a person's behavior was not necessarily to understand him any better. They made prediction possible, but this was different from the understanding of an experi-

[20] L. Binswanger, "Verstehen und Erklären in der Psychologie," *Zeitschrift für die gesamte Neurologie und Psychiatrie*, Bd. 197, H. 5, 1927.

ence in terms of its "rational appropriateness" to the specific motive of a concrete individual.[21]

In connection with this last point he specifically rejected as inappropriate for psychology both Dilthey's *geisteswissenschaftliches Verstehen* and Weber's concept, adopted by Jaspers, of *Verstehen* on the basis of ideal types. The former was an attempt to understand the individual in terms of supra-individual meanings, as exemplars of objective historical *Geistestypen*. Weber's ideal types were also depersonalizations of individual experience, not only because they were confessedly idealized abstractions from reality but because they overstressed rationality in the sense of rational behavior modelled on market activity (*Zweckrationalität*)[22] and, as Binswanger had insisted, "the irrational, never the rational, ought to be the starting point and goal of psychology."[23]

Binswanger also now distinguished between inner perception, or direct knowledge, and psychological understanding. The first was the act of ascertaining the presence and manifestations of another self, the second the grasping of their meaningful contents. To be presented with the other as person meant to be presented with the problem of understanding him, but not necessarily with its solution, though, in the first instance, conventions of behavior common to observer and observed might give his behavior an immediate intelligibility. It was, however, precisely on the basis of the initial intentional directedness toward the other as person, as engaging in interpersonal discourse, that a preliminary judgment of unintelligibility was possible. Nevertheless, the phenomenological method carried with it the demand to drop the normative attitude to human behavior which equated unin-

[21] *Ibid.*, p. 678.

[22] Binswanger was referring to Weber's position in "Einige Kategorien der verstehenden Soziologie," but even in his later work, where Weber included the possibility of ideal types of irrational behavior, he claimed a higher degree of intelligibility for rational behavior in the sense defined by Binswanger.

[23] Binswanger, *Einführung*, p. 301.

telligibility with meaninglessness and to realize that "the person expresses something about himself in every single experience."[24] To discover that something was the job of psychology.

Even before the *Introduction* was published, Binswanger used the conclusions he had arrived at in a first philosophical confrontation with psychoanalysis. At the Sixth International Psychoanalytical Congress held at The Hague in 1920, he delivered a paper on "Psychoanalysis and Clinical Psychiatry." The signs did not augur well for an enthusiastic reception. As early as 1917, Binswanger had sent Freud a 200-page draft of the book; it was received with polite interest and a sharp question. "What," Freud had asked, "are you going to do about the Ucs. or rather, how will you manage without the Ucs.? Has the philosophical devil got you in his claws after all? Reassure me."[25] That Freud was not reassured by the 1920 paper, Binswanger immediately realized. "After I finished and sat down next to him, he said only these two words: 'Very clear.' Apparently he had expected more."[26] The reasons for Freud's response are obvious. Nevertheless, the paper was interesting as one of the earliest efforts at a systematic conceptual analysis of psychoanalytic theory.

Binswanger recognized a three-tiered structure in psychoanalytic theory, the "personalistic," mechanical, and biological levels. The first level alone marked its superiority to contemporary clinical psychiatry and academic psychology. Unlike the former, which generally began with isolated symptoms and defined them only negatively as deviations from some norm, usually biological, psychoanalysis began with the whole person. Unlike the latter, psychoanalysis did not divide the personality into discrete functions and faculties; its very conception of the centered personality as valuing, as actively

---

[24] L. Binswanger, "Über Phänomenologie," *Ausgewählte Vorträge und Aufsätze*, Bd. I, Bern, 1947, p. 48.

[25] Binswanger, *Erinnerungen*, p. 77.

[26] *Ibid.*, p. 82.

judging the world and itself, made possible the perception of inner conflict as its key insight. Accurate as this assessment was, Binswanger's characterization of this inner conflict was, both in language and emphasis, quite foreign to Freud's thought, and as will be seen, significant for his own: "How man turns and twists in conflicts of conscience . . . how he wishes to stand 'pure,' worthy and righteous before himself, God and the world and yet continuously becomes aware of his 'impurity,' worthlessness, and unrighteousness, how he deceives God, himself and the world to seize at last the phantom of purity—this and nothing else is the basic theme of psychoanalysis."[27]

However, Binswanger continued, Freud was not content with a descriptive psychology; he wanted to go beyond this to develop an explanatory "physics of the mind" [*Seelenmechanik*]. Binswanger did not take the energy model as seriously as Freud himself did. Despite his recognition of its explanatory purpose, he argued that Freud's mechanistic model was different from the systems of Descartes, Hobbes, Spinoza, and Leibniz, which had sought on general metaphysical and methodological grounds to apply the principles of mechanical causality to the mental sphere. For Freud, quantitative or economic considerations were essentially a fictional construction to help conceptualize the radically different functioning of the conscious and unconscious minds. They were secondary and subordinate; they merely served to clarify empirical psychological material and their existence was justified only in those terms. Though there was some warrant for this position in Freud's own writings,[28] it certainly did not accurately picture either the genesis and real content of Freud's theory of meaning, as chapter one has already indicated, or Freud's own explanatory intentions. At the time Binswanger delivered the paper, however, the Fliess correspondence had not yet been discovered and Freud had not

[27] L. Binswanger, "Psychoanalyse und klinische Psychiatrie," *Vorträge*, Bd. II, p. 51.

[28] See, for example, Freud's remarks on theory, *S.E.*, Vol. XIV, p. 117.

yet openly reaffirmed his commitment to physicalistic explanation.[29]

More interesting to Binswanger was the third, the biological, level of psychoanalytic theory. Here, he saw the link with psychiatry and the means by which a value system, a definition of health, was inserted into the purely descriptive psychology of psychoanalysis. The energy of Freud's *Seelenphysik* was that of the biological organism. Thus his economic considerations were biological and teleological rather than psychological, because they were concerned not with the purposes of individual persons but of "nature." Nature's purposes in the distribution of energy in the psychic apparatus were directed toward the procurement of pleasure and the avoidance of pain. These purposes were embodied in the instincts, Freud's key biological concept, whose job was to bridge the metaphysical gap between body and soul. Instinct in Freud's definition was a borderline concept between the psychic and somatic sphere, linking body feelings and desires; through the notion of disturbance of instinctual functioning he sought to explain how psychic conflict could have physical effects. However philosophically unsatisfactory, it was an attempt any branch of psychiatry must make if it were to deal with illness.

Binswanger was unequivocal in his judgment of this form of theorizing in psychology: "I consider it a violation of the idea of personality if it is depersonalized by the application of teleological or natural-law points of view."[30] However, psychiatry was not only psychology; like medicine, it had to have norms of health, and these had to be supplied by biology. The introduction of norms of instinctual performance served both to measure psychic health and to establish a heuristic principle for the investigation of the causes of deviations from it. Thus, in psychoanalysis, illness was determined neither by subjective feelings of lack of well-being nor by deviations from statistical averages of normal behavior. Nor

[29] Freud, *S.E.*, Vol. XVIII, p. 179.
[30] Binswanger, *Vorträge*, Bd. II, p. 56.

did the mere fact of repression by itself determine illness, since it was omnipresent. What mattered was the context in which the mechanisms of repression operated; whether they appeared in harmless activities of everyday life or "in the most important individual or social activities . . . is what distinguishes health from illness . . . rather than the variety or vigor of the symptoms."[31] Thus psychoanalysis, through its biological concepts, introduced constructions that transcended the purely psychological data, but these were necessary for any psychiatric system. Psychoanalysis was the very model of how a scientific psychiatry was constructed.

Binswanger criticized Freud's psychology on only one point in his paper—on Freud's biological characterization of psychic conflict as one between the sexual and ego instincts. This criticism, and its implications for his concept of the person, represented the one concrete consequence of his methodological work.

By and large, the force of his theoretical considerations up to this point had been negative. The exhortations to psychiatry to drop its exclusively critical, judgmental attitude to "symptoms," and to adopt a phenomenological method in order to understand the bizarre utterances and behavior of the mentally ill as expressions of a person, did not lead to any substantive new insights (except for a few isolated, though fascinating, examples of interpretations of individual symptoms).[32] On the whole, Binswanger's concept of the person remained a methodological, hence formal, category, generated by the attack against positivistic thinking in psychology rather than by concrete therapeutic problems.

There was, however, an important exception to this. The phenomenological method demanded the pure description of the phenomena of consciousness, free of any theoretical pre-

---

[31] *Ibid.*, p. 161, quoted from Freud, *The Psychopathology of Everyday Life*.

[32] See, for example, the articles "Welche Aufgaben . . ." and "Über Phänomenologie," cited earlier.

suppositions. Each type of intentional act was autonomous and irreducible to some more fundamental one. It was illegitimate, therefore, to reduce morality to, or derive it from, instinctual impulses. The person was as much a spiritual and ethical as an instinctual creature:

"In psychoanalysis . . . the specifically spiritual in man, his receptivity to the world of values and his attitude towards it, is derived from the purely mechanical conception of the pleasure-unpleasure principle: on the one hand, that is, the concepts of value and pleasure are identified, and on the other hand, the phenomenologically fundamentally different acts of comprehending and sustaining objective values are confused with states of pain and pleasure. This can already be seen in Freud's conception of the essence of the ethical in man as a pleasure-laden striving for a narcissistic ideal of perfection projected beyond the self. With such a conception one can indeed give a genetic explanation for inauthentic ethical attitudes, which is of course of the greatest importance psychologically, but one cannot understand in this way the completely new and qualitatively different aspects which mark off the intentional forms . . . of consciousness constituting the realm of values, from feelings of pain and pleasure."[33]

Binswanger had a valid conceptual point here. But in the context of the times the stress on the moral ego as the essence of personality was a profoundly conservative notion. In this respect, Binswanger typified a major thrust of the idealist revival of the last part of the nineteenth century, most particularly Neo-Kantianism and phenomenology. For all their opposition to one another, both stressed the universal and a priori nature of ideal values. Husserl's phenomenology itself had been born of an attempt to combat psychologism, and relativism in general, by demonstrating that our concepts contained elements of universality, unity, timelessness, and necessity that made them irreducible to empirical generalizations about thought processes or the merely contingent and

[33] Binswanger, "Welche Aufgaben . . . ," p. 143.

ephemeral determinants of historical conditions. Husserl's earlier students applied the phenomenological method to law, ethics, aesthetics, and religion in an attempt to establish the objective and universal validity of concepts and beliefs in these areas.[34] The most influential of them, Max Scheler, aimed at a phenomenological reconstruction of the theory of value generally and ethical theory in particular that would make ethics immune to psychological, sociological, or historical relativism. The phenomenological focus on the direct perception of experience as it was immediately given, undistorted by any theories, functioned in somewhat the same way as the later Wittgensteinian analysis of concepts: the meaning of the particular concept in question was to be found in its particular use, in its intentional form (e.g., as ethical intending), and nothing more was needed to account for it. It could not be critically judged from a standpoint external to it, for that would be to violate its nature as given by pure phenomenological description.

That this general approach had a concrete socio-historical bearing has been effectively demonstrated by Ringer and others.[35] It represented the defense by a beleaguered European bourgeois intellectual stratum of a humanist culture of spiritual values and striving that was coming under attack from within and from without. In this movement Binswanger was a secondary but representative figure. So far as psychoanalysis was concerned, however, his emphasis on the conceptual autonomy of moral concepts and beliefs meant retrogression; it meant a surrender of Freud's insights into the integral relation of morality to repressed desires—indeed, its development in reaction to certain "instinctual" desires—and into the way it embodied the continuation of

[34] H. Spiegelberg, *The Phenomenological Movement*, 2nd ed., The Hague, 1965, Vol. I, pp. 168 ff.

[35] There is an increasing literature on the subject. See, inter alia, J. R. Staude, *Max Scheler, An Intellectual Portrait*, New York, 1967; A. Mitzman, *The Iron Cage*, New York, 1970; and Ringer, *The Decline of the German Mandarins*.

submissive love and parental authority into adulthood. So long as Binswanger's critique remained within this traditional framework, it was unlikely that it would have any fruitful issue, no matter how philosopically sound certain of its elements were. Heidegger's book *Sein und Zeit*, published in 1927, altered or, more accurately, expanded this narrow moralistic view and put the problem of the "person" in a much wider and more fundamental perspective.

BEING AND TIME

There are many ways of characterizing the meaning and significance of Heidegger's *Being and Time*. For our purposes, two are of special importance. From the perspective of intellectual history, *Being and Time* represented the climax of the philosophical current of subjectivism in European thought that had begun in the 1880's, a strange climax, however, which subverted the central intention of the work that preceded it. Heidegger's work also put forward a new concept of irrationality and—however strenuously he would have repudiated this description—a theory of motivation to explain it. The two perspectives are closely connected.

Thinkers such as the Neo-Kantians, Dilthey, Bergson, Weber, Husserl, and Scheler had been concerned to affirm two things against the assumptions and procedures of contemporary science: first, that human subjectivity played a fundamental role in the investigation of the objective natural world and, second, that human subjectivity was itself unique as a possible object of scientific investigation. They had argued that values and concept-formation played vital roles in the natural sciences and all the more so in the human and social sciences. They had challenged the ability of the abstracting and generalizing methods of empiricism, whose aim was to subsume human experience under generalizations and causal laws, to do justice to the individuality, particularity, meaning, and concrete fullness of psychological and cultural expressions, and called instead for one or another form of descriptive method in history, sociology, and psychology. Their critiques took the form of methodological and epistemological treatises. But, in their technical considerations, these men thought they were doing more than methodological criticism: in showing the existence and role in human experience of moral and religious beliefs and intentions, or of aesthetic values, they thought they were also showing the objectivity and universal validity of these beliefs, concepts, or interests. Bergson's intuition, Weber's *Verstehen*, Husserl's *Wesensschau* (intuition of essences), Scheler's *innere Wahrnehmung* were methods that not only ascertained meaning and purpose in experience rather than explain it in terms of external deterministic forces and laws; they were also privileged modes of cognition that established the ideal values and beliefs they ascertained as necessary constituents of human meaningfulness. With these methods the dangers of association and physiological psychology, Darwinism and Marxism, which threatened to reduce the expressions of spiritual life to more basic material or utilitarian substrata, could be overcome.

Heidegger's work presupposed the conclusions of his predecessors. He too began from the idea of the subjective origin of meanings and concepts; indeed, as he saw it, a major purpose of his book was to lay the necessary philosophical foundations for the earlier work of the idealists. But in his hands the Husserlian idea of the subjective origins of the ideal of objectivity[36] turned against the intentions and conclusions of its originator. The deeper exploration of subjectivity shattered any notion of universal, timeless objective meanings, whether prescriptive or descriptive, independent of man's activity in history. If man was necessarily involved in establishing the conditions of meaningfulness, a concept of objectivity that entailed the view of his own role as that of passive observer or supplier of a priori universal categories was false, and its persistence in need of explanation.

Yet, though Heidegger defined his own enterprise at one

[36] See fn. 15.

point as the clarification of the Cartesian *sum*[37]—that is, the clarification of what it means to say "I am"—he rejected any imputation that he was concerned with the self as subject. There were two reasons for this. "Every idea of a 'subject,' " he wrote, "still posits the *subjectum* along with it, no matter how rigorous one's protestations against the 'soul substance' or the 'reification of consciousness.' The Thinghood itself which such reification implies must have its . . . origin demonstrated if we are to be in a position to ask what we are to understand positively when we think of the unreified *Being* of the subject, the soul, consciousness, the spirit, the person."[38] Even the phenomenological conceptions of Husserl and Scheler, according to which a person was not a substance or an object but a "performer of intentional acts which are bound together by the unity of a meaning," did not escape the taint of reification, since behind them lay the preconceptions of classical or Christian anthropology. The idea of man as a "rational being" or as a "transcendent being" still suggested that man was an entity, possessed, like a thing of a determinate nature, with fixed qualities. Hence Heidegger rejected any terms for the self with thing-like connotations and chose instead the term *Dasein*, the ordinary German word for existence, but one whose grammatical form suggested ongoing and directed activity.

In the second place, the notion of subjectivity was traditionally connected with the specific formulation of the epistemological problem in philosophy: how does that which exists, which is given, get known by the subject? To Heidegger, the epistemological question concealed an invalid assumption—that there existed something with a fixed, determinate meaning that was external to the isolated knowing subject, that the knowing subject had somehow to internalize. But to know

[37] M. Heidegger, *Being and Time*, trans. J. Macquarrie and E. Robinson, London, 1962, p. 72. I have felt free to modify the translation where clarity and context seemed to demand it. All such modifications are indicated.

[38] *Ibid.*, p. 37.

was to know something *as* something, i.e., in terms of some concept; knowledge itself depended upon prior interpretation. "A *commercium* of the subject with a world," wrote Heidegger, "does not get *created* for the first time by knowing, nor does it arise from some way in which the world acts upon a subject."[39] This *commercium* was designated by Heidegger as "Being-in-the-world," and his book was the explication of its meaning.

Heidegger began with an interpretation of our experience of the world rather than with the self because, he pointed out, self-knowledge was not in the first instance direct but rather implicit in the way we understood the world. Since, however, the world of nature, the highly specialized world of the pure "things" of natural science, masked the meaning of Being-in-the-world, it was necessary to examine it in the context of everyday experience. Our everyday world was present to us most generally as a world of entities defined in terms of purpose and serviceability, in terms of their "usefulness for" something or other; we experienced these qualities as constituting these entities, as defining them or being them, no less objectively than their purely spatial and measurable qualities. Heidegger labelled this aspect of our orientation to entities "readiness-to-hand" (*Zuhandenheit*, i.e., availability for some purpose) in contrast to the "presence-at-hand" (*Vorhandenheit*) of things understood as matter or substance, as pure extension. The point of the distinction was to establish that these two categories were independent and complementary ways of perceiving the world. A chair, for example, was not initially or essentially conceived of as a collection of certain physical-mathematical properties subsequently "subjectively" endowed with usability for sitting. Normally its function-meaning was primary; it was first and foremost a "tool for sitting." "*Readiness-to-hand,*" insisted Heidegger, "*is the way in which entities as they are 'in themselves' are defined....*"[40]

This preliminary emphasis on the objectivity of utility definitions, however, was deceptive and one-sided. For when our

[39] *Ibid.*, p. 90.   [40] *Ibid.*, p. 101.

definitions of things in terms of functionality—their "usefulness for . . ."—were followed back to their end-point, it became clear that at the end of the chain of "what for?" refer-
ences stood the human self and its purposes, the source, the
necessary condition for the objective qualities and meanings
that the world disclosed: "A hammer . . . is for hammering;
hammering is for making something fast; making something
fast is for protection against bad weather; and this protection
'is' for the sake of providing shelter for Dasein—that is to
say, for the sake of a possibility of Dasein's being . . . the
structure of an involvement [i.e., of a reference relationship]
leads to Dasein's Being as the sole authentic 'for-the-sake-of-
which.' "[41]

Zuhandenheit as a category represented a context of meanings and relationships, a network of significance of a particular kind that was made possible by a specific orientation or
interest of the self in the world: "This 'a priori' letting-some-
thing-be-involved is the condition for the possibility of encountering anything ready-to-hand. . . . In understanding a
context of relations . . . Dasein has assigned itself to an 'in-
order-to' and it has done so in terms of a potentiality-for-
Being for the sake of which it itself is."[42]

Thus the relationship between the self and the world was
not that between the world and an inert photographic film.
The world was disclosed to man only in terms of the questions he asked of it and the purposes with which he addressed
it. In *this* sense there could be no objective meaning to which
man could passively surrender himself to discover the ultimate truth of the universe; man always established the particular frame of reference within which anything could be considered as known and could never know anything without
such a frame of reference. This was the meaning of Heidegger's paradoxical assertion that "Whenever we encounter
anything, the world has already been previously discovered."[43] In the case of the world of the ready-to-hand, the

41 *Ibid.*, pp. 116-117. (Translation modified.)
42 *Ibid.*, pp. 117, 119.   43 *Ibid.*, p. 114.

condition for the possibility of encountering functional objects was the self's involvement in goal-directed activity that caused it to address the world and question it from this point of view. Other points of view, and hence other "worlds," were equally possible. The world of natural science, the world of the Cartesian ontology in which existents were defined in terms of their purely measurable attributes, was one, but only one, such "world," and Heidegger pointed out how specialized and sophisticated an act of looking was required to see the world in this way. However, though he lauded philosophical idealism over realism for having seen the role of subjectivity, he insisted on dissociating his position from certain variants of idealism. It was not the material existence of a real world but its Being, the universals or categories in which particulars were organized and by which alone they appeared in a meaningful way to the self, that was dependent on the self and its involvement in some form of activity.

On the level so far discussed, *Being and Time* could be seen as a continuation of the methodological work of the Neo-Kantians and the phenomenologists that broadened the conception of subjectivity from consciousness to the pre-theoretical and non-cognitive dimensions of human existence. Many of Heidegger's readers were to take his work as an analysis of the philosophical foundations of the human sciences, a prolegomenon to any future anthropology, sociology, or psychology—as indeed Heidegger intended it to be. He could be seen as attacking the paradigms that had prevailed up to then in the human sciences by differentiating man's way of being, the way he related to the world, from the way of being of inanimate objects and of organisms ("life"). An object simply *was*, its attributes given, interacting mechanically with other objects; man *existed*, bringing a world into being for himself in terms of meanings through action and sustaining meanings only so long as a particular kind of involvement prevailed. An animal *lived*, pursuing a prescribed range of activities blindly, completely at one with them; man *existed*, choosing among possibilities, able to take an attitude even

95

toward the inexorable demands of his own body, the necessity of death, and the unchangeable past, thus giving them different meanings and a degree of freedom in relation to them.

Heidegger was not concerned primarily to establish new categories for the sciences of man. What basically engaged his attention was the fact that, for the most part, the self was completely unaware of its own role in establishing frames of reference or significance. Indeed, and this was the crucial point, the very character of objective "Being" that our concepts and categories seemed to have was a denial of the self's role, precisely because it was the ascription to those categories of an absolute nature *an sich*, a nature that concealed the fact that they existed relative to the purposes and thematizing activity of the self. The result was a *de facto* subordination of the self to things, which seemed to dictate their own imperatives because of their natures; Heidegger spoke of this as Dasein's "fascination" with or "absorption" in its world. In many respects, this analysis seemed to hark back to the Hegelian-Marxist conception of reification, though a comprehension of Hegel, not to speak of Marx, in these terms was neither fashionable nor widespread at the time.[44]

But Heidegger developed a new element in the idea of subjectivity. Dasein was characterized by what he called *Jemeinigkeit*, "mine-ness," the radical individuality of selfhood:

[44] Lucien Goldmann pointed out the similarities between the thought of Heidegger and Lukács, who refurbished the idea of reification in *Geschichte und Klassenbewusstsein*, which was published in 1923, four years before *Being and Time*. (L. Goldmann, *Mensch, Gemeinschaft und Welt in der Philosophie Immanuel Kants*, Zurich, 1945, pp. 241 ff.) Accepting Heidegger's statement in *Being and Time* that he had already worked out and lectured on the major themes of the book in 1919, Goldmann did not claim priority for Lukács, though he insisted on the common parentage of their main ideas in the work of Rickert and Lask; he did claim, however, that *Being and Time* is above all an argument with Lukács, an attempt to combat the Marxist approach to the problem of reification with a philosophy of death and anxiety. Heidegger's own approach will be discussed later in this section, and the differences between Heidegger's existentialism and Marxism will be examined in chapter seven.

Dasein was always mine or yours. Individuality, however, was not just an inert property of the self, like an attribute of a thing; it was something which the self had to live in one way or another: "Dasein has always made some sort of decision as to the way in which it is in each case mine."[45] Dasein, in fact, had the possibility of either being itself or not itself; it could be either authentic or inauthentic. And Heidegger declared, "When Dasein is absorbed in the world of its concern ... it is not itself."[46]

To illuminate the paradox of a self that was simultaneously itself and not itself, Heidegger presented a phenomenology of the inauthenticity of everyday life. The specifics of his description were so clearly taken from contemporary urban civilization, from what has come to be called mass society, that he was later criticized for universalizing, in the most abstract terms, what were concrete and historically delimited conditions. In fact, Heidegger was not at all oblivious of the immediate referent of his categories; he chose to ignore their specificity because he felt that the condition he was describing transcended the features of any one historical society. "[Inauthenticity] has . . . various possibilities of becoming concrete . . . the extent to which its dominion becomes compelling and explicit may change in the course of history."[47]

Everyday Dasein, when questioned as to its identity, had some understanding of itself as a self, as itself; it could say "I." This "I," however, was for the most part an abstract and empty point of self-reference, indicating no real differentiation of the self from others, no real individuation. Our everyday experience of a world of objective givens with their preordained meanings and functions was accompanied by the experience of other selves for whom these things existed and who employed them in specific ways. These other selves were given in immediate experience as co-agents, producers and consumers of the social world. They did not have to be interpreted as other selves through a process of empathy;[48] on the

45 Heidegger, *Being and Time*, p. 68.
46 *Ibid.*, p. 163.   47 *Ibid.*, p. 167.   48 *Ibid.*, p. 162.

contrary, rather than their deriving identity as persons from an observed similarity with me, I derived my identity through my similarity with them. "By 'Others' we do not mean everyone else but me. . . . They are rather those from whom for the most part one does *not* distinguish oneself—those among whom one is too."[49] The "I" was simply another self among those selves which as a matter of course did what was done and used things in prescribed ways. Everyday Dasein did not act in accord with criteria for which its sole warrant was itself, but in accord with the behavior and criteria manifested around it, which it took as prescriptive for itself. "Dasein, as everyday Being-with-one-another, stands in *subjection* to Others. It itself *is* not; its Being has been taken away by others."[50] This subjection was not a coerced submission against which a self-conscious "I" rebelled either openly or clandestinely. The self slid into the "usual," "correct" way of doing things quite naturally, accepting them implicitly *de jure.* "What is decisive is just that inconspicuous domination by Others which has already been taken over *unawares* from Dasein as Being-with. *One belongs to the others oneself* and enhances their power."[51] This abstract self, its individuality dissolved into a common public identity and consisting solely in being an exemplar of the universal, Heidegger labelled "*das Man*"—the anonymous "one," or the "they self."[52]

"*Das Man*" guided itself by "what was done" and "what was said" in society, as proclaimed by public opinion. The essential feature of this anonymous individual was the negation of the existential fact that values and ways of life existed for him only to the degree that he continued to sustain them in being, only to the degree that he went along with them. By this rejection he disburdened himself of any responsibility

---

[49] *Ibid.,* p. 154.   [50] *Ibid.,* p. 164.   [51] *Ibid.* Italics added.

[52] The Macquarrie-Robinson translation uses the term "the 'they'" for "*das Man*," since the most idiomatic English rendering of the impersonal "*man sagt*" in the active voice is "they say." In this chapter somewhat more flexibility is used in rendering it where other terms seem more suitable. All such changes have been indicated.

for his actions. "Because every judgment and decision is presented as being made by 'them,' the particular Dasein is deprived of its responsibility. . . . 'They' can be responsible for
everything most easily because 'they' are not someone who
needs to vouch for anything. It was always 'they' who did it
and yet it can be said that it has been 'no one.' "[53] Dasein
took the given way of doing things as the only way, unaware
of other possibilities or unable to entertain other possibilities
as living options for itself. In existential *truth*, Dasein's characteristics were only possible ways for it to be, among which
it had to choose. But the inauthentic anonymous self did not
relate to its own ways of existing as one set of possibilities
among others; it took itself as a determinate being with fixed
characteristics, an entity differing from things present-at-
hand only by being endowed with an I-consciousness.

In a later chapter we shall be interested in comparing the
existential and the Freudian concepts of identification. For
the moment the point to be stressed is that Heidegger was
interested not in the "contents" but in the "form" of selfhood.
He was not at all unaware of the historical origins of the specific ways of being of selfhood—indeed, as we shall see shortly, the historical nature of the self was a central point of his
analysis—but the essence of inauthentic selfhood was that it
was based on a set of implicit but incorrigible and hence irrational beliefs to the effect that there was only one set or
legitimate way of doing, being, or believing, the objective
warrant for which was embodied in authorities beyond the
self. In effect, the inauthentic self was committing an existential form of the naturalistic fallacy, deriving an "ought" from
the practice around it. Hence, while the concrete characteristics of the inauthentic self as described by Heidegger—
averageness, levelling down, and publicness—were obviously
derived from modern mass civilization, inauthenticity as a
general category was applicable in any case where an external
entity—God, tribe, class, nation—was allowed to stand as the

[53] Heidegger, *Being and Time*, p. 163. Translation modified.

99

objective warrant, explicitly or implicitly, for the self, taking all responsibility for its actions and beliefs. Thus, for example, Heidegger wrote of technologically less advanced societies, "Primitive Dasein . . . has a specific everydayness of its own."[54]

Beyond establishing the fact of inauthenticity, however, *Being and Time* also presented a theory of motivation to explain it. Heidegger's constantly reiterated assertion that Dasein's Being was an issue for it meant that the categories of authenticity and inauthenticiy were not an external criterion imposed on Dasein and used to judge it, but were in fact derived from the action of Dasein itself in falsifying the true nature of its own activity. The use of the phenomenological method was crucial in this context. As a purely descriptive method, its purpose was to expose the falsification in belief and behavior itself, to show the motive at work in the subject's pre-theoretical, pre-reflective consciousness. The nature of the motive could be understood only by a description of the way in which experience was falsified and of what the falsification accomplished for the self.

The explicit analysis of Dasein's reasons for inauthenticity was contained in the book's relatively brief discussion of anxiety. "Falling" into inauthenticity was grounded in anxiety, the anxiety generated by the fact that man was not a necessary but a contingent being, his mode of being *merely* possibilities or contingent necessities rather than decreed necessities. In the sense of being born into a setting with purpose and direction provided in advance, man was *not* at home in the world. "When falling we flee *into* the 'at-home' of publicness, we flee *in the face of* the 'not-at-home'; that is, we flee in the face of the uncanniness which lies in Dasein. . . ."[55] This uncanniness, the feeling of not being at home in an ultimate sense, was occasionally experienced directly, in attacks of anxiety in which the world around us literally became meaningless, denuded of significance. In these moods, the

[54] *Ibid.*, p. 76.   [55] *Ibid.*, p. 234.

world ceased to matter anymore; it no longer said anything to us. Much more commonly, however, uncanniness appeared indirectly through our attempts to escape it. Anxiety manifested itself in our very "comprehension of Being," the basic theme of *Being and Time*. Our comprehension of Being was the very badge of our inauthenticity; it was not the passive understanding of a fact but the manufacture of an illusion. It was in reality a quest for identity.

This word must be understood in the strictest possible sense. Inauthentic Dasein's interpretation of the world as one of determinate meaning, and of itself as a being with fixed, objectively given characteristics, enabled it to *be* something. In truth, at any given time the self was nothing but that with which it was concerning itself, a finite, future-directed realizing of one or some of its many possibilities. Nothing guaranteed the continuity of the self or of its world of meanings; nothing but its own adherence to past modes of activity, loyalties, and traditions guaranteed stability and order. Yet by projecting Being—determinacy, permanence, and objectivity independent of the self's choices and decisions—onto the meanings of entities in its world or onto its own values, purposes, and activities, the self was able to think of itself as unified and substantial. "The [inauthentic] 'Self' . . . is what maintains itself as something identical throughout changes in its Experiences and ways of behavior, and which relates itself to this changing multiplicity in so doing. Ontologically we understand it as something which is in each case already constantly present-at-hand, both in and for a closed realm. . . . As something selfsame in manifold otherness, it has the character of the *Self*."[56]

Heidegger's language on the subject of identity did at times also seem to refer to a particular historical form of society: "At first and for the most part Dasein understands itself in terms of that with which it is customarily concerned. 'One is' what one does."[57] But it was not the fact that in modern so-

[56] *Ibid.*, p. 150.   [57] *Ibid.*, p. 283.

ciety Dasein's identity was derived from its socio-economic role, its place in the division of labor, that interested Heidegger so much as the way in which Dasein, in giving itself an identity, interpreted its own factual experience. "Being" was what man aimed at when he elevated a specific, temporally bound social determination to the level of a destiny, or when he attempted the integration of his manifold activities by positing a unified and substantial self different from them and underlying them. Being was a protection against the chaos of relativity and of diffusion that the nature of man's being as existence implied. There was nothing necessary or ultimate in any of man's possibilities and choices. Even his "facticity," the contingencies, some of them unchangeable, of the conditions into which he had been thrown by birth, were not absolutes dictating courses of action; they were merely there. Conferring "Being"—objective necessity—on one's nationality, religion, or even sex, was an attempt to absolutize them and derive from them guidelines for action, thus concealing from oneself that nothing was ordained and that there was always something else that the self could be beyond what it "was."

This concealment hid from Dasein the truth of its own finitude and tranquilized it. It was accomplished through such modes of everyday experience as "idle talk." Idle talk was the publicly held conventional wisdom that served as expertise in lieu of genuine personal experience. "Idle talk . . . having seen everything, having understood everything, develop[s] the supposition that Dasein's disclosedness . . . can guarantee that all the possibilities of its Being will be secure, genuine and full. . . . The supposition of the 'they' that one is leading and sustaining a full and genuine 'life' brings Dasein a tranquility, for which everything is 'in the best of order' and all doors are open."[58]

Heidegger did not pursue in any detail the concrete forms that the quest for identity could take. He was not, he claimed,

58 *Ibid.*, p. 222.

interested in the particular forms but in the general features of existence, and he left it to others to apply them in concrete studies. A more important reason for the paucity of living description in his work, however, was that despite his disclaimer, Heidegger was a moralist intent on preaching the possibility of authentic existence. Contrary to some later misconceptions, *Being and Time*, for all its concern with anxiety, death, and guilt, was not morbid or pessimistic in its basic thrust. Anxiety, by breaking down the false beliefs of everydayness, was a liberating experience that brought Dasein back to its own individuality. Our awareness of death and guilt were potentially privileged experiences that, when seen rightly, attested to Dasein's underlying authenticity and opened to it the possibility of living authentically.

It was at this point that the fundamental tension within *Being and Time* emerged. There was a serious question as to whether the shift in emphasis from the nature and causes of inauthenticity to the possibility of authenticity was plausible or even admissible in the framework of Heidegger's assumptions in *Being and Time*. This problem will concern us in some detail later. For the moment, the focus will be on those aspects of Heidegger's analysis which were of psychological significance.

Heidegger's notion of the unique potentiality for self-liberation in the experience of coming to grips with the fact of one's death may not carry conviction. Sartre thought Heidegger wrong to single out this phenomenon, though a literary evocation such as Gide's portrayal of Michel's crisis in *The Immoralist* is a dramatically convincing illustration of the kind of case that might be made for Heidegger's position. This aside, however, for Heidegger the significance of man's anticipation of death was that death was the symbol, the epitome, of human finitude. Ultimately, anxiety was about death, for in anxiety "Dasein finds itself *face to face* with the 'nothing' of the possible impossibility of its existence."[59]

[59] *Ibid.*, p. 310.

Anxiety about death was the breakthrough of the awareness that the self could in fact cease to be, that indeed this possibility was a certainty of existence. Death brought home the nothingness of human existence, its evanescence, its final insignificance.

Heidegger conceded that anxiety was not usually consciously understood in this sense, but he argued that our concrete affects and moods, with their concrete intentional objects, were "fallen" or disguised expressions of basic anxiety. Fear *of* something, for example, was fear *for* the self, for its continued existence, and hence an implicit awareness of its possible nonexistence and insignificance; but we were not aware of this dimension of the experience because, in fear, the value of life was taken for granted while attention was focused on the external threat. Emotions were "disclosive submissions to the world out of which we can encounter something that matters to us";[60] they precluded the reflective awareness that it was only our valuing, our choice of life, that made things matter, that structured situations as threats.

Heidegger's interpretation of guilt and conscience contained a number of interesting features. For one thing, it clearly showed the usefulness of the phenomenological method in avoiding the opposite pitfalls of reductionist criticism and idealist apologia. "The ontological analysis of conscience . . . lies outside . . . of any biological 'explanation' of the phenomenon (which would mean its dissolution). But it is not less distant from a theological exegesis of conscience or any employment of this phenomenon for proofs of God or for establishing an 'immediate' consciousness of God."[61]

So, for example, on the one hand, Heidegger insisted that the fact that the demands of conscience were experienced as

[60] *Ibid.*, p. 177.

[61] *Ibid.*, p. 343. One important aspect of the historical significance of the appearance of existentialism is its role in mediating the polarization established in the debates between the attackers and defenders of traditional culture. It aimed at restoring the surface texture of experience destroyed by such reductive explanations as Darwinism and Marxism while maintaining their critical perspective. See chapter four.

coming from "beyond the self" was an integral part of the phenomenon of conscience, not to be explained away. On the other hand, the phenomenological evidence gave no support to the attempt to prove the existence of God as the source of the alien power dominating the self. That someone felt called by a higher power was no evidence for the existence of that power. The caller was in fact none other than Dasein itself, in disguised form.

Heidegger's version of the meaning of the message of conscience is extremely difficult to understand and, to the degree that it is intelligible, highly dubious. Roughly, the argument was that, in feeling guilty about something, the self was really faced with the truth of its own freedom. By committing or omitting an act prohibited or demanded by conscience, the self revealed itself in guilt as a source of negation, since by its choice it had broken what was presented as an absolute, unbreakable injunction. Though the moral law presented itself as a universal, binding necessity, the phenomenon of guilt revealed the reality of choice and finitude and hence opened up the possibility of authenticity. By its choice, Dasein had necessarily opted for one possibility and ruled out others. This was the essence of freedom.[62]

More illuminating, however, was Heidegger's interpretation of the everyday phenomenological experience of conscience as an objective alien power that was universally binding. This experience, he suggested, represented an escape from authenticity because it couched what were in fact the demands of the self on the self in the impersonal, indefinite form of the "they." The very form of conscience, the categorical imperative, was therefore a fleeing from responsibility since it entailed the existence of a priori norms; its point was to secure the self against the abyss of choice by the establishment of universal obligation. However onerous was obligation, however tormenting was guilt, the norms that were their source offered the haven of a secure set of guidelines for behavior.

[62] Heidegger, *Being and Time*, pp. 330-331.

For Heidegger, the ultimate key to the proper interpretation of Dasein's authentic being and of the form inauthenticity took was the concept of temporality. The basic features or "existentialia" that characterized human existence were seen by Heidegger from the perspective of man as the being who creates time by living it. Existence was a process of "projecting possibilities"—of living for, though not necessarily consciously positing, goals, and of realizing them: Dasein existed "for the sake of a potentiality-for-Being of itself."[63] As such, Dasein was always oriented to the future; it was always "ahead of itself." "Self-projection upon the 'for-the-sake-of-oneself' is grounded in the future," Heidegger wrote, "and is an essential characteristic of *existentiality. The primary meaning of existentiality is the future.*"[64]

The possibilities for the sake of which Dasein existed, however, came from the past, from Dasein's "thrownness." That is to say, they were furnished by the environment into which Dasein was born and in which it found itself engaged at any given time. Heidegger was never specific about the elements of "thrownness." Above all, as we shall see later, they included the historical context of existence, but they also seemed to involve man's physical and biological nature, as the discussions of the purposes of utilitarian activity (providing shelter) and of death suggested. "Thrownness" comprised the totality of the givens of man's situation that he willy-nilly was always reacting to, taking a position towards, even if only by way of avoidance. Dasein's goal-directed activities were determined by the possibilities and contingencies furnished by his natural and his historical makeup.

It was this circumstance which governed the nature of inauthenticity. Since Dasein's possibilities were constituted by the environment, it could well appear, to a being looking for identity and permanence, that they were predetermined, and that choice, evaluation, and individual appropriation played no role in their assimilation by the individual. The result was

[63] *Ibid.*, p. 416. [64] *Ibid.*, pp. 375-376.

a purely passive attitude to events: "That which will come tomorrow is 'eternally yesterday's.' "[65] The future was not made; it was *awaited*, because the goals of action were seen not as intentions, purposes, and ends sustained by the individual but as preexisting in the nature of things.

In this way Heidegger explained the power of the past over the present and the future. In effect, Dasein absolutized the past, the environment of its "thrownness": "From the world it takes its possibilities, and it does so first in accordance with the way things have been interpreted by the 'they.' This interpretation has already restricted the possible options of choice to what lies within the range of the familiar, the attainable, the respectable—that which is fitting and proper. This levelling off of Dasein's possibilities to what is proximally at its everyday disposal also results in a dimming down of the possible as such."[66]

To escape freedom, Dasein turned the actual, the present contingency, into the necessary. Though Heidegger did not construe his analysis genetically, his theory of motiviation entailed the universalization of the historical, which could account for the child's perpetuation of his early environment as the model for all later activity.

[65] *Ibid.*, p. 422.   [66] *Ibid.*, p. 239.

CHAPTER THREE

The Existentialist Critique of Psychoanalytic Theory

IN *Being and Time*, Heidegger's description of Dasein's "essential structures" and the analysis of the problem of authenticity were part of a single enterprise; indeed, the definition of the first in terms of the second gave the book's argument what Heidegger frankly acknowledged to be its circular character. The two elements, however, could be separated because the categories of his analysis of Dasein could be seen to be in opposition to certain prevailing paradigms in the human sciences and could be thought of as an extension of the methodological debate about their nature. While denying that *Being and Time* was an attempt at a philosophical anthropology, a general empirical characterization of human nature, Heidegger had himself insisted on the indispensability of his ontological investigation for any properly based, philosophically sound, study in the human sciences.

Historically, a split along these lines did take place. One group of Heidegger's followers focused on the purely formal description of existence as being-in-the-world as a methodological starting point for combatting mechanistic and biological reductionism in psychology and psychiatry. Jean-Paul Sartre, on the other hand, followed Heidegger in developing the concept of existence as the basis for his analysis of selfhood, freedom, and bad faith. This division makes for a certain difficulty in exposition. Among the first group were the two psychiatrists, Ludwig Binswanger and Medard Boss, who became identified as the founders and leaders of existential analysis in the field of psychotherapy and who were the main existential critics of Freud. They regarded their work not as an alternative depth-psychology or psychotherapy to psychoanalysis—both of them had been trained as orthodox psychoanalysts[1]—but as a metapsychological correction of the positivistic theoretical foundations of psychoanalysis, which left Freud's empirical and clinical insights largely intact. This assessment has been accepted by most commentators on existential analysis.[2] There is an element of truth in it, though the claim is somewhat disingenuous, since the philosophical critique resulted in the rejection of the libido theory and the unconscious. More significantly, the philosophical and methodological critique was in fact the expression of important substantive differences with psychoanalysis. Existentialism and psychoanalysis have very different concepts of the roots of selfhood; moreover, these different concepts reflected in part significant historical developments, both intellectual and social, in Europe in the late nineteenth and the twentieth centuries. In order to deal with the various levels of significance, we shall first examine the existential criticism of psychoanalytic metapsychology and then look at its underlying historical significance.

A further complexity in the definition of "existential analysis" makes a prefatory note necessary before we can begin discussion of the existential critique of psychoanalytic theory. Ludwig Binswanger was the first psychiatrist to attempt to apply Heidegger's philosophy to psychiatry and psychotherapy. In a series of articles and case studies published between 1930 and 1935, he began to define an independent existential approach to theoretical and clinical problems. It was Binswanger who transferred the word and concept *Daseinsanalyse*, existential analysis, into psychiatry, in obvious parallel to psychoanalysis, and in the following decades he became the recognized leader of that orientation—it was never organized or codified enough to be called a school—in European psychiatry.

[1] Binswanger's training was not formal, neither training analyses nor courses having been institutionalized in his time.

[2] See, for example, J. Needleman in *Being-In-The-World*, p. 59.

His position, however, was challenged in the 1950's by Medard Boss, a Swiss psychiatrist teaching and practicing in Zurich, who, under Heidegger's direct guidance, attacked Binswanger's interpretation of the philosopher's work. A generation younger than Binswanger,[3] Boss had been able to receive formal psychoanalytic training in a movement far broader and better organized than it had been during Binswanger's apprenticeship. He had met Freud only briefly, but had undergone a training analysis in Zurich, and had subsequently studied with Ernest Jones at the London Psychoanalytic Institute and with Karen Horney and Otto Fenichel at the Psychoanalytic Institute of Berlin. Boss seems initially to have had no outside philosophical interests and certainly, unlike Binswanger, no early serious theoretical reservations about psychoanalysis. His first published work was thoroughly orthodox in theory and language on such issues as the meaning of dreams and the nature of the unconscious and transference;[4] only a few hints of the equivocations that were to lead to later developments could be detected.[5]

It was under the influence of Jung that Boss first moved away from psychoanalytic orthodoxy and through Binswanger's work that he encountered Heidegger and got his first impression of existential philosophy. Boss's first existentialist writings were heavily indebted both to Binswanger's interpretation of *Being and Time* and to Binswanger's own philo-

[3] Binswanger was born in 1886, Boss in 1903.

[4] The models of the actual- and the psychoneuroses presented in this book were crude and simple versions of the conversion of energy dammed up and prevented from discharge by external obstacles or internal repression into the physical sphere. M. Boss, *Körperliches Kranksein als Folge seelischer Gleichgewichtsstörungen*, Bern, 1940.

[5] For example, Boss defended psychoanalysis against the charges of reductionism by insisting that while observation and not psychoanalytic projection had shown that religious feeling derived its energy and often its form from the earthly and egotistical love of the infant for its parents, there was no warrant in psychoanalysis for the thesis that the higher human capabilities were nothing but primitive drives. Boss, *Körperliches Kranksein*, pp. 105-107.

sophical anthropology.[6] Almost immediately after the publication of the first of his books to take an existentialist approach, however, Boss began a personal collaboration with Heidegger that resulted in an increasing divergence from Binswanger's mode of expression.

In the decade following his first major philosophical writings, Heidegger's thought had undergone a radical transformation. In his own view, this development represented not a reversal of the positions he had taken in *Being and Time* but their completion. As a result of this change he became greatly concerned to guard against what he claimed to be "subjectivist" misinterpretations of *Being and Time*. Binswanger's work represented just such a misinterpretation, and by making himself available to Boss for the clarification of his own work and for general philosophical guidance, Heidegger hoped to furnish a corrective for it in the field of psychotherapy. Heidegger not only met with Boss for private philosophical instruction but appeared at his seminars for psychiatric residents at the University of Zurich Medical School. Thus Boss was able to establish himself as something of an authorized interpreter of Heidegger and to criticize with the official imprimatur the defects in Binswanger's comprehension and application of Heidegger's philosophy.

The change that took place in Heidegger's thought and the resulting differences between Binswanger and Boss are of significance both for the evolution of existentialism specifically and for the intellectual history of Europe in our period. We shall explore them in some detail in a later chapter. For the purposes of examining the critique of psychoanalysis, however, they may by and large be safely ignored. Even while criticizing Binswanger for his misinterpretation of Heidegger, Boss seconded his critique of psychoanalysis, calling it his most important contribution and acknowledging that he had said everything essential on the subject.[7] This acknowledg-

6 See chapters five and six.

7 M. Boss, *Psychoanalyse und Daseinsanalytik*, Bern und Stuttgart, 1954, p. 102.

111

ment was in effect later qualified when, in the English-language version of his book on existential analysis, Boss gave his own detailed account of how existentialism transformed many key psychoanalytic doctrines, but here again the differences with Binswanger are not crucial; Boss's work represented continuation of Binswanger's point of view in a more systematic way and into areas not covered by Binswanger.

The existential critique of Freud was not always coherent or clear. It was nevertheless concerned with genuine issues, some of which have been addressed more lucidly by English and American philosophers who, however, often fail to appreciate the clinical reality underlying the philosophical difficulties. Increasingly, these issues have even been taken up by "orthodox" analysts, though with a good deal more circumspection than the existentialists and without their well-defined alternative conceptual starting-point.

For a better understanding of the force of the existentialists' criticisms, it is necessary first to recapitulate briefly the conclusions of the first chapter. The historical outline of the development of Freud's theory of meaning makes it clear that a certain conventional account of his achievement will not do. It is not correct to say that Freud reclassified or redescribed aspects of our behavior in terms of intention, emotion, and belief where none was hitherto thought to exist and then proceeded to explain that behavior with theories of infantile sexuality and of repression. There was no such clearcut distinction between description and explanation in psychoanalytic theory; rather the psychoanalytic theory of meaning, the theory of unconscious phantasy, collapsed the two together. The result was threefold. In the first place, the basic motivational terms of the theory were not intentions and purposes but instinctual impulses, a concept that itself embodied an explanation of behavior. Secondly, where wishes and impulses were in fact referred to, they had no current context or meaning in the needs, self-definitions, or beliefs of agents; they were literally resurrections of the past. The explanatory theory of infantile sexuality thus provided the vocabulary for the description of the very facts the theory was supposed to explain, and did so via a reification of psychic processes which "spatialized" time. In reacting oedipally to a woman, for example, an adult male was not simply repeating a past pattern or structure of relations but was re-enacting as if pictorially in his mind a childhood scene with his mother. I say "as if pictorially" because it is not at all clear just what Freud conceived to be going on when someone was acting out of unconscious phantasy, what type or level of event was taking place.

This leads to the third point. Insofar as the neurotic was acting on or fulfilling an unconscious wish, or defending against it, the process was not equivalent to ordinary wish-fulfillment or defense, where steps appropriate to or believed appropriate to the goal aimed at are taken. But it is not enough to say that the difference was precisely what Freud was pointing to in his distinction between primary and secondary processes. The point is that primary process functioning was not in action terms a mental or psychological process at all but an energic process. The theoretical link between motive and behavior was a physicalistic one, not one of subjective meaning.

Given their insistence on the primacy of meaning, and their belief in the inappropriateness of conceptualizing meaning in terms either of the functioning of a mental apparatus or of biological instincts, the existentialists had three problems with regard to psychoanalytic theory:

(1) how to give an account of the meaning of neurotic symptoms without recourse to concepts such as conversion, displacement, dream work and symbolism, which depended upon explanation in terms of a psychic apparatus and psychic energy;

(2) how to understand the connection between the past and the present without theoretical constructs such as repression, which established a causal connection by dissolving the present into the past;

(3) how to classify and describe behavior that did not fit into instinctual categories.

113

The first two problems struck at the heart of the psychoanalytic theory of the unconscious; the third at the theory of the libido.

The existentialists were hampered in their task by an inadequate understanding of the philosophical problems of causal explanation. They did not attack psychoanalysis only for conceptualizing the self and its meaning-relationship to the world in terms appropriate to physical objects; they attacked the very idea of causal explanation itself. This was because they equated causal explanation with an illegitimate reductionism that did violence to the phenomena it was explaining by replacing them with a set of events of a different conceptual order. This equation is false; it is in principle possible to give non-reductionist causal explanations of action, even referring to physical events as necessary conditions, if appropriate autonomous action descriptions are given first.[8] But the idea that meaning and cause were mutually exclusive was generally a feature of the causal approaches that the antipositivists were criticizing, and their position, if too much the mirror image of the one they opposed, was a step towards the establishment of the need for proper descriptions of meaning prior to causal explanation. Behind the existentialist rejection of Freudian causality lay Freud's use of topographic and economic language both as a description and an explanation of psychic processes; the failure of the existentialists to make distinctions between the two paralleled Freud's own. Nevertheless, this failure caused them to reject more than they had to, and proved embarrassing when they themselves fell back on causal ideas.

THE SELF AS THING

In general terms, apart from particular criticisms of causality, the existentialists assailed the basic conceptual language

[8] A. MacIntyre, *Against the Self-Images of the Age*, New York, 1971, pp. 191-230.

of psychoanalytic metapsychology for characterizing meaning processes in terms relevant to physical objects. Binswanger dismissed the proto-physiological thinking underlying Freud's topographic and economic models of mental functioning as totally inappropriate to psychology: "We have known for a long time that the logical or moral value of an 'idea,' an action, a character cannot be explained in terms of the intensity of a physiological function, that we have here rather two categorically incommensurable 'levels of discourse,' two completely incompatible conceptual worlds. In our time such a gross violation of the psychic facts, such a distorting retranslation of questions of psychological, logical and ethical values into questions of biological-physiological intensity, can be found only in Freud's work."[9]

What was involved in the Freudian conversion of questions of meaning into questions of energy cathexis was at best a conflation of two very different concepts of energy. While it was quite proper in ordinary language to ascribe greater or lesser energy to people or actions, or to differentiate between more and less intense emotions, these terms referred to dispositions to act, location in a hierarchy of possible actions, types of action or emotion, or even quantitative measures of the duration of a reaction or number of actions per unit of time; but this language had nothing to do with measurable physiological quantities and could be used whatever the proper physiological descriptions of changes accompanying emotion or action.

Boss went even further, to reject the psychological reification of mental processes that had made plausible the translation of psychology into neurology, with ideas corresponding to individual neurons. Modes of existence, meaning-disclosing involvements with the world, could not properly be thought of as thing-like entities, whether as "ideas" in a non-material "psychic apparatus" or as structural divisions of a self. Psychoanalytic metapsychology distorted psychic phenomena as

9 L. Binswanger, *Über Ideenflucht*, Zurich, 1933, p. 4.

115

they were given in experience by dehumanizing them, reifying them, and characterizing them as a set of autonomous activities independent of either a self or a world. "If man," Boss wrote, "did actually consist of originally isolated somato-psychic telescope-like apparatuses . . . not even one single 'act of consciousness' would be possible. . . . No theory which pictures man as an object . . . will ever be able to explain human perceiving, thinking and acting."[10]

Ultimately, according to Boss, the concept of a "psychic apparatus" had its roots in Cartesian philosophy, which furnished the metaphysical foundation of modern science generally and psychoanalysis in particular. The Cartesian concept of mind as *res cogitans*, non-material substance, made it into a peculiar kind of place or location. Only out of such a conception of mind could there develop the notions of "psychic topography," of a realm of consciousness containing quality-less "excitations" and verbal images, and of an unconscious as a psychic locality and system, an independent entity with its own properties and laws.

The idea of a "psychic apparatus" was thus a contradiction in terms. In regard to the unconscious, however, the distortion of subjectivity involved in the psychoanalytic conception was even greater. As a system, the unconscious was in principle, as Freud himself had admitted, beyond immediately observable phenomena. It was a theoretical entity, a "psychic 'black box' " in which "All the manifold psychic transformation processes which Freud assumed behind the immediately given phenomena" take place.[11]

Boss recognized that Freud's assumption of an undemonstrable entity, the unconscious, arose from the need for explanation of the observed phenomena, and he argued that the existential approach, through proper description of them, made such an explanation unnecessary. But, aside from this,

---

[10] M. Boss, *Psychoanalysis and Daseinsanalysis*, New York, 1963, pp. 79, 93. This is a much revised and enlarged version of the German work of the same name; to all intents and purposes it is a new book.

[11] *Ibid.*, p. 92.

the conception of the unconscious as an entity was incompatible with the idea of human subjectivity. "Freud abandoned his central aim and violated his own brilliant innovation of seeing human phenomena in a meaningful historical perspective when he interpolated assumed [unconscious] processes. . . . Nothing is gained for the understanding of *meaningful* connections, which are in fact hidden from view from the beginning in such an approach. . . ."[12]

Binswanger put the point most sharply when he charged that Freud, by making the unconscious into an "it," had betrayed his own most profound and revolutionary insight: "It was after all precisely Freud who taught us that the 'I can't' of the patient must always be understood as an 'I won't,' in other words that the 'I-not I' relationship must be understood as an 'I-I myself' relationship . . . psychoanalysis in general has its justification only insofar as this translation is possible or at least meaningful. Yet Freud transforms—with a literally suicidal [*selbstmörderischer*] intention—the 'I will not' to an 'it can not.' "[13] In this way psychoanalytic theory mirrored the state of mind of the neurotic.

The same objection lay at the heart of Sartre's rejection of the unconscious in *Being and Nothingness* a decade later. Unless, Sartre argued, the self were conscious of the impulses it wanted to repress, neither repression nor resistance would be possible. The self had to know its impulses, and to know them as its own, in order to resist the interpretations of the analyst as they threatened to expose what was hidden. But this was to say that the self was not divisible, like a thing, that the unconscious was *also* the self and could not be conceived as a non-subjective entity lying outside the boundaries of selfhood.

Sartre, however, defined selfhood as consciousness, and was thus, after having exposed the psychoanalytic concept of the unconscious as contradictory, himself left with a paradoxical description of the self-consciousness of the censor; the cen-

12 *Ibid.*
13 Binswanger, "Über Psychotherapie," *Vorträge*, Bd. I, p. 154.

sorship was "consciousness [of] being conscious of the drive to be repressed, but *precisely in order not to be conscious of it*."[14] How this differed from hypocrisy, from which Sartre specifically wanted to differentiate bad faith, was not evident; he evaded the problem. Binswanger and Boss, however, were not caught in this dilemma. Since they started with Heidegger's concept of Dasein rather than Husserl's concept of consciousness, they were not put in the position of having to affirm a uniform consciousness, transparent to itself, as the necessary consequence of rejecting the idea of the unconscious as a locality or energy system.

IRRATIONALITY AND THE MEANING OF DREAMS AND SYMPTOMS

In ruling out mechanistic reduction, the existentialists were also ruling out the causal explanation of "symptomatic" behavior. This did not cause them concern, however, for they rejected the original Freudian premise that irrationality demanded the abandonment of a meaning-approach to behavior and the shift to another level of discourse and theory. In turn they tried to work out alternative accounts of psychoanalytic "mechanisms" of the unconscious.

(1) *Conversion and the Mind-Body Problem*

Freud's Cartesianism, however qualified by his early attempts to materialize mind, left him with the problem of explaining how the mind could influence the body in hysteria. Among the early observations that led to the discovery of psychoanalysis was the fact that the physical symptoms of hysteria did not correlate with the facts of anatomy and physiology but with popular ideas about the units of physical action. When he realized that unacceptable ideas, wishes, and emotions lay behind the symptoms, Freud theorized that the latter were defenses against the former. The theoretical prob-

---

[14] J.-P. Sartre, *Being and Nothingness*, trans. H. Barnes, New York, 1956, p. 53.

lem, then, was to explain how physical symptoms could appear in place of repressed ideas. The theoretical bridge was the concept of conversion, according to which the energy that accompanied ideas and that gave them their conscious affectual charge was stripped from them and converted into somatic manifestations, rendering the ideas themselves unconscious.

As the existentialists pointed out, Freud himself was unsatisfied with this idea, and confessed that the leap from the mental to the physical involved in it remained a mystery, implying as it did the transmutation of one substance, mental energy, into bodily manifestations.[15] Moreover, the dualistic conception turned the repressed ideas into external and thus contingent causes of physical manifestations; on the theoretical level there was no intrinsic meaningful connection between them. Yet clinically Freud often treated physical symptoms as expressions of behavior rather than caused physical events, attributing definite purposes to them.

These difficulties could be obviated, the existentialists argued, if the Freudian mind-body dualism were rejected, if purposiveness and ideation were not considered to be matters of "cathected" ideas in a mind-container and if the body were not considered merely a thing and its actions a set of physical events. Certainly the body was a physico-chemical structure, but from the psychological and existential view it was a sphere of existence, an independent form of human self-expression. Man, Binswanger asserted, not only had a body, he was a body and expressed himself in body language,[16] indeed never more "audibly" than when he withdrew from the customary verbal form of communication. Binswanger described the case of a young girl who suffered from loss of appetite and attacks of vomiting and aphonia after her mother forbade her to see the man with whom she was in love. Her inability to keep food down was the bodily expression of her fury at her mother, her inability to "swallow" her mother's

[15] Boss, *Psychoanalysis and Daseinsanalysis*, p. 134.
[16] Binswanger, *Vorträge*, Bd. I, p. 146.

119

prohibition—and this, Binswanger argued, was not just a metaphor, but a description of what the girl was expressing in her bodily behavior. Rejection, revolt, and anger were not simply mental acts but the behavior of the unified mind-body self; swallowing was not simply a physiological process metaphorically applied to the psychic assimilation of information or commands but was itself a meaningful act of acceptance (or in the case of vomiting, rejection), and therefore an attitude toward the world. Similarly, the girl's withdrawal from communication was expressed in her loss of speech. This was not simply a willful mental act that would have left the body at the free disposal of conscious volition; the girl was not pretending to be unable to speak.

It was when the body took over in this way that an important dimension of selfhood became apparent. Selfhood was not disembodied consciousness, mere verbal articulation or formal decision-making, though it could appear this way when there was no inner conflict. It was a body-soul unity that showed up the emptiness and helplessness of mere "will" when it was arrayed against the deepest desires of the self. On the other hand, body language took over, to the exclusion of words and therefore of conscious decision, when the individual was not able to face his own desires and feelings. Body language was thus a way of acting out those desires *without representing them to oneself in language.*[17] This was one form at least of what Freud called the unconscious. There were not preexisting ideas somewhere in an unconscious cut off from association with an "I"; the unconscious desire or emotion existed *only* as it was expressing itself in the body, and if and when it was verbalized, the linguistic mode would be something entirely new. Freudianism was too rationalist in its as-

[17] Cf. M. Merleau-Ponty, *Phenomenology of Perception,* trans. C. Smith, London, 1962, pp. 160-164, 296. Merleau-Ponty tried to mediate between the positions of Binswanger and Sartre in this way. Experience was always experience of a self and in this sense there could be no unconscious, but experience was not equivalent to representation and there was no need to posit a suppressed representation.

sumptions about unconscious mental content being in the form of ideas. "Thus it does not in our opinion adequately meet the case," wrote Binswanger, "when one merely explains that a mental impulse of defense 'is converted into the somatic sphere.' Rather one must realize that the 'somatic realm' [das Körperliche] or corporeality [die Leiblichkeit] is only a special form of human existence. One must realize and try to understand why it is that under certain circumstances it remains the only form of expression left to people, and that people henceforth use its language, i.e., instead of scolding and raging, they sob, belch, screech and vomit."[18] Physical symptoms were thus not merely negative, *substitutions* for behavior or language, but a different form of them that could be described in their own terms.

On the basis of Binswanger's concept of corporeality, Boss developed a far-reaching and radical theory of psychosomatic illness.[19] Psychosomatic symptoms were not effect signs of something hidden, but themselves the events they were supposed to replace. Thoughts, ideas, and phantasies were different ways of existing from bodily ones; neither was reducible to or derivable from the other.[20] Thus for Boss, body language was not always mutually exclusive with verbal language and its use not limited to what in psychoanalysis would be cases of repression. Body symptoms manifested themselves either when certain "world-relations were prevented from being able to be realized appropriately in an intentional, interpersonal manner" or when a "narrowing" of the whole existence of a person occurred such that it was reduced more or less exclusively to one kind of relation to the world,[21] which was expressed in body events as well as interpersonal behavior.

Boss's working out of the implications of *Leiblichkeit* re-

---

18 Binswanger, *Vorträge*, Bd. I, p. 149.

19 M. Boss, *Einführung in die psychosomatische Medizin*, Bern und Stuttgart, 1954; *Psychoanalysis and Daseinsanalysis*, pp. 133-177.

20 Boss, *Einführung*, pp. 77 ff.

21 Boss, *Psychoanalysis and Daseinsanalysis*, p. 144.

vealed more clearly the radical position inherent in Binswanger's concept. His critical foil was Franz Alexander, one of the founders of the psychoanalytic theory of psychosomatic illness. Alexander had distinguished between two types of symptoms. True hysterical conversion symptoms occurred in the realm of the voluntary neuro-muscular or sensory-perceptive systems, and were the symbolic expressions of emotions and desires. "Vegetative" neurosis involved the psychogenic dysfunction of organs that were not under the control of the voluntary neuro-muscular systems; they were somatic end-results of neurotic conflict but not themselves the concealed expressions of wishes. The reason for Alexander's distinction was the belief that a change in organs of the body not under "ordinary" voluntary control could not be directly attributed to ideas, i.e., could not be an action. Pointing to the phenomena of hypnosis and the physical feats of Eastern and Western saints and mystics, Boss argued against Alexander's line of division: "Even [the] most 'material' and rigid media of the somatic realm . . . participate in the occurrence of human existence. Even there, the relations to the world which constitute Dasein exert their directive power."[22] So, for example, the hyperactive stomach and duodenum of patients with peptic ulcers were manifestations of the same attitude or "world-relation" of seizing and overpowering as the patients manifested in their relations to people and things.

Though in fact Freud did not follow Alexander's line of division between the voluntary and autonomic nervous systems, Boss's psychological or meaning theory of psychosomatic symptoms was more radical than that of Freud. In the first place, Freud's psychogenic theory of somatic illness did not (as a causal theory) preclude physical causes, and Freud often argued that the hysteric made use of areas of the body already sensitized by physical illness, giving them an overlay of psychological significance. Boss totally ignored physical contributions and took the position that if the patient could

[22] *Ibid.*, p. 142.

open up his constricted world of functioning, he need no longer suffer from such illnesses as colitis and migraine.[23] Treatment and cure were thus completely psychological.

Secondly, for Freud, the psychic meaning of physical symptoms depended upon the hysteric's beliefs about the nature and function of the physical processes or part of the body he was exploiting for the production of symptoms, even if those beliefs were erroneous. Boss, on the other hand, extended the notion of physical event as behavior into spheres of physiological functioning of which the patient could not have any knowledge.

Finally, it appeared that for Boss body language could be read off with the same certainty as verbal language, so that it was not necessary to know its meaning to the subject. Indeed, body language was more easily read since it was not social or conventional. "At a particular time," Boss argued, "those realms of the body will predominate which belong to the particular relation which is carried out, those realms of the body . . . which this particular relation is, insofar as it shows itself somatically."[24] Thus he did not deal with the problem posed by the fact that the physical and physiological manifestations of very different emotions were often quite similar. This made implausible the hypothesis that they were unique world-disclosing relationships in and of themselves independently of the beliefs and wishes of the subject.

(2) Displacement and Symbolism: The Problem of Symptoms and Dreams

While the Freudian explanation of psychological symptoms involved no obscure transition from a mental to a physical sphere, it had other difficulties. Symptomatic behavior was defined as behavior that was unintelligible according to conventional criteria of appropriate behavior or irrational insofar as the beliefs that generated it were distortions of reality. For Freud this meant that the language of intention and belief was not applicable to the behavior in question. Thus the

[23] *Ibid.*, p. 154.   [24] *Ibid.*, p. 168.

explanation of how the neurotic moved from unconscious desire A to inappropriate behavior B was not one referring to beliefs about the best way of either carrying out the wish or defending against it, but one that referred to the laws governing energy flow in a mechanical system under such concepts as displacement, i.e., primary process functioning.

This kind of explanation was ruled out for the existentialists. By definition, the concept of being-in-the-world meant that experience was always to be interpreted in terms of its meaning to a self. What appeared to the subject was a function of his orientation to the world, the "possibilities" he was realizing or the "mood" of his "attunement." In principle, then, it should be possible to understand someone's world, no matter how apparently bizarre its appearances or behavior, by referring it to the subjective orientations—needs, concerns, and emotions—that made them possible. Conversely, since the self was, as Binswanger, quoting Hegel, put it, "what its world, as its own world, was,"[25] it should be possible to understand the concerns of the self from its experience of the world—its coloring, its spatial qualities, texture, coherence, the way people appeared in it, and so on.

Existentialism thus undercut Freud's starting point. There was no such thing as a given "reality" of which neurotic perception was a distortion in need of explanation. "World," Binswanger claimed, "is not a reality existing 'in itself' which can simply be copied and imitated perceptually or conceptually . . . but a *universum* of constituted transcendences."[26] Consequently, all judgments about the inappropriateness of a reaction to an event that was "harmless in itself" were invalid; there were, in fact, no such "events-in-themselves" independent of their meanings for us. "In 'reality' . . . no event is ever an unambiguously determinate self-contained happening, insofar as 'the same event' *means* something totally different for intellectual abstraction."[27] Such judgments, therefore, had no empirical content; they simply indicated a

[25] Binswanger, *Ideenflucht*, p. 53.
[26] *Ibid.*, p. 52.   [27] *Ibid.*, p. 25.

disjunction between two types of experience. The world of the "insane" was a world of meaning, even if not our meaning. "Whenever we call such a 'querulous' man deranged [*verrückt*, literally displaced] or mentally ill," Binswanger wrote of one of his patients, "it is above all because we feel him as removed [*entrückt*] from our world. Now, however, he has a different world from us."[28]

Binswanger thus conceded that we must, in dealing with mental illness, still begin from our meanings and sense of reality. His point, however, was that we must not equate our meanings with meaningfulness per se; the unintelligible was not meaningless. This admonition would appear quite superfluous directed at psychoanalysis, which could indeed claim to have originated the maxim; Binswanger was still fighting the battle against orthodox psychiatry and tended at times to confuse his targets. But it is also the case that Freud arrived at his concept of meaning via the kind of conceptual detour criticized by Binswanger. It is a measure of the implications of the different approaches to meaning that Binswanger was led, not in the direction of the past to find an explanation of the present, nor to the level of energic event from which such concepts as displacement could emerge, but in the direction of trying to understand the *current* conditions for the possibility of abnormal experience.

This is, in fact, just how Binswanger characterized the enterprise of existential analysis as compared with phenomenological psychiatry. Phenomenology was concerned with understanding individual experiences, using the methods of psychological understanding and empathy. Its goal was to accumulate as many single psychological observations as possible: "We, on the other hand, seek in the first place neither the specification of the factical experience nor that of the process of experiencing, but rather that something which stands 'behind' or 'above' both. We seek, namely, the mode of being-in-the-world that makes possible such experience, that, in

28 *Ibid.*, p. 18.

other words, makes such experience understandable."[29] That is, existential analysis sought to discover the overarching unifying subjective concern, what Needleman, accurately reflecting Binswanger's Kantian language, has called the "existential *a priori*,"[30] which structured a person's world and underlay a wide variety of emotions and perceptions. Phenomenological investigation might reveal the existence of a particular fear or desire; the point of existential analysis was to discover what made that fear or desire possible, i.e., its wider context, its deeper meaning.

As an example, Binswanger cited one of his own earliest psychoanalytic cases: a young girl who at the age of five experienced an attack of anxiety and fainting when her heel got stuck in her skate and separated from her shoe. Psychoanalysis revealed that behind the girl's fear of the separating heel lay the fear of separation from her mother.[31] Binswanger acknowledged that the heel separation "symbolized" the girl's fear of separation from the mother, which was experienced by everyone as the arch-separation in life. But how could the breaking-off of a *heel* "stand for" the loss of the *mother*? The answer was that it did not, at least in the psychoanalytic sense. What linked the two events in the mind of the girl was the experience of continuity and discontinuity that was the basic structure of both. The girl's association of the skate incident to the mother revealed that what underlay her dependent need for her mother was her precarious sense of the continuity of her own existence, and correspondingly that of her world. This was the fundamental issue that determined how she would experience the world; as an all-consuming concern it was the criterion to which all perceptions were submitted in order to be admitted to her world as observables. The child, and later the adult, could brook no events that suggested a rupture in continuity, a break, or a sudden change,

[29] Binswanger, *Being-in-the-World*, p. 128.
[30] *Ibid.*, pp. 25ff.
[31] R. May et al., *Existence, A New Dimension in Psychology and Psychiatry*, New York, 1958, p. 203.

and would have to run away or faint. Thus the heel-anxiety was not a displacement of her mother-anxiety; it was an independent instantiation of the basic anxiety over continuity.

It would seem, then, that Binswanger was contradicting himself, since, on the one hand, he insisted on the independence of the two events and, on the other, acknowledged that one symbolized the other. Part of the difficulty can be removed by using another approach to clarify the point of Binswanger's Kantianism, but part of it has to do with an error in his thinking. Actions and emotions are properly characterized not by one but by a hierarchy of descriptions in terms of intentions, or in the case of emotions, intentional objects, and beliefs. For example, to the question "What is he doing?" the answer "Chopping wood" is true but insufficient, for someone may chop wood to take exercise, make a fire, earn money, or perform a moral duty. Similarly, an answer to the question "What is he afraid of?" requires not just a reference to the object of the fear but must include a reference to the danger feared from the object. When Binswanger claimed that explaining the anxiety over the loss of the heel as anxiety over losing the mother was not sufficient, he meant that it was still necessary to discover the point of the fear of losing the mother such that the heel-anxiety could be a form of it and associatively related to it. But in arguing that the abstract meaning category of continuity-discontinuity was primary, and that anxiety over separation from the mother did not cause the heel anxiety, Binswanger was abstracting from the experience of the girl, for whom continuity of existence was *defined* in terms of attachment to the mother. This was after all the justification for Binswanger's own admission that separation from the mother was symbolized in the heel episode.

Binswanger's reason for going too far in this direction and abstracting the issue of continuity from the mother-relationship was connected with the specifically biological meaning that separation-anxiety had in psychoanalytic theory. Organically related to the methodological point about the need for a meaning connection between event and symbol was the rejection of Freud's basically biological theory of motivation. Separation anxiety was anxiety about the continuity and permanence of personal identity, not about the need for nourishment and survival. This was revealed in an accurate phenomenological description of the object of the original anxiety—the break in continuity.

Binswanger regarded his categories of experience as "individual modifications" of the essential structure of being-in-the-world. Boss criticized this idea as an illegitimately subjectivist interpretation of Heidegger's ontology. Being-in-the-world was shorthand for the basic structure of human existence as meaning-disclosing and not therefore subject to individual "modification."[32] Boss, as we shall see, had specific reasons for denying the subject a role in the specific determination of meaning, reasons having to do with problems inherent in the existential concept of authenticity and health. He could not, however, escape the need for relating meaning to the specific orientation or concern of the self, and, instead of talking about a priori categories, talked about Dasein's "attunement" or "mood" as determinative of what appeared in the world of the self. The idea, however, was the same. Thus, for example, Boss criticized Freud's explanation of phobias and other so-called displacement phenomena. The animals that were the object of anxiety in phobias were not substitutions for someone or something other than themselves, substitutions brought about by "displacements of perceptual content" or by projection of an affect that was internal onto something external. The animals were what they were: aggressive, sensual, evil, or whatever; their importance to the subject resulted from his attunement to those aspects of existence which corresponded to his own emotions and desires. It was not necessary to get behind these objects to the reality they "symbolized"; that reality was in them and was ascertainable through phenomenological description of their meaning for the subject.

[32] Boss, *Psychoanalyse und Daseinsanalytik*, pp. 95-96.

The different implications of the Freudian and existential approaches to meaning were made dramatically clear in their respective approaches to dream interpretation. The distinction between manifest and latent content was a necessary one for Freud's theory. The manifest content of the dream was, in terms of logic and conventions of meaning, bizarre and irrational. Therefore, the true meaning of the dream could lie only in another text whose relationship to the manifest one was causal; the latent content was an entity separate from and temporally antecedent to the manifest content. Theoretically, at least, there was no intrinsic or meaning relationship between the two; the manifest content was the effect of a causal process involving an energy flow between ideational representatives, not the result of psychic processes involving beliefs, subjective symbolic equivalences, metaphorical language, and so on. If the energy process was law-governed, its results from the standpoint of meaning were arbitrary.[33] Hence the manifest content was unimportant in itself; it furnished only a series of isolated starting points for the retracing of a chain of mechanically determined associations. This is why Freud asserted that the paths of association traversed during a dream interpretation were, with minor exceptions, the actual paths followed by the mental energy in the creation of the dream.

The existentialists rejected the Freudian conception of dream work. There was no need for it, they argued, if there were no initial presumption about the "essential" meanings of objects and actions; if certain limited or conventional meanings did not get theoretical priority; and if, instead, the question were asked as to the meaning of a dream element for the dreamer in the context of his life and current needs. Binswanger began very modestly by suggesting a renewed focus on the manifest content of the dream: "By steeping oneself in the manifest content of the dream—which since Freud's epoch-making postulate concerning the reconstruction of latent dream thoughts, has receded all too far into the back-

[33] Freud, *S.E.*, Vol. v, p. 644.

ground—one learns the proper evaluation of the primal and strict interdependence of feeling and image, of mood and pictorial realization."[34] Boss, however, in his monograph *The Analysis of Dreams*,[35] no longer even conceded the distinction between manifest and latent contents. There was no legitimate reason to connect causally the beginning and end points of free associations to dream elements.[36] Free association simply revealed the full subjective meaning of the dream contents. Freud's recourse to causal and symbolic explanation resulted from his considering "the essence of things in themselves as much too impoverished."[37] If the criteria of judgment of the rationality of dream contents were that of positivism—i.e., the order of the world of natural science—then the "aberrant" significations of dream components would of course have to be brought to them from outside, as their contingent causes. But, in fact, for the dreamer these significations were intrinsic to the elements of the dream. Properly understood, interpretation did not replace one text with another but unfolded what was already given in the dream contents.

A vital corollary of this approach was the rejection of wish-fulfillment as the exclusive meaning of dreams. While granting that dreams could indeed be wish-fulfillments, Boss denied the legitimacy of making the structure of one particular type of dream the prototype of dreams in general.[38] As many kinds of activity as went on in waking life were to be found in dreams as well. For Freud, as we have seen in chapter one, the idea of wish-fulfillment was a conclusion derived from the postulates of his neurophysiological model. On the basis of phenomenology, however, it was not possible, according to Boss, to define a criterion whereby the essence of our dream life as a whole could be distinguished from waking

[34] Binswanger, *Being-in-the-World*, p. 231.

[35] M. Boss, *The Analysis of Dreams*, trans. A. J. Pomerans, New York, 1958.

[36] *Ibid.*, p. 34.   [37] *Ibid.*, p. 100.   [38] *Ibid.*, p. 36.

life,[39] except for the fact that dream life did not show the same historical continuity as waking life. It was certainly not correct to regard dreams as hallucinations and then define hallucinations as wish-fulfillments. This was to ignore the richness and diversity of dream contents, which showed the same variety of concerns and interests as daily life. As with daily life, the proper approach to the dream involved interpreting it from within and then raising the questions, "What kind of existence, what kinds of needs and fears would allow such figures, objects, and activities to appear in the world of the dreamer? What kind of problem was the dreamer concerned with?"

The existential approach to interpretation had the attractiveness of simplification. It proposed to sweep away a set of cumbersome metapsychological hypotheses, whose conceptual foundations were untenable, and replace them with a descriptive approach. However, existentialism created certain obvious problems of its own. Most seriously, it seemed to raise the question of the necessity of interpretation, if, as it held, meaning was on the surface of things, immediately given in our experience of them. On this score, Boss was in one sense more radical than Binswanger. Binswanger was equally opposed to the notion of dreams or symptoms as the intrinsically meaningless effects of underlying mechanical causal processes, but he had no trouble with the idea that they might be indirect or "symbolic" expressions of meanings, desires, and emotions. The metaphorical or concrete language of symptoms and dreams functioned in just the same way as body language to conceal from the neurotic the articulated verbal content, the general conceptual meaning, of his wishes and fears. It did this through the particularity, the individuality, that differentiated the symbol from the thing symbolized. It was, for example, the very concreteness of the phobic girl's anxiety about heels that "concealed," by concretizing it, the girl's anxiety about separation. Thus, wrote Binswanger, "the

[39] *Ibid.*, p. 208.

self has to be freed from its . . . imprisonment in the images *in* which it always in some way lives."[40]

For Boss, however, there were not two layers of meaning but one, since he rejected the language of symbolism; dream elements and the intentional objects of fears, obsessions and the like carried their meanings in themselves. Clinically, he was fully aware of, and insisted on the reality of, "conceal-ment" and defense—the unavailability to the neurotic of cer-tain of his own impulses and feelings. Indeed, he was, as we shall see, rather closer to Freud on this issue than was Bins-wanger, because Binswanger's understanding of concealment was non-dynamic while Boss's rested on conflict. Upholding the reality of concealment, however, seemed to contradict his insistence that manifest contents did not symbolize anything. According to his interpretation, for example, the presence of animals in dreams and as objects of phobias revealed the existence of "animalistic" impulses in the subject; but neither the impulses themselves, nor their real objects, nor the reasons for them, were known to the agent.

(3) *The Unconscious*

Here, then, was the dilemma for the existentialists. Mean-ing was the way in which things appeared to us, the necessary context of any behavior or relationship to the world: the idea of unconscious meaning seemed therefore a contradiction in terms. On the other hand, as working therapists, they were well acquainted with the clinical realities of defense. Over thirty-five years after Freud had asked Binswanger how he was going to get by without the unconscious, Binswanger an-swered him retrospectively, "Of course I never 'got along' without the unconscious . . . in psychotherapeutic practice, which is indeed impossible without Freud's conception of the unconscious."[41] What *was* impossible was Freud's theoretical understanding of unconscious processes, which omitted the

40 Binswanger, *Vorträge*, Bd. I, p. 157.
41 Binswanger, *Erinnerungen*, p. 77.

dimension of subjective meaning in deriving the link between the concealed and the overt form of its manifestation.

The concept of being-in-the-world at least suggested a way of understanding this link. The self was the condition of meaning in the sense that its concerns and interests determined the meaning-schemes in terms of which the world of things and people would be experienced and described. Potentially, the individual could become reflectively aware of these concerns and meaning-structures as his own. Often, however, these meaning-schemes were rigidly inflexible and not available to reflective awareness, conscious appropriation, or modification. In such cases, one could be obsessed or fascinated with objects, images, or persons without being able to understand or verbalize the relationship of their characteristics to one's subjective needs and desires.

One of Boss's patients "saw" writhing masses of snakes and worms whenever she closed her eyes. Boss encouraged her to describe the kind of world and the possibilities of behavior the snakes embodied. They were, she said, low, bestial, loathsome, instinct-driven creatures that could appear suddenly out of the darkness of the earth, attack dangerously, insinuate themselves into someone unawares through the tiniest opening, and poison and pollute.[42] The modes of existence that the snakes embodied in their meaning to the woman were the unacknowledged and unassimilable possibilities and desires of the patient herself: that was why the snakes could appear to her, but that was also why they had to appear as alien. Another of his patients, a nineteen-year-old girl, suddenly developed a hysterical paralysis of the legs as she walked past a handsome young gardener who attracted and excited her in a way that she found quite bewildering. The attraction was there in the girl's behavior itself, Boss argued, in her quite conscious fascination with the gardener, and not in unconscious ideas or images in the mind; but the girl could not become aware of the gardener's oppressive presence in a reflected and articulated way because she could not accept

[42] Boss, *Psychoanalysis and Daseinsanalysis*, p. 150.

her own sensual possibilities. "The girl," Boss wrote, "could not even think, 'It is not permitted to love the man erotically' because even a prohibition points to the thing which one is not allowed to do."[43]

There was, however, an important difference in the ways in which Binswanger and Boss conceived of the restricted scope and unavailability to consciousness of the neurotic's mode of being-in-the-world. Binswanger's treatment was static and epistemological, Boss's dynamic and closer to the Freudian conception of conflict. For Binswanger, the "existential *a priori*," as the condition of all possible experience, by definition set the limits of experience. Within the framework of a given meaning-structure, there was no perspective from which its criterion could be characterized or relativized, because so long as it prescribed the field of description there was no standpoint outside of it on the basis of which it could be accepted as just one meaning among others. In the case of the girl with the heel phobia, for example, this meant that all experience could be seen by her only in terms of its bearing on the issues of continuity and discontinuity. All experience had to conform to the norm of continuity; she could not assimilate experiences of discontinuity or separation and had to escape them. "Becoming conscious" of the category would involve expanding the horizon of possible experience so that she could gain a vantage point from which it could not be the form of experience itself but one possible mode of experience. What such a process of expansion would entail, however, was left unclear because Binswanger had no explanation of how a particular category came exclusively to dominate or constrict the patient's world. For Boss, however, the permitted existential schema of possibilities did not exclude the *existence* of others for the patient; it excluded the possibility of integrating them as self-conscious possibilities into the individual's self-definition because the latter was closed and exclusive. This meant that they could lead only a strangulated existence, emerging as alien processes or objects of concern.

[43] *Ibid.*, p. 119.

The "unconscious" could not be known because it could not be done. The conceptual scheme that governed the beliefs and possibilities of the neurotic was a set of rules for meaning and behavior maintained by needs and fears; only if the needs were to some extent satisfied and the fears to some extent lifted could they even be recognized as rules.

PAST AND PRESENT: THE INFANTILE ORIGIN OF SYMPTOMS

Just as the existentialists attacked the validity of conceiving the beginning and end of a chain of free associations as a causal relationship in dream interpretation, they also attacked the Freudian reasoning that made remembered childhood events the causes of the symptoms to which they had been associated. It is possible to understand what they had in mind only if one recalls the peculiar nature of psychoanalytic "description-explanations." Had Freud simply asserted a correlation between, or even a law-like generalization connecting, separately described childhood events and adult behavior, the existentialists would have had no quarrel with him. Boss, for example, asserted rather simple causal relationships between oppressive, puritanical family milieus and sexual repressiveness in adults. In the "heel phobia" case, Binswanger accepted without demur the idea that the young woman's anxiety originated in a traumatic event in childhood. What Binswanger objected to was the reduction of adult behavior to a stage-specific event in childhood such that the behavior could be explained—or described—only as a repetition of that childhood event. Freud's designation of adult behavior as infantile was not meant as an illuminating metaphor but literally. This conception was made possible by the hypotheses underlying the concept of unconscious phantasy.[44] The meaning of behavior in the present was the event in the past that it replicated; it had no significance, no proper description, in a contemporary context. The deeper significance

[44] See chapter one.

135

of this conception, as of the conception of primary process, has yet to be explored; we shall see its importance both for Freud's concept of irrationality and for his concept of health. It was, in any case, this formulation of unconscious phantasy with which the existentialists took issue.

The point of the existentialists' position has already been adumbrated in the case of the heel phobia. Binswanger insisted that the extension of the phobia and the separation anxiety it represented into the girl's adult life was possible only because of the persistence of her preoccupation with the issue of the continuity of her existence. He did not try to explain why the girl's existence was so precarious to begin with and why she could not become an autonomous human being. He was trying to show that the causal effectiveness of the traumatic event in the past on behavior in the present could be understood only in terms of a motive in the *present* that lent that event its continuing significance in her adult life.

Binswanger's critique was more explicit in the case of Freud's derivation of character traits from infantile sexuality. Psychoanalysis saw in a character trait such as miserliness an "unintelligible basic motive [*Befindlichkeitsmoment*]," that is to say a purely irrational manifestation.[45] It then proceeded to explain that behavior as a substitute formation for infantile anal erotism. But how was it that parsimony could function as a substitute for anal erotism? Freud had argued that in this syndrome gold was equated with feces, but, despite his citation of numerous examples from literature of the existence of such an equation, he had not indicated how gold could come to have such significance. That is, in Freud's explanation, no subjectively meaningful connection existed between the two; there was no understanding of how hoarding feces could be satisfied by hoarding gold.

Binswanger accepted the psychoanalytically discovered equation because of the associative evidence. But what made the equation possible *for the subject* was the common denominator in both activities of filling up an emptiness. The

45 Binswanger, "Geschehnis und Erlebnis," *Vorträge*, II, p. 168.

miser's passion for filling boxes with gold, just like the child's concern with losing his feces, was a response to the danger of becoming empty of substance, losing part of oneself: "Thus filling is the *a priori* bond which furnishes a common denominator for gold and feces; only on this basis does there arise the possibility that in the course of development of the individual gold addiction can 'originate' from retention of feces. *In no way, however, is the latter the 'cause' or the motive of miserliness.* This motive lies, as we have said, deeper than and behind both. We must always convert psychoanalytic derivations or genetic interpretations in this way."[46]

The equivocation between "cause" and "motive" in this passage is significant: it testifies to some awareness on Binswanger's part of the peculiar logical structure of psychoanalytic explanation. On the one hand, he was arguing that it was not the impulse to retain feces *per se* (i.e., physical retention of the *substance*) that was manifested in miserliness, but the defense against the feeling of emptiness or the danger of losing something that was vital to the integrity of the self. Otherwise, no meaning sense could be made out of the idea that in hoarding gold the miser was "really," i.e., literally, hoarding feces (unless Freud wanted to say that the miser unconsciously *believed* that money was feces. As we have seen, however, Freud's symbolic equivalences were the results of energic primary processes, not mental or psychic processes). On the other hand, Binswanger was also arguing that in causal terms the historical fact of anal retentiveness in childhood was not by itself sufficient to explain the existence of the need to fill in adulthood. The adult act had meaning in its own terms (defending the integrity of the self) and not just with reference to a past historical event (anal retention). A *type* of conflict that had originated in childhood continued into adulthood, though its form of expression was different. Psychoanalysis, however, did not *explain* the persistence of the early conflict; it only noted it.

We can see now that in criticizing genetic explanation,

46 Binswanger, *Vorträge*, Bd. I, p. 169.

Binswanger was actually compressing two criticisms into one. In questioning the reduction of behavior to the literal significance of the infantile past, he was simultaneously attacking the instinctual and the physical interpretation of the infantile past itself.

"The derivation of illness and character traits from the over-accentuation of certain erotogenic zones acquired in the course of inner and outer life-history seems to me impossible to carry out, because in such derivations, anthropological-structural and life-historical motives are confused, or rather the first are completely absorbed in the second. If one designates what psychoanalysis doubtlessly saw correctly, but interpreted too historically and genetically (stressing the early infantile as a genetic condition) as quite generally an oral or anal 'characteristic' in the total structure of a human being, which can only be strengthened or weakened through accidental historical motives; and if one gives up the materialistic-positivistic point of view, according to which the body is seen as existing first and only afterwards invested by mind, the essential core of the doctrine is retained. . . . Orality, anality and so on are then [seen to be] onesidedly somato-dynamic and somatographic expressions for fundamental features of human behavior understood as a mind-body unity."[47]

Thus Binswanger accepted the idea of infantile sexuality with two very serious qualifications. In the first place, sexuality involved more than organ-pleasure or physical gratification but a whole attitude to the world encompassing the very meaning of selfhood. Secondly, he argued that the so-called "anthropological structures," or basic needs and conflicts, embodied in infantile sexuality were general human characteristics that expressed themselves one way in childhood but another way in adulthood; the typical error of psychoanalysis was to interpret the later form as if it were a recurrence of the earlier form, rather than as a different instantiation of the same more general structure. The existential approach re-

47 Binswanger, *Ideenflucht*, p. 26.

138

fused to reduce the present to the past by describing the present as a mere repetition of a "life-historical moment," but at the same time it was able to see in the present event a meaning-structure that linked it to the past.

As to why a particular characteristic would be "intensified" or "exaggerated" by specific historical events in the life of the individual so that it would recur later, Binswanger had no general explanation. Indeed, this kind of explanation, as he saw it, was specifically the task of psychoanalysis or scientific psychiatry, not existential analysis, which was content with showing how past and present were linked by a common meaning structure in a way that avoided the genetic reductionism of psychoanalysis. He had, however, in effect argued that in fact psychoanalysis itself had no full explanation for the persistence of the past, either, that it simply identified continuity of concern or behavior between childhood and adulthood without giving a sufficient explanation. What Binswanger was driving at was what Freud himself conceded on a number of occasions, most significantly, as will be seen, in *The Problem of Anxiety*: there was no *psychological* explanation in psychoanalytic theory for the problem of fixation.

Boss remained closer to Freud than did Binswanger in his interpretations of the significance of neurotic impulses and in his genetic thinking. However, like Binswanger, he rejected the version of unconscious phantasy that described present behavior as the disguised substitute or phantasy fulfillment of infantile wishes. Moreover, he also rejected the concept of repression insofar as it served in psychoanalytic theory to explain the link between past and present. Repression was a mechanical doctrine according to which a wish was buried in a psychic compartment, and reappeared later as somehow the same wish, though distorted or attached to different objects. The concept, however, gave no account in meaning terms (in terms of purposes and beliefs) of *why* a certain impulse, prohibition, or self-definition would be sustained by the individual from childhood to adulthood. Nor could it explain how desires or emotions felt towards parent figures could attempt

139

to fulfill or repeat themselves by being directed at completely different people.

Thus, even though Boss disagreed with Binswanger about the meaning of anality, his version of it made the same conceptual point. Boss criticized "those theorists who attempt to generalize the anal-erotic relationship to the world into the *formal* modalities of holding-on and expelling" for abandoning Freud's crucial discovery that these modalities always concerned the spheres of what the neurotic considered as being filthy.[48] But Daseinsanalysis differed from Freud in that it could not "think of a child's relation to his excrement as being the cause and origin of his 'retentive' behavior toward all other things as well. Daseinsanalysis may fully agree that a child's handling of his feces is often the first instance of this kind of relationship, but objects if psychoanalytic theory turns a sequence in time into a causal connection."[49] An explanation both of "fixation" and of the generalization of the prohibition against feces into one against a sphere or category of filthy things was still necessary.

Boss did try to explain the persistence or intensification of certain needs and impulses found in childhood. For example, he argued that certain desires that appeared in childhood must be satisfied at the appropriate time or they would continue unabated in later life, hindering further development. The theory on which this argument was based was not explicit or fully worked out in Boss's work; it was only hinted at. In his view, "child-like behavior," dependency on trusted, loving, and open adults, for example, was a prerequisite to the development of a confident, autonomous, and flexible self. "A parent-child relationship . . . whose openness is sufficiently in accord with all of the child's genuine nature is the only realm into which his possibilities of existing can come forth in a healthy way."[50] If the child's dependency needs were not satisfied at the right time (the result either of lack

[48] Boss, *Psychoanalysis and Daseinsanalysis*, p. 184.
[49] *Ibid.*, p. 185.
[50] *Ibid.*, p. 207.

of parental love or of the child's "exaggerated sensitivity" and "excessive love requirement"), he would continue to try to satisfy them as an adult, constantly restructuring dependency relationships, setting up authority figures for himself, and running away from demands for autonomous, independent behavior. The adult "Oedipus complex" was a manifestation of just this kind of behavior. Of one of his cases, a young man whose mistress was an older married woman, Boss argued that it was wrong to explain his love for her as "actually" meaning his own concrete mother. "His mistress fitted admirably into this existential world openness as the actual motherly woman she was without any 'meaning' or 'symbolizing.' "[51] Even if he were to have dreamed of actually having intercourse with his mother, it would not have proved that the mistress "was" the mother. Dream and event would be autonomous occurrences, corresponding in their similar structure to the patient's "world-openness" of dependency.

Dependency needs, however, were not so easily satisfied. The neurotic often defeated his own purposes and was unable to accept the love and acceptance he desired. If in his early relationships certain needs and impulses (including perhaps dependency) had been regarded as evil or otherwise impermissible, he would "fall prey" to the attitudes of his parents and adopt them as his own. His own needs would thus turn against him, making him unacceptable in his own eyes and therefore necessarily in the eyes of others.

"Falling prey" was Boss's version of identification; its explanation was essentially in Heideggerian terms. Particular historical events—in this case the interaction of parent and child—had the effect of conditioning the "world-openness" of the patient by limiting and restricting his existential possibilities. The definitions and prohibitions of the family milieu were taken as absolutes and generalized into universal categories of meaning and perception that were relatively irrefutable as the child developed. Certain types of behavior were in effect ruled inadmissible, officially unrecognizable, and

[51] *Ibid.*, p. 201.

attraction to them would necessarily lead to a self-condemnation that itself could not be articulated; other forms became generalized norms of experience so that their concrete historical origin was lost.

Thus a dependency wish was not necessarily aimed at the mother, though its frustration in childhood may have been the main cause of its persistence and its later manifestations bore structural similarities to early experience. Inhibitions against sexuality did not derive from the fact that the sexual wish was really directed at the mother but from the generalized definition of sex as dirty, and of decent women as not desiring it. The prototype of the decent woman was the mother and the prohibitions were generated as a result of childhood sexual play, but they were communicated as or transformed into general schema relevant to all experience. It is obvious that Boss could not and did not dispense with the concept of repression insofar as it denoted the unavailability of memories and impulses to conscious verbal appropriation. He rejected it, however, for purposes of explanation because it begged the psychological question of why the meaning-schemes of the past lived on or why the individual was animated by impulses similar to those in childhood but with different objects.

Instinct and Meaning

So far, we have considered the existentialist criticism of the causal relationship asserted by psychoanalysis between the meaning behind an act or a symbol and the act or symbol itself, a relationship conceived of as mechanical and predicated on the presumed intrinsic irrationality of the manifest act or symbol under its conventional description. For Binswanger, this criticism was inseparable from another and to him, at least, even more important one; the meaning that psychoanalysis did find behind symptoms was either misconstrued or interpreted too narrowly because it was squeezed within the confines of an instinctual theory of behavior and motivation.

In his first paper on the subject of biologism, Binswanger had seen it as a level complementary to psychological description and one necessary to convert psychology into psychiatry by the insertion of a norm of health. Under the influence of existentialism he changed his mind about the basic conceptual structure of psychoanalysis. In a paper delivered in 1936 at a meeting in honor of Freud's eightieth birthday, Binswanger argued that "To understand Freud's great ideas correctly one must not . . . proceed from psychology—a mistake that I myself made for a long time."[52] For Freud, psychology was always in principle a biological natural science; the "pictorial language" of psychology—the language of meanings and motives—was a temporary substitute for a language that would describe the real underlying organic forces more simply and more directly. In the interim, the concept of instinct, important, but, as Freud admitted, obscure, served to indicate the relation between the somatic and the psychic spheres. The psychic component of instinct was not descriptive but theoretical, representing "effects stemming from within the body and carried over to the psychic apparatus."[53] Freud's instinctualism was his way of keeping psychoanalytic psychology a *natural* science, a body of thought whose basic explanatory scheme was materialist. As an explanatory concept, the idea of instinct subsumed psychoanalysis under the "founding charter" of modern psychiatry: Griesinger's dictum that because of their organic base, psychic phenomena ought to be interpreted only by natural scientists, as functions of organic processes.

Binswanger rejected this as a viable theoretical base for a study of man, even mentally ill man. The conception of man as an organism was no doubt necessary for psychiatric and psychoanalytic theorizing, since only in the event of causal

[52] Binswanger, *Being-in-the-World*, p. 195.
[53] *Ibid.*

143

links between body and mind could cure be possible.[54] Nevertheless, this conception could also be dangerous if it were allowed to usurp the whole field of human experience, if it were based on a *"destruction* of man's experimental knowledge of himself . . . that is of anthropological experience": "Health is doubtless one of man's greatest goods and its protection one of the noblest tasks of civilization. But man has even more to protect than his physical and mental health. The many-sidedness of his being must be adequate to the many-sidedness of his struggles."[55] Only a method that did not reduce man a priori to the lowest common denominator of "life" could be faithful to human diversity and to the variability of human meaning. For all its insight and power, psychoanalysis was by its basic conception limited to what Binswanger called *"homo natura"*—man as an extension of the natural world, man as a natural creature. This philosophical anthropology underlay Freud's elevation of the pleasure principle to the position of sole motivating factor in human behavior. Logically, however, it was an inadequate conception: "To confuse the unmasking of a *particular* hypocrisy with the destruction of the meaningfulness of human existence in general is to fall into the grave error of *interpreting a priori or essential potentialities of human existence as genetic developmental processes, the error, in short, of interpreting existence as natural history*. It results in 'explaining' the religious mode of existence by the anxiety and helplessness of childhood and early manhood . . . the ethical mode of existence by external compulsion and introjection, the artistic by the pleasures of beautiful semblance, etc."[56]

Binswanger's point against psychoanalysis was conceptual,

---

[54] It is curious that in passages like these Binswanger minimized the resources of psychotherapy and showed himself to be far more wedded to the biological doctrines of orthodox psychiatry than was Freud. This was a consequence of his emphasis on existential analysis as a purely descriptive endeavor that had no intention of usurping the legitimate function of "scientific," i.e., physical, explanation.

[55] *Ibid.*, p. 166.   [56] *Ibid.*, p. 175.

not empirical. "Excessive" moralism did frequently conceal impulses to the very act condemned by the moral prohibition. But the idea of obligation or duty itself could not be derived from utilitarian or prudential considerations. The concept of conscience as the introjection of parental authority begged the question of how that which was external and coercive could become internal, universal, and *legitimate*.

Sometimes Binswanger wrote as if he accepted the circumscribed validity of the concepts of instinct and pleasure for the types of cases Freud studied.[57] At other times he attacked the adequacy of biological interpretations of Freud's own clinical discoveries. Thus he did not either ignore or reject the data that came under the general heading of sexuality, but he argued that "sexuality" meant more than physical sensations and the gratification of physical desires. He proposed, as has been indicated, to revise Freud's picture of the stages of sexual development by reinterpreting them in terms of broader and deeper significance than those associated with instinctual theory, meanings with both physical and "spiritual" dimensions. "Orality," for example, Binswanger saw as a basic mode of relatedness to the world and to other people, a way in which the individual expressed his feeling about the integrity of his selfhood in relation to the external world, whether in the forms of reciprocal exchange, defensive rejection, or needy assimilation. As in the case of the hysterical girl who had lost her voice and her appetite, it was the mode of communication with others or withdrawal, acceptance, or rejection of the impact of others and of the world on her. Assimilation or rejection were embodied most graphically in the functions of eating and speaking, but they could be the meaning of other activities as well.[58] In another case study, Binswanger characterized the grandiose flights of ideas of manic psychosis with the slang expression "having a big mouth" (*Grossmauligkeit*) to indicate a specific "anthropological" trait. Psychoanalysis, he wrote, appropriately classified such

57 *Ibid.*, pp. 168, 169, 173.
58 Binswanger, *Vorträge*, Bd. 1, pp. 150 ff.

an individual as an "oral type," but here orality could be properly understood only as a mode of self-presentation to the world, a mode in which the excess of self-glorifying words covered up a deficiency of selfhood.[59]

Binswanger did not limit himself to reinterpreting the modes of experience discovered by psychoanalysis; in his opinion, these were far from exhausting the range of general meaning contexts available to man. In his essay "Dream and Existence" he analyzed a number of dreams containing images of falling and rising in terms of their "anthropological" significance. These vectors had their own basic meaning as existential directions, referring to the happy, harmonious, soaring cycle of life, on the one hand, and the unhappy, constricted descending cycle, on the other. In psychoanalytic theory, Binswanger noted, dreams of flying and falling were often thought to be connected with erotic moods and sexual wishes. This was perfectly compatible with his own interpretation, which aimed at "uncovering an a priori structure of which . . . the erotic-sexual themes are special, secondary contents."[60] The question here thus was "What was the meaning of sexuality itself?" and this could be known from the way it was embodied or symbolized in the dream, e.g., as a form of "falling existence." Sexuality as a physical act was not the irreducible datum. Binswanger's general approach to the issue of sexuality was more succinctly formulated some years later by Merleau-Ponty, whose interpretation of psychoanalysis was heavily influenced by him:

"In so far as a man's sexuality provides a key to his life, it is because in his sexuality is projected his manner of being towards the world, that is, towards time and other men. There are sexual symptoms at the root of all neuroses, but these symptoms, correctly interpreted, symbolize a whole attitude, whether, for example, one of conquest or of flight."[61]

Neither Binswanger nor Merleau-Ponty made any system-

[59] Binswanger, *Ideenflucht*, pp. 117-119.
[60] Binswanger, *Being-in-the-World*, p. 228.
[61] Merleau-Ponty, *Phenomenology of Perception*, p. 158.

atic analysis of the "basic attitudes" symbolized by sexuality; nevertheless, as we shall see, Binswanger's "existential *a prioris*" or "anthropological structures" all had an underlying common tendency that in effect made them a unified alternative to Freud's concept of libido.

Medard Boss's monograph on sexual perversions represented a special application of Binswanger's critique of biologism in psychoanalytic theory. The first edition of the book came at the peak of Binswanger's influence on Boss, before the latter began his collaboration with Heidegger. It reflected not only the critical aspect of Binswanger's work but the constructive part as well, his major book on philosophical anthropology that developed a concept of love as a mode of interpersonal relationship in contrast to Freud's concept of libido.[62]

In *Meaning and Content of Sexual Perversions* Boss attacked the psychoanalytic theory of perversions as fixations of, or regressions to, infantile "partial impulses" or component instincts. There were a number of problems with this formulation. Causal reduction of adult behavior to infantile impulses made it impossible to understand the meaning of the perversion for the present life of the adult. The interpretation of perverse impulses as instincts relating to specific erogenous zones of the body or as biological preliminaries to the sexual act that had somehow become autonomous (for example, sadism) distorted the actual nature of the desires as experienced by the "pervert" and made it impossible to see them as expressions of his whole personality. Finally, the notion of instinct as essentially autoerotic, inherently unconcerned with the outside world and only secondarily attached to objects, was based on an untenable concept of human relatedness to people.

In place of the psychoanalytic doctrine, Boss argued that perversions could be described as distorted attempts at human relatedness by people suffering from "loss of personal-

[62] L. Binswanger, *Grundformen und Erkenntnis menschlichen Daseins,* Zurich, 1942.

ity."[63] "At the bottom of all concrete love- and sex-distur-
bances . . . we find that the fullness of the loving mode of
existence is limited by the mode of being as an isolated, auto-
cratic, petty, and fear-laden individual."[64] Free, loving relationships with others were blocked and constricted by a number of different factors—horror of sexuality, fear of women,
obedience to social conventions, feelings of inadequacy and
impotence before the objects of desire, and so on. Perversions
were stratagems designed to circumvent or overcome the barriers to contact without actually getting rid of them. They
were thus responses of a whole, if stunted, self to a relationship with another embracing but transcending physical sexuality. Fetishism, voyeurism, and kleptomania were different
ways of touching someone at a distance, indirectly or sym-
bolically, without the danger of a direct encounter with the
other person. Exhibitionism and sadism were assaults out of
fear; their purpose was to tear down the forbidding autonomy and otherness of the love object and to increase the pervert's own sense of power and effectiveness so that he could
surrender to the vulnerability of his own need for love. Perversions were not original instinctual impulses but defenses.
Moreover, they were defenses against desires that could not
be fitted into the biological category of instinct.

In some of Boss's case studies the clinical evidence was
clearly at odds with his own theoretical categories. The dependent, symbiotic love that the sado-masochistic patient
both desired and feared was far from the idealized "I-Thou"
love relationship described by Binswanger.[65] Nevertheless,
this did not alter the force of the criticism of psychoanalytic
biologism. This emerges from perhaps the most interesting
of Boss's reinterpretations of the most Freudian of categories
—the incest taboo, Oedipus complex, and castration fear.

These psychic facts discovered by psychoanalysis were

[63] M. Boss, *Meaning and Content of Sexual Perversions*, trans. L. L.
Abell, New York, 1949, p. 30.
[64] *Ibid.*, p. 37.
[65] *Ibid.*, pp. 79-114.

intelligible as concrete manifestations of existential anxiety: man's basic anxiety about being-in-the-world as an individuated self. The incest taboo expressed the truth of man's fate, the "commandment" that human earthly life exists in myriads of separated individual particles. Only gods and kings at the dawn of history had the right of incest, marking their ability to achieve eternal, unseparated existence; they could continue to exist in their incest-procreated sons while maintaining their own identity. Mortals, however, were threatened with castration for violating the incest taboo; and the weight of this retaliation served as a measure of man's anxiety about accepting the destiny of a separate existence. "It seems that nothing less than the tremendous threat of castration forces man to overcome this fear and to prevent him from withdrawing and escaping into the spaceless and timeless incestuous cosmic entirety."[66] At the same time, however, castration fear also embodied man's anxiety about the possibility of human existence as a separate individual.

Like Binswanger, Boss insisted that though the fundamental instinctual categories of psychoanalysis had to be replaced, existential analysis was not only compatible with psychoanalysis, but no substitute for the painstaking historical investigation of psychoanalytic therapy: "We look upon our work as being the foundation to these 'central complexes' of psychoanalytic theory; however, we must not mistake it as a substitute for the therapeutic necessity to work out and make conscious to the individual these complexes through the process of psychoanalytic treatment. *For general existential constituents become personal experience only in their concrete individual form.*"[67]

Boss was, as we have suggested, closer to the clinical descriptions and genetic analyses of psychoanalytic theory in his reinterpretations than was Binswanger, whose "existential *a prioris*" often seemed lifeless and abstract, detached from individual development. For example, Boss agreed that the theoretically inadequate psychoanalytic concept of orality jus-

---

[66] *Ibid.*, p. 46. [67] *Ibid.* Italics added.

tifiably referred to the period when the infant's relationship to his world consisted almost exclusively of sucking. That sucking, however, could not be understood in strictly biological terms as sensuous gratification or a need for food; it also represented a need for a receptive, confirmatory environment and through it the child was getting nourishment for his self-hood as well as for his body. Nor could orality be seen as phase-specific in the biological sense that seemed to entail that it was automatically outgrown in the course of maturation, since it was a function of the biological helplessness of the child. On the contrary, a proper "oral-erotic" infant-mother relationship was a condition of the development of mature autonomy; without it, a dependent, "sucking" relationship to others would be the individual's continuing dominant mode of relating to the world.

Another criticism of instinct theory followed from this view. Aside from its inadequacy in describing the full contents of desire, it was wrong in its solipsistic implications. As Freud had defined it, instinctual pleasure was in essence concerned with the internal economy of the organism and had no necessary reference to other selves; it was only contingently that it came to be attached to external objects. Hence Freud could conceive of an initial stage of total autoeroticism or primary narcissism. From the existential viewpoint, however, existence was always a "being-with" others, a primary "object-relatedness" incompatible with Freud's concept of instinct. The object was not, as Freud had said, separable from the impulse or emotion directed toward it; an impulse could not be properly specified without a description of the object toward which it was directed. Primary narcissism did not exist; from the outset the infant was directed towards others.

In Boss's later work, the use of Binswanger's anthropological categories virtually disappeared and he laid greater stress on the sexual aspects of love that were inhibited in the life of the neurotic and were to be liberated by psychotherapy.

But he continued to insist on the equal status of other needs and their non-derivability from biological instincts or infantile libidinal fixations.

DETERMINISM AND FREEDOM

Closely connected with the existential insistence on the primacy of meaning and the attack on causal and biological explanation was another important issue—the problem of freedom. One of the major reasons for the existentialist rejection of causality was the implication of determinism. The heart of existentialism was the idea of choice and responsibility. It was, however, not only as existentialists but as psychoanalysts that Boss and Binswanger recoiled from Freud's determinism. The enterprise of psychoanalysis was one of psychotherapeutic liberation; its purpose was to free individuals from the compulsion to repeat, to enable them to bring their lives under their own conscious control, and to open their world to greater variety and flexibility. These were Freud's own professed aims, but they seemed incompatible with the theory itself and with his programmatic announcements about the nature of science.

The existentialists did not quarrel with the idea that human existence had in it a quality of "drivenness," of determinateness. Moreover, this was as true for normal as for neurotic existence. Neurotic behavior was certainly commonly marked by a repetitiveness that appeared almost mechanical in its rigidity and in the inability of the neurotic to change it at will. But, beyond this, man was also unquestionably circumscribed by his biological nature and the impulses that were part of it. The psychiatrists rejected Sartre's excessive claims for freedom and argued with Heidegger that the range of human choice was limited by the "thrownness" of human existence, i.e., by the contingent necessities of the human and individual situation. "Man as a creature of nature," wrote Binswanger, "is revealed in the thrownness of the

151

Dasein, its 'that-it-is,' its facticity. . . . The Dasein . . . has . . . not itself laid the ground of its own being. . . . Consequently it is not 'completely free' in its world-design either."[68]

This, however, was not the whole story. Despite the influence of the past, therapy proved that it could be shaken off or reduced so that genuine change and choice were possible. The possibility of course depended on the patient's ability to transcend the transference, the repetitive patterns of the past, and enter into communication with the analyst as a free individual. He had to be able to accept, not simply see, feelings and impulses hitherto denied as his own or not even allowed to appear in his world. As for man's bodily nature, Dasein had the capacity to " 'distance' itself from its bodily involvement, its thrownness, in order to be fully free as 'spirit.' "[69] The very idea of repression and conflict depended on this kind of distance, not to speak of on the Freudian idea of sublimation, where the instinctual aspect of behavior virtually disappeared.

Descriptively and clinically, psychoanalysis not only had to acknowledge these facts; it made them the basis of its practice. Psychoanalytic theory, however, had no way of talking about them or conceptualizing them. A complete anthropology had to account for both aspects of human existence—freedom and constraint—and Heidegger's ontological analysis of being-in-the-world seemed to lay the groundwork for such an anthropology. Human existence was the disclosure of significance in the world through the projection of human possibilities. Repetition or necessity stemmed from the self-alienation that reified norms and meaning structures and made them an objective part of the world rather than the product of a self-world interaction; in this form they remained rigid and unchangeable because they were believed to be so. It was this that gave the past its power; what happened to the child as a matter of contingent fact was taken

68 Binswanger, *Being-in-the-World*. p. 212.
69 *Ibid.*, p. 216.

by him to be a matter of metaphysical necessity. Freedom lay in the possibility of abandoning this belief and therefore of breaking the exclusive hold of the closed meaning-structures that determined how the world would be experienced. Even where the meaning scheme was rooted in the biological structure of human nature, however, more flexibility towards it and about it could be achieved simply by recognizing and accepting it as human; and the option of distancing and self-control was always open.

The issue of freedom and determinism in psychoanalytic theory was more confused and complex than even the existentialists realized. For one thing, Freud frequently used the word "determinism" when he was really talking about meaning; thus, when he claimed that all behavior was determined and not produced arbitrarily or by chance, he meant that all behavior was meaningful, not that it could be causally explained. But it is certainly also the case that for Freud the idea of freedom was incompatible with a scientific approach to human behavior, which depended on invariant causal laws. Here it can be argued that the issue that bedeviled nineteenth-century positivism and its critics was a false one, that there is no incompatibility between freedom and causal explanation because causality does not imply determinism. To show that an action has causes is not necessarily to show that it had to happen, that the agent could not alter what he did. Discovering causes for events helps to reveal how the events in question can be inhibited as well as produced, since intervention in the causal chain may be possible.[70] Indeed, psychoanalytic therapy depended on just such an assumption. If the hidden motives and beliefs that produced neurotic symptoms could be revealed, they could be counteracted by other beliefs and intentions so that their force would be lessened or even dissipated. This is indeed how Freud sometimes spoke about the process of cure in psychoanalysis.

On the theoretical level, however, this model did not work.

[70] MacIntyre, *Against the Self-Images of the Age*, p. 208.

Since the explanation of symptom formation was in terms of a proto-neurological mechanical energy system, its implications were necessarily determinist unless some way could be specified to intervene in the system. Given the ambiguity of the existential referent of the metapsychology, it was not at all clear what such intervention could mean; Freud had long since abandoned any claim to be giving actual physical explanations for psychological events. This made it impossible to conceptualize the possibility of psychotherapeutic cure. Freud's scientific determinism was indeed incompatible with psychotherapeutic liberation.

There are, however, two aspects of Binswanger's attack on determinism that must be differentiated. In traditional German idealist fashion, Binswanger appeared to regard the body itself and its passions as the realm of unfreedom or drivenness. Hence freedom was equivalent to "spirituality," rising above mere bodily needs, or, as Binswanger put it, "distancing" oneself from one's bodily involvement. Despite a certain basic contempt for sexuality stemming from the same cultural tradition,[71] Freud did not essentially regard the body, or freedom, this way. Freedom meant conscious control, liberation from unconscious compulsion, not from the body, and in terms of his theoretical categories the body was preeminently the sphere of pleasure and spontaneity. From the viewpoint of psychoanalysis, Binswanger's philosophical position was reactionary, just the attitude that had been unmasked by Freud's discovery of spirituality as a defensive rationalization against sexuality. However, by determinism Binswanger also referred to infantile, dependent modes of action and to the repetitive and hence imprisoning patterns of behavior characteristic of neurosis. In criticizing Freudian theory as deterministic in this context he was on better ground, for there was no way in psychoanalytic theory of conceptualizing the autonomous selfhood that could rise above infantilism and break the stereotyped patterns.

[71] P. Rieff, *Freud: The Mind of the Moralist*, New York, 1959, pp. 169-170.

THE NATURE OF THERAPY

Existential criticisms were directed not only at psycho-analytic theory but at Freud's conception of psychoanalytic practice as well. The existentialists insisted that they had no quarrel with many of Freud's suggestions on technique; on the contrary, they accepted them as unsurpassed for thera-peutic treatment. Boss, however, argued that there was a con-flict between Freud's theoretical presuppositions and the prin-ciples actually underlying the analytic procedure, a conflict eliminated by existential analysis. It therefore provided a bet-ter understanding of the meaning of Freud's technical recom-mendations than his own theory. There were, however, a few important points where theory had deleterious effects on Freud's ideas about technique, and these needed revision.[72] But Boss himself underestimated the differences between the existential and the psychoanalytic interpretations of the ther-apeutic process, and this was in part because he himself mis-described what he perceived was happening in it.

The best way to approach the issue is to begin with the dilemma noted by Freud in his attempts to explain what brought about change in an analysis. For this, a brief sketch of the development of Freud's ideas about therapy is necessary.

Freud's first formula for therapy stemmed from the period of the *Studies on Hysteria* and the abreaction theory. The dis-solution of symptoms was accomplished by making the un-conscious conscious through remembering, i.e., by relating the alien, compulsive aspects of behavior to the event in the past from which they originated. The explanation of why con-scious remembering worked was essentially in terms of energy theory. Repression at the time of the original traumatic event prevented an appropriate discharge of energy because the event was cut off from the associative process. The result was the formation of symptoms—the damming up of energy through false connections and inappropriate responses. Re-

[72] Boss, *Psychoanalysis and Daseinsanalysis*, p. 237.

membering made possible the associative reintegration of the past events and hence a proper response, release of affect, and dissolution of the symptom.

Many changes were to take place in Freud's ideas about therapy, but the notion of making the unconscious conscious through knowledge was never modified. When he realized that repression was concerned primarily with impulses rather than memories, and the abreaction theory was dropped, he could give an explanation of the workings of cure through conscious knowledge in terms of intention and meaning. Symptoms existed because they functioned as concealments of or defenses against impulses; revelation of the actual nature of the impulses behind a symptom rendered the symptom untenable since its ability to disguise was lost.[73]

Almost from the very beginning, however, the idea of making the unconscious conscious as the road to therapy was qualified by Freud himself. The use of free association led to his discovery of the patient's resistance, not only to remembering but to assimilating the interpretations of the analyst. "Making conscious" could not be equivalent to the analyst's simply informing the patient of the meaning of his behavior, because conscious knowledge could co-exist side by side with unconscious impulses without making any difference in behavior.[74] Freud quickly gave up the method of telling the patient the meaning of his symptoms as soon as he himself discovered it, in order to work on the resistances. This, however, did not solve the basic problem: removal of the resistances was also a matter of the analyst's interpretation. There seemed to be no reason why interpretations of resistance could not also co-exist with the unconscious without making any difference to behavior.

A further step was taken with the discovery of transference. Freud used the term to describe the patient's emotional interest in the analyst—his impulses towards him and his beliefs about him. The term itself drew attention to the element of distortion present in the patient's attitude to the analyst,

[73] Freud, *S.E.*, Vol. XVI, p. 435.   [74] *Ibid.*, pp. 281, 436.

the fact that his feelings towards and his beliefs about the analyst were not warranted by the objective situation. They were, in fact, Freud saw, derived from elsewhere, repetitions of earlier situations.

At first, he saw the transference—whether "positive" (feelings of love) or "negative" (hostility)—exclusively as resistance to the work of memory. He soon came to appreciate its crucial place in therapy. Transference represented past memories in live form, the acting-out of the past in the present. Through transference the analysand could gain a real conviction of his unconscious phantasies and wishes as he lived them out with his analyst. The primary goal of analysis thus became working through the transference relationship via interpretation.

However, the same question existed with respect to interpreting the transference as with interpreting the resistances. What would ensure that assent to these interpretations would not be merely intellectual? Freud's answer was—the transference, that is, the positive feelings for the analyst that were not resistance but the patient's response to the analyst's therapeutic concern and help. The patient believed the interpretations of the analyst not through intellectual assent but through his love for the analyst and his consequent acceptance of the analyst's authority.[75]

This left Freud with an obvious problem that he was quick to face. Depending on the analyst's authority raised the specter of suggestion and put into question both the evidential value of the patient's assent for the truth of the analyst's interpretations and the need for truth as a therapeutic agent. If the credulity of the patient was ultimately what mattered, any interpretation would do, provided it had the desired consequences. Freud's answers to this dilemma were not really satisfactory. It was not adequate to argue that only those interpretations would work which were true, even if false ones were also accepted.[76] Under transference suggestion, interpretations were not believed rationally, and hence there was

[75] *Ibid.*, p. 445.   [76] *Ibid.*, p. 452.

no criterion enabling the patient to distinguish between true and false ones. Nor was it satisfactory to claim that ultimately the transference was superseded and what was left were the rational convictions of the patient in the truth of the interpretations.[77] For then it was difficult to see why love was necessary in the first place, since rational assent was ultimately the therapeutic agent. But if this were the case, one was back to the original problem—how to achieve "real" as opposed to merely "intellectual" cognition.

The primary explicit disagreement of the existentialists was with Freud's conception of transference and with the idea of cure as resulting from a making conscious of the unconscious. Binswanger in some scattered comments argued that psychoanalytic cure depended upon a human relationship of trust and mutual respect between analyst and patient, and hence upon the personality of the analyst and the freedom of the patient. The so-called "transference" relationship was not merely repetition but "an independent new form of communication . . . a new intertwining of destinies . . . not only in reference to the doctor-patient relationship but also and above all in reference to the pure relationship to a fellow human being in the sense of a genuine being-with one another."[78] The question of "resistance" was thus not simply one of a patient's inability to overcome his resistance to the father-image transferred to the doctor but whether his resistance could be overcome with this particular doctor, that is "whether the rejection of *this* doctor as a human being, and therefore the impossibility of a genuine communication with him, did not constitute the obstacle against breaking through the 'eternal' return of the resistance to the father."[79] Cure also depended upon the freedom of the patient, which Binswanger referred to as "spirit," the ability of the patient to "raise himself to the level of 'spiritual communcation' with the physician [and thus] gain insight into the 'unconscious instinctual drive' in question and be enabled to take the last

---

[77] *Ibid.*, p. 453. [78] Binswanger, *Vorträge*, Bd. I, p. 142.
[79] *Ibid.*, p. 143.

decisive step toward self-mastery."[80] Only a conception of reciprocity could get the concept of cure out of the bind that Freud's concept of transference-love created; the patient was in some way dependent on the personality of the therapist to gain the freedom to break through his defenses.

The new relationship emphasized by Binswanger was, in fact, not in place of but alongside the transference; it was in some ways similar to what contemporary analysts have come to call the "therapeutic alliance."[81] Boss, however, went further, to criticize Freud's conception of transference proper. It was a mistake to regard the transference as merely repetition, a projection of unconscious infantile feelings that did not originate in the current situation and did not really concern the analyst. Transference feelings were genuine interpersonal relationships to the analyst, even if they involved distorted or restricted perceptions of him.[82] Such distortions were functions of the limited types of relationship available to and desired by the patient. These were indeed formed by his early experiences. But these possibilities of relating were the contemporary structure of the patient's personality and his world, not separated ideas and impulses pertaining only to early scenes and figures.[83] Thus transference distortions were sustained by currently operating needs.

[80] Binswanger, *Being-in-the-World*, pp. 182-183.

[81] E. Zetzel, "Current Concepts of Transference," *International Journal of Psychoanalysis*, 37, pp. 369-376; R. Greenson, *The Technique and Practice of Psychoanalysis*, New York, 1967, pp. 46, 167-169.

[82] From the patient's frame of reference, his perceptions might not even be distortions. The paranoid delusions of a hostile world ready to destroy one, Boss pointed out, were often experienced by people who were so immature, weak, and dependent that they experienced as threats to life itself the most ordinary requirements and demands of adult interpersonal relationships, no matter how benevolently intentioned. From their point of view, they were threats. *Psychoanalysis and Daseinsanalysis*, p. 126.

[83] Freud had also insisted that "we must treat [the patient's] illness not as an event in the past, but as a present-day force." Nevertheless, he inevitably ended in contradiction because of the peculiarities of the psychoanalytic theory of meaning. Thus the sentence just quoted was im-

It followed from this that even correct genetic interpretations would not by themselves bring about the cessation of neurotic behavior or transference. Thus "the patient will hate his analyst," Boss argued, "as long as he is still (because of his childhood experiences) open only to a child-father or child-mother relationship which limits his perception of adults to frustrating experiences."[84] Knowing that he was repeating would do no good if his human condition remained so infantile and undeveloped that no other kind of relationship was possible for him. "No actual convincing evidence has ever been presented as to the effect of this kind of remembering as such. On the contrary, Freud's conviction that the mere remembering of the occasion when neurotic behavior was first produced and stamped on a child's existence will itself stop the compulsive repetition of such behavior is based on laws which can be applied only to physical objects."[85]

Remembering was insufficient if it left the old needs and impulses in place or if it left unchanged the norms that enforced repression. In fact, the existential position was stronger than this; remembering was really impossible so long as old norms and needs remained, and unnecessary if they changed. The point for the patient was not to remember the past but to change it by maturing in the analysis, by accepting the idea that the values and inhibitions adopted in the parental world were not universally valid or universally binding, and that there were other possibilities of conceiving the world and of existing that were live options for him.

Such maturation and learning did not take place in a vacuum, any more than did the original developmental inhibitions or repression of needs and impulses. Human existence was from the beginning a primary relating to others;

---

mediately followed by the assertion that "while the patient experiences [his present illness] as something real and contemporary, we have to do our therapeutic work on it, which consists in a large measure in tracing it back to the past." "Remembering, Repeating and Working Through," *S.E.*, Vol. XII, pp. 151-152.

[84] *Ibid.*, p. 240. [85] *Ibid.*, p. 243.

one's sense of self and of permitted and forbidden possibilities was always defined in a social context. Neurosis thus could never be adequately conceptualized as internal conflict or in terms of the economy of the libido alone. "No psychopathological symptom will ever fully and adequately be understood," Boss insisted, "unless it is conceived of as a disturbance in the texture of the social relationships of which a given human existence fundamentally consists."[86] The achievement of authenticity, or autonomy, was a joint venture of the individual and his milieu, just as both cooperated in the formation of submission and neurotic conflict.

In essence, the therapeutic process, as Boss saw it, was a reversal of the original failed process of maturation. The analyst played an active and direct role in it. To begin with, he permitted, and indeed encouraged, a good deal of "acting-out" in the transference. Freud had been wrong to regard acting-out only as resistance and repetition. In many cases it was the first real expression of hitherto buried emotions and impulses of positive developmental significance. Regression to an infantile dependence on the part of the patient might be his first genuine experience of that kind; its indulgence and gratification by the analyst might be the first real confirmation of the patient's needs and worth. The analysand's dependent love for the analyst was the first sign of that trust in a protecting, nurturing, and loving figure which was a prerequisite for autonomy.

Boss's case studies were full of striking examples of how he himself indulged and responded to regressive behavior on the part of his patients, to the point of bottle-feeding one of

[86] *Ibid.*, p. 56. Hence Boss's appreciation of the tradition of American social psychology and psychiatry. In the German edition of his book on existential analysis, Boss credited Harry Stack Sullivan with breaking the atomistic orientation of psychoanalytic theory and recognizing man's original nature as the product of the action of the environment on him through "reflected appraisal." Boss related this self of reflected appraisal to Heidegger's "Man-sein," the being of the anonymous self, though for Sullivan there was no counterpart notion of an "authentic self." *Psychoanalyse und Daseinsanalytik,* p. 33.

them. "The child-like modes of behavior which sprout for the first time in the analysand-analyst relationship," he wrote, "should be valued as the precious starting-point from which all future developments will arise. The analysand's being-himself will mature into ever more differentiated forms of relating if (and only if) the more primitive forms of relating are first permitted to unfold themselves fully."[87] On this issue Boss directly criticized Freud's prescription that the analyst be passive and mirror-like. At first Boss had thought that it stemmed from Freud's respect for the unique individuality of the analysand, which was to emerge without violation by the doctor's personality.[88] Later, however, he came to feel that Freud's recommendation was the counterpart of his belief that the analyst played no real interpersonal role in the therapeutic process, that he was the catalyst to a totally internal reaction. Against this, Boss quoted Freud himself, in a letter to Binswanger, on the need to give affect to the patient, and indeed occasionally a great deal of it, though never from the unconscious.[89]

Permissiveness, however, did not include gratifying or indulging the patient's "neurotic" demands, by which Boss meant those which functioned as defenses against his more basic desires. Erotic demands on the analyst, for example, frequently concealed the need for reassurance that one was loved, and aggressive impulses were reactions against dependency needs, anxiety-provoking impulses of affection linked with low self-esteem and fear of the analyst's control. Here the analyst's job was both interpreting the defenses and sanctioning the underlying needs—the only way, indeed, in which interpretation of the defenses could be rendered efficacious, for the patient's own reactions against his needs had to be counteracted before the needs could be admitted. In part this was accomplished by persuading the patient to tolerate his "infantile" and "evil" impulses as intelligible and

---

[87] Boss, *Psychoanalysis and Daseinsanalysis*, p. 241.

[88] *Ibid.*, p. 49.

[89] *Ibid.*, p. 256.

even to a degree acceptable human reactions to excessive need for affirmation in childhood or excessive frustration of this need.

Acknowledging dependency needs was only the first step. The next was the progressive growth, testing out, and adoption of new, self-motivated forms of activity and interpersonal relationships with a corresponding abandonment of dependent needs. In this process, too, the analyst played a central role, affirming the new possibilities emerging in the patient's life, supporting the patient against the anxiety of abandoning previous absolutes, and in general using the authority granted him by the patient to counter old authorities and bestow the recognition necessary for a positive sense of selfhood in which the need for all authorities would whither away.

Boss thus understood the process of undoing the effects of repression as overthrowing or at least modifying the absolutes that made overt recognition of the repressed content intolerable to the individual. Interpretation had to be not only cognitive, but deliberately aimed at expanding the patient's sense of possibilities. "What matters most, therapeutically, is not the recalling of the occasion when a neurotic pattern of relating to fellow men was acquired in childhood, but finding the answer to two questions: Why has the patient remained, right up to the present time, caught within this same restricted way of communicating? What is keeping him a prisoner of his neurotic patterns right now? The general answer to these all-important questions is that neurotic patients usually cannot even imagine that another way of relating to people is possible."[90]

It can be argued that Boss's version of therapy was not so much a substitute for or correction of Freud's as it was a supplement, designed for far more disturbed patients than would be accepted for classical analysis. There is some truth in this assessment. Though Boss made no basic distinction between the techniques suitable for neurotic and psychotic or pre-psychotic patients, most of the patients described in the case

[90] *Ibid.*, p. 243.

studies fell into the latter category. Boss acknowledged that the Daseinanalytically modified handling of transference was nowhere more decisive therapeutically than with schizophrenic patients[91] and that it was to them that the extreme characterization of people who had remained small children at the very core of their existence seemed most appropriate. It was significant also that Boss completely rejected Freud's conception of psychosis as a regression to primary narcissism that made transference, and hence analysis, impossible. Rather, he agreed with H. S. Sullivan that schizophrenics were capable of nothing else but transference. This meant that it was impossible to expect the patient to be detached enough or sufficiently aware of the doctor-patient relationship to be able to interpret his own transference. This model would not be appropriate for patients with greater maturity or ego strength, whose autonomy and ability to tolerate insight would be underestimated from such a perspective.

These objections, though of some validity, miss the crucial point. Even with less disturbed neurotic patients, conscious insight demanded a transformation of the personality, and the analyst's authority played a causal role in bringing it about. Freud had himself said at one point that the unconscious could not become conscious until the ego was made "conciliatory to the libido,"[92] until, that is, the censorship was replaced and the self permitted to recognize its impulses, and even to gratify some of them. This reconciliation was accomplished by what Freud cryptically called the analyst's "instruction" in the therapy.[93] Though instruction apparently differed from interpretation, Freud never clarified just what it involved. It appears that with this idea he introduced factors going beyond the explanation that therapy was a matter of conscious insight. By encouraging insight, the analyst was using his authority to counteract that of early figures and to sustain the patient's self-esteem against the forces of repression. Even the success of classical psychoanalytic interpretation, when it was

91 *Ibid.*, p. 244.   92 Freud, *S.E.*, Vol. xvi, p. 455.
93 *Ibid.*

successful, could be understood only in these terms. Interpretation relativized the patient's operative norms and beliefs by showing their historical roots and thus dissolving the beliefs in their necessity and universality, but it could do so only if the patient and analyst could build a new relationship, replacing and correcting the old. In a substitute-parent milieu, the patient gained the self-esteem necessary to advance beyond the dependent experience. Under the analyst's tutelage, which might consist simply of the acceptance implicit in both silent non-condemnation and helpful interpretation, the patient revised certain values that supported suppression of impulses or refusal to acknowledge them, or both. From the analyst's behavior, which might simply be non-intrusiveness, the patient would revise expectations of disaster upon following or even facing his impulses.

Thus, despite the fact that Boss's explicit emphasis in describing the therapeutic process was on the patient's potential for authenticity, and a freer, more open, stance to the world, the real thrust of his interpretation pointed towards the basic dependence of the patient and the role of the analyst as an authority to whom subjection was paradoxically a necessary precondition of autonomy. Freud had seen this, but had not known how to integrate it into his interpretation of therapy, which rested fundamentally on belief in the patient's autonomous capacity for rational insight. This brings us to the basic underlying difference between existentialism and psychoanalysis.

CHAPTER FOUR

The Historical Significance
of the Existential Critique

THERE have been a number of different assessments of the significance of existentialism within psychotherapy in general and in relationship to psychoanalysis in particular. It has been suggested that existential analysis was primarily a vehicle for the introduction of religious consolation into therapy, an attempt to use the phenomenological method to buttress faith by appeal to "experience as given" against reductive reason. Freud thought so, and gently chided Binswanger for his illusions. Boss was militant in his defense of the "numinous" quality of religious experience. A number of his case studies described a therapeutic progression from the liberation of sensuous and aggressive possibilities to the awakening of spiritual and religious ones, a progression that mirrored Boss's own intellectual development from Freud to Jung. Ideally, in his view, cure was an acceptance and integration of these different "modes of being." To an important degree, Boss often used religion as a traditional moralistic check on the sexuality that therapy liberated in his patients. Thus he wrote of one of them, "With her growing open acceptance of these potentialities in life came a real danger that on the plane of direct, volitional interpersonal relationships she herself would completely capitulate to this 'animal' relatedness to the world and would, in short, become a whore."[1] From this point of view existential analysis was a rearguard action fought by the spiritual reactionaries of European culture against the onslaught of demystifying secular rationalism and cultural anarchy, or, more accurately, an attempt to defend a

[1] M. Boss, *Psychoanalysis and Daseinsanalysis*, p. 153.

The pioneering and standard account of the crisis of rationalism in late nineteenth- and early twentieth-century Europe is H. S. Hughes' *Consciousness and Society*. Hughes has described the generation of European intellectuals after 1890 as having embarked upon a "critique of the Enlightenment,"[3] though not so much in its eighteenth-century rationalist form as in its late nineteenth-century travestied reincarnation—positivism. Thus the innovative philosophers and social thinkers of the period attacked the reductive determinism of positivist modes of thought—orthodox Marxism, Darwinism, mechanism, and environmentalism in general—in order to vindicate the rights of "the freely inquiring mind."[4] At the same time, however, many of these thinkers were also critical of Enlightenment assumptions about the rationality of human motivation and thought. Nevertheless, the most important ones remained "loyal" critics who, while skeptical about the possibilities of Enlightenment rationalism, sought to restate the tradition in more convincing terms.

Hughes has emphasized that any simple phrase or label for the orientation of the intellectual critique of the post-1890 period must necessarily be unsatisfactory. His characterization of its central thrusts are important contributions to our understanding of the period. However, his interpretation presents a number of problems. For one thing, his own description suggests that the critique of positivism and the critique of rationalism had different, indeed opposite, implications. The attack on positivism was ostensibly a defense of human freedom, while the criticism of the Enlightenment implied an attack against the rationalist assumptions of human autonomy and rationality. This introduces a seemingly fatal complexity that defies any attempt to see the 1890's critique as a homogeneous movement.

One solution would be to take a more nominalist approach and reject any effort to link the two critiques. Closer investigation, however, shows that some link between them does

[3] H. S. Hughes, *Consciousness and Society*, New York, 1958, p. 28.
[4] *Ibid.*, p. 39.

169

exist. For the same contradiction that is apparent between the two critiques is reproduced within each of them. Such critics of positivism as Mosca, Weber, and Sorel, for example, did indeed attack certain kinds of causal explanations for eliminating the role of subjective intentions and ideals in understanding behavior and belief, but their notion of subjectivity was in important ways antithetical to the rationalist ideal of autonomy and rational thought—one need only think of Mosca's concept of the propensity to submission, Weber's notion of charisma, and Sorel's concept of myth. The most radical critics of positivism, the neo-idealists, in rejecting external causal determinants of action in favor of absolute objective values, introduced yet another limitation or constraint upon human freedom. As Talcott Parsons pointed out: "Eternal objects have the same fixity independent of the observer as the empirical facts of the positivist, a similar objectivity is possible with reference to them."[5] Hughes does not reconcile the contradiction between the idea of a critique of positivism whose purpose was to defend the rights of the freely inquiring mind and the conclusion of that critique in a view of human motivation that equated human spontaneity with the abnegation of freedom. On the other side, such thinkers as Durkheim and Freud who were most critical of certain of the assumptions of the Enlightenment—individualism, autonomy, rationality—were ardent, even militant, positivists. If positivism was a later development of rationalism that in some way preserved Enlightenment beliefs, there is another contradiction to be explained.

These unresolved difficulties suggest the need for a more differentiated and nuanced picture of the crisis of rationalism after 1890. Such a picture emerges from a detailed analysis of the structure of Freud's theory, the criticisms of the existentialists, and the later vicissitudes of existentialism. While much work would have to be done to substantiate the more

[5] T. Parsons, *The Structure of Social Action*, 2nd ed., New York, Vol. I, p. 445.

general thesis, it can be argued that Freud was representative of a great many social thinkers, philosophers, and creative artists, intellectually and emotionally rooted in the rationalist tradition, who made discoveries about human motivation and belief incompatible with their own previous conceptions. Nevertheless, they tried either to explain these discoveries through, or incorporate them within, their original rationalist intellectual-moral framework. The result was an unstable and conceptually tenuous synthesis between rationalism and irrationalism that in different ways undercut the thrust of the new insights into irrationality. The specific form of this tenuous synthesis varied, especially between thinkers with roots in utilitarian and positivist thought and those with roots in idealism. The situation is complicated by the fact that, for socio-historical reasons, the latter group sometimes displayed an ambivalent sympathy to irrationality. Without denying the importance of these differences, however, it is still possible to ascertain a pattern of conceptual ambivalence across the whole range of the post-1890 analyses of rationalism.

The general argument is that the pre-war critique of rationalism was incomplete because frequently its theoretical terms of reference did not allow for the full intellectual assimilation of its own empirical discoveries. It was only after the First World War that the synthesis proved untenable for many thinkers and broke down. A number of them faced, for the first time, the full implications of the pre-war insights into the flight from autonomy, the relativism of norms and values, and irrationality of belief. Others fled from these now inescapable discoveries back to a strict form of rationalism that either recognized the irrational but claimed that nothing could be understood or said about it because of the very nature of language, or tried to resurrect an older objective Reason to which the mind could appeal. Even at this point, however, many of those who looked most deeply and clearly into the implications of the pre-war critique of rationalism and developed concepts to do justice to its insights were unable to accept the ultimate conclusions of their own thought. The

171

result was a desperate attempt to find a way out beyond the pessimism and despair of the anti-rationalism to which they had been driven.

The themes just sketched out are epitomized in the work of Freud and the existentialists. With regard to Freud, it will be shown that it was precisely through his positivistic meta-psychology—the energy model and the instinctual and biolog-ical-developmental model—that he preserved intact the ra-tionalist conception of selfhood and its understanding of the relationship between the individual and society. Thus, espe-cially in the period before 1914, there was a contradiction between his clinical discoveries and the presuppositions about motivation and rationality built into the metapsychology. In the metapsychological innovations after 1920, Freud at-tempted to square the metapsychological with the clinical theory, explicitly and implicitly recognizing certain implica-tions of his clinical work that he had originally denied.

In attacking Freudian metapsychology through neo-ideal-ism and phenomenology in the early 1920's, Binswanger was not simply, as he thought, concerned with problems in the philosophy of the social sciences. He was, in fact, advancing a concept of subjectivity that implied a theory of motivation at odds with the rationalist presuppositions of Freudian meta-psychology. It was, however, only in Heidegger's work that the radically anti-rationalist implications of the phenomeno-logical notion of subjectivity were exposed. In applying Hei-degger's ontology to concrete psychological problems, the other existentialists developed a view of man based on a com-pletely different set of motivational premises than those im-plicit in Freud; they were thus able to address a range of psy-chological and conceptual problems not really dealt with in classical psychoanalysis.

However, none of the existentialists were either fully aware of or fully accepted the negative, pessimistic conclusions of their own work. When Heidegger and Sartre faced them head on, at different times and for different reasons, they reached an impasse in their thought that caused them to abandon their initial existentialism. Binswanger never accepted Heidegger's work as fully definitive of the human condition, and from the very beginning tried to supplement it with a view antithetical to the spirit of *Being and Time*. Boss came under Heidegger's influence only after he had modified his work to escape the original existentialist impasse. Thus the existential therapists evaded full consciousness of the dilemma of existential philosophy—an evasion that was crucial if existentialism were to be applied to psychotherapy at all.

In what follows, the concept of selfhood central to Freud and embodied in the metapsychological theory will be examined in some detail. To appreciate it, however, will be to see how one-dimensional was Binswanger's assessment of the underlying spirit and purpose of Freud's psychoanalysis. Binswanger was one of the first to try to discern a central animating view of man, a philosophical anthropology, in Freud's work. According to him, the unifying vision of man in psychoanalysis was in the idea of *homo natura*, man as a creature of the physical needs that made him part of nature. Freud's basic discovery was the fact that all too often man tried to live psychologically beyond his means by denying his animal nature and concealing it behind a façade of spirituality. Binswanger conceded that the one-sided concept of *homo natura* was a legitimate natural scientific construct abstracted from the totality of human reality; its ultimate purpose was medical and therapeutic. By conceptualizing man as part of nature, and hence subject to laws and causality, Freud made feasible the project of classifying irregularities of behavior, discovering mechanisms at their root, and repairing the mind. Conceiving man as totally free and undetermined would have obviated any possibility of obtaining the kind of knowledge necessary to effect changes in his behavior. But however practically justifiable and partially true the idea of *homo natura* was, it did distort the concept of man. It forced all experience within the straight-jacket of an a priori theory, subsuming observed phenomena under merely hypothesized biological and mechanical forces and altering them in the process. It divested man of his freedom to choose, above all the freedom to assume responsibility for himself and make his life meaningful in terms of some absolute purpose or value.

Binswanger was correct in his assessment of the importance of Freud's belief in material determinsim as the necessary foundation for a science of the mind. Freud, like Binswanger, worked within the dualistic idealist-materialist dichotomy that equated freedom with the unconditioned will, causality with the body and its drives, and posited an absolute opposition between them. Freud simply opted for the other side of the opposition. Since freedom meant independence from all external or antecedent forces, a science founded on regularities of occurrence and causal explanations could not admit it—even if in practice Freudian therapy finally depended in some undefined way on the strength of the will in overcoming resistances. One can even agree with Binswanger's later assertion that in a basic philosophical sense Freud's central interest was not man but nature. Freud always subsumed individual psychology under more general biological principles beginning with the hard-headed scientific concept of the constancy principle and ending with the Romantic cosmic forces of Eros and Thanatos.[6]

But Binswanger was wrong in his judgment that psychoanalysis ignored the problem of selfhood as a whole. The conception of man as an instinctual creature never meant for Freud that man was unfree. Freud was certainly ambivalent towards sexuality and the ethic of psychoanalysis did put a premium on self-control and sublimation. For him, however, these were not goods in themselves but necessities enforced by reality. Whatever cultural rewards sublimation brought were functions of the degree of libidinal energy still possible in sublimated activities. Freud did not accept the idealist concept of the body as the limitation of human freedom. Binswanger was not completely off the mark when he wrote of

[6] L. Binswanger, "Mein Weg zu Freud," *Der Mensch in der Psychiatrie*, Pfullingen, 1957, pp. 37-63.

psychoanalysis: "Freudian doctrine is diametrically opposed to the teachings of Augustine and Fichte in that in it the 'good,' the ethical, is nothing but a negative, i.e., a limiting constricting, condemnatory and oppressive force that possessed no essentially positive i.e., liberating or creative effectiveness."[7]

The statement was, of course, far too extreme, for it ignored Freud's equation of civilization and repression, but it correctly suggested that in the metapsychology, repression and self-denial were not valued as such but only as means to serve the instincts better in the face of reality. Freud's instinct theory itself embodied a specific conception of human freedom. If the existentialists failed to appreciate this, it was not only because of their concern with the issue of the proper philosphical foundations of psychology; it was rather because for them the problem of freedom had shifted from what it had been for Freud.

The view of man in Freud's metapsychology derived from what will be called here the rationalist tradition of freedom in modern European thought. The term "rationalist" rather than individualist, empiricist, or utilitarian is stressed because, though Freud's theoretical assumptions about man were obviously individualist and utilitarian in essence, individualism and utilitarianism were themselves a variant or subspecies of a broader intellectual tradition with characteristic beliefs about human nature, reason, and the relationship of the individual to society. It is important for our purposes to emphasize this broader current because the existential critique of Freud cannot be finally understood simply as a quarrel between "Western European" modes of thought—such as empiricism, utilitarianism, and positivism—and "German" neo-idealism. The rationalist concept of freedom underlay a range of otherwise conflicting philosophical and social theories. It must be remembered that existentialism, for all its roots in idealism, was as critical of idealism as it was of positivism; the ultimate existential challenge to Freud struck at elements common to both of them, above all a shared concept of human freedom. What was so radical about the existential critique of Freud was that it denied certain cherished assumptions of progressive European thought since the Enlightenment and thus testified to the profundity of a crisis of rationalism that cut across ideological, philosophical, and national lines.

The central tenet of the rationalist concept of freedom was a view of the human being as free or autonomous. According to this view, the individual's thought and action were his own, spontaneous and self-generated, not determined by agencies or causes other than his own will or outside his control. Different thinkers conceived the sphere of this autonomy in different ways, focussing on narrowly specific areas of political, economic, or moral activity, or generalizing it, as did Rousseau, Hegel, and J. S. Mill into an abstract ideal of authenticity, self-realization, or the overcoming of alienation. Common to all of them, however, was the belief in a sphere in which the individual was completely self-determining, acting on motives that were genuinely his own and for ends that he had freely chosen.

Autonomy was both an ideal and a way of conceiving the individual, and the distinction between the two was not clearly made in rationalist thought. This was a consequence of the historical context in which the modern idea of freedom developed. It grew out of the struggle with traditional hierarchical society, as an affirmation of the right of the individual against religious, social, and political authorities to control the conditions of his own life, to choose what activities to pursue and what to believe. However, autonomy was not affirmed in the rationalist tradition merely as a value, a goal to be achieved.

To begin with, the existence of a degree of individual autonomy was the precondition for whatever success had already been achieved in the expansion of knowledge and in ideological, economic, and political emancipation. Moreover, the idea of autonomy as a wish for the future was insufficient as a weapon against the reality of continuing social, political, and ideological domination. Hence, rationalism posited the existence of freedom as rooted in human nature, as an established fact of human behavior. This was expressed in a number of different and even conflicting forms, from the a priori state of nature argument of seventeenth- and eighteenth-century thinkers, through the utilitarian psychology of Bentham, for whom the pursuit of pleasure meant self-activated behavior as opposed to behavior governed by ascetic or "arbitrary" principles; the Kantian principle of autonomy expressed in the Categorical Imperative, according to which each individual was his own legislator; to the Marxist anthropological notion of man's "species being" as free, sensuous, non-alienated labor. Whatever form it took, autonomy was conceived as a pre-given reality, in contemporary terms, the key term in a universal theory of motivation. Even the rationalists arguing out of a historical tradition, who ostensibly saw individual autonomy as an historical product and not an a priori category, presupposed the drive to autonomy as the motor of development of the historical process.

A corollary of the rationalist concept of autonomy was that individual unfreedom—which of course rationalists acknowledged as existing—was explicable only in terms of external forces, that is, some form of environmental coercion. If men were "born free," unfreedom could not be the product of the will, but only of coercive institutions and men, perhaps supported by error and ignorance on the part of the oppressed. The paradigmatic explanation of freedom so far as individual psychology was concerned was Hegel's master-slave dialectic, which explained willing submission to authority as the surrender of freedom in a clash between initially free selves, each trying to assert its own mastery and hence freedom over the obstacle apparently presented by the other. It was the greater fear of death on the part of one of the combatants that led him to succumb and then to try to rationalize his submission. Generalized, this explanation rationalized all willing subordination as utilitarian or instrumental insofar as it served some

177

other purpose of the autonomous self. It could not, however, account for submission as an end in itself, i.e., as legitimate according to some non-utilitarian transcendental sanction or belief.

Original freedom, then, was the first element of the rationalist tradition, even though historically men were not necessarily free. To the extent that they were able to free themselves from environmental coercion, however, and pursue their own ends, their actions were seen to be governed by what may be called second-order rationality—means-end rationality and rationality of belief. In their actions they chose the means best suited to attaining their ends, and their choices were determined by an assessment of the objective conditions of action, that is, by an adequate testing of reality. A rational norm of efficiency and an empirical or objective attitude to reality were thus part of the rationalist tradition. As we shall see, the objective conditions of action included not only the facts of the natural world but of the social world as well. The rationalists believed that the social world was either law-governed, like the natural world, or governed by rules that had the same objective status as the laws of nature. These laws or rules were assimilated to the objective conditions of action and men had only to know them in order to act rationally. Within the rationalist tradition, mind or thought was held to be equivalent to rationality in the sense of instrumental action and a cognitive stance to reality in the sense just defined. It followed that if men failed to behave rationally in pursuit of their ends, it was the result of a failure to adequately assess the conditions of action—i.e., intellectual error.

It thus also follows from what has been said that the belief in the original autonomy of the self was only one pole of the rationalist idea of freedom. Historically, that belief had grown out of the conquest of the natural world through the scientific and economic revolutions—through the development of mathematical and empirical techniques that provided certain knowledge about and control over the physical world

178

through natural science as well as rational economic activity and productive achievement. Autonomy was thus predicated on the ability of man's unaided reason to furnish him with the knowledge, power, and security formerly provided by authority and tradition, and this in turn was based on the belief that nature was a law-governed process, subordination to which enabled man to turn nature to his own purposes. By analogy, rationalism also posited the existence in the moral and social sphere of a pre-established harmony of individual wills, an objective social good, moral law, or socio-political order that was not merely contingent but universal and a priori, an objective basis of social action. Like the rationalist concept of autonomy, the notion of a pre-established objective harmony took very different forms in the different variants of rationalism.

But whether thinkers held to the belief in a natural identity of interests, a General Will, a Categorical Imperative that reconciled autonomy with the universalizability of a command to treat others as ends in themselves, an Absolute Idea that hypostatized the identity of subject and object, particular and universal, or a species-being that harmonized the free, sensuous labor of each with the needs, interests, and potentialities of all, the idea of an objective order reconciling individual freedoms, to which men must subordinate themselves insofar as they were rational, was fundamental to rationalism. Empiricists and utilitarians might stress harmony from the individualist standpoint, as the consequence of individuals' pursuit of their private ends (though this was accompanied by a belief that reason or inclination dictated concern for the rights of others); idealists might insist on the need to will, over and above individual freedom, a transcendent objective good. Though these were important differences which led historically to significant conflicts and diverging ideological developments, the two tendencies had a common thrust. The belief in the a priori harmony of individual freedoms, of particular and universal, of subjective and objective, was the guarantee not only of the social safety of individual auton-

179

omy, but of the fact that autonomy itself was written into the structure of rational social action insofar as it was based on knowledge of objective reality. Thus it is in fact impossible to separate out the poles of autonomy and universality in the rationalist tradition. The second was the foundation of the first and incorporated the first within it. Subordination to the universal was not alienation but the fulfillment of freedom, both because the objective order guaranteed it and because it provided for the mutual recognition of individuals so that others would not constitute obstacles to one's own self-realization.

The rationalist belief in an objective, universal order, it can be said in summary, fulfilled three functions: it guaranteed the empirical conditions for the possibility of individual freedom; it ensured society against anarchy and disruptive conflict; and it provided a metaphysical assurance that freedom was ordained by the structure of the universe.

With all of this emphasis on the way in which reconciliation was built into the beliefs of the rationalists, however, we do not mean to argue that the rationalists were blind to the reality of conflict. Quite the contrary, even as their concepts hypostatized the identity of individual and universal, they grappled with the problem of conflict. The very need to posit harmony was the inevitable outcome of a concept of autonomy whose starting point was essentially negative or asocial, defined in terms of individual liberation from alien control and pursuing one's own goals or interests. Thus most rationalists accepted the reality of conflict on some level and felt the need for coercive institutions to reinforce the objective harmony, institutions, that would, in Rousseau's paradoxical phrase, force men to be free. Those who did not see conflict as inevitable simply went further than others in assuming the natural harmony of men. This distinction is obviously not a trivial one in intellectual history, since it marked the difference, for example, between liberals and socialists. For our purposes, what is relevant is that in all variants of the rationalist tradition, the starting point of autonomy meant the need to recognize conflict either explicitly or implicitly, by positing an objective reconciliation beyond conflict.

Positivism, particularly the radical positivism that informed Freud's conceptual framework, was a derivative of the rationalist tradition that introduced modifications designed to deal with some of its difficulties. Positivism can be broadly defined as the elimination of all consideration of human action in terms of subjective intentions and beliefs and their conceptualization as passive functions of antecedent causes—environmental, mechanistic, or biological. Parsons has shown how radical positivism altered consideration of the ends of human action from manifestations of spontaneous autonomy, ultimate data without further explantion ("random ends," as he called them), into determined products of law-governed causal processes. He saw this shift as the result of an inherent instability within the premises of utilitarian individualism. From the point of view of this work, we can understand it as resulting from the need to deal with three problems faced by the rationalist tradition in its confrontation with social and historical reality in the nineteenth century: the problems of continuing individual unfreedom in society, of persisting irrationality of behavior and belief in the instrumental and cognitive sense, and of continuing conflict and social disorder.

On the level of motivational theory, determinist theories replaced the view of individuals acting according to freely chosen ends. Though action was thus seen as determined by, or equivalent to, physical facts, these facts were seen as predisposing the individual in the same direction as the original concept of autonomy. Energy theories of mental functioning, for example, which, following the principle of conservation of energy, made energy discharge the function of action, equated discharge with pleasure and thus, as we have seen, with self-motivated purpose. Instinct theory, in its Darwinian form, redefined autonomy both as a procreative drive, which aimed simultaneously at the gratification of the individual

181

and the benefit of the species, and as a drive for individual self-preservation. Darwinian biology thus gave scientific grounding to the rationalist assumption of autonomy while at the same time affirming the identity of individual gratification with the ultimate welfare of the species. However, it did so at the cost of institutionalizing conflict as the motor of species development. Insofar as Darwinism was applied to social theory, the ultimate benefit to the species came from a competitive struggle for survival within any contemporary population. Thus the necessity of conflict was affirmed and scientifically justified, but at the same time given a progressive rationale.

Reducing the purposes of action to determinist terms also made possible a different approach to irrationality. Deviations from second-order rationality, as was pointed out earlier, were explained within rationalism as the results of error or ignorance. When action and belief were conceptualized as the effects of material causes, deviations from a rational norm of efficiency or objective cognition could be explained in causal terms. So, for example, irrationality could be explained as the product of environmental or biological factors or in mechanistic terms as the results of malfunctions of the physical substratum of the mind or psyche. Such an approach, we saw in chapter one, was used by Meynert and incorporated by Freud. While all mental and psychic processes were conceptualized in physicalistic terms, it was the norm of rationality that was invoked as the implicit criterion for recourse to physicalistic explanations; that is, it was felt necessary to turn to such explanations when rationality broke down.

One of the most important types of causal law to which appeal was made to explain deviations from rationality was evolutionary theory. Insofar as behavior in human society did not meet rationalist norms, it could be seen as not yet having reached the end point of a developmental process whose *telos* was the achievement of these norms. J. W. Burrow has argued that the insight at the core of the emerging evolutionary sociology of the nineteenth century was that the social order was primarily maintained neither by man's rational appreciation of its advantages nor by coercion but by irrational customs and habits obeyed for fanciful reasons or no reasons at all.[8]

To this can be added the impetus derived from the perceived discrepancy between expectations of liberty and social harmony and the persistence of irrational domination and disruptive social conflict. Evolutionary doctrines dealt with these difficulties by positing a force moving society "by a power far above human wills," in Spencer's words, to the desired rationalist end state. Unfreedom, irrationality, and conflict were thus the residues of an incomplete evolutionary process, forms of social structure that had at one time been adaptive to existing conditions but that were so no longer. Their persistence was not further explained. It was considered sufficiently explanatory to locate them on an evolutionary spectrum and characterize them as residues. Evolutionary thinking protected rationalism by seeing its norms as the end point of an inevitable process, not itself dependent on rationality, and explaining all intermediary forms of behavior as necessary adaptations to existing conditions. Thus aberrations from ultimate rationality could be admitted, but as stages surpassed in the normal course of development.

Automatic developmental laws were applied to the different elements of the rationalist tradition to account for the existence of both past and present irrationality. Comte's Law of the Three Stages posited a necessary development in the direction of scientific thinking traversing the irrationality of religious and metaphysical thought, which, however, were seen as appropriate to human development at earlier stages of maturation. Spencer's evolutionism posited a necessary cosmic progress from a state of non-differentiation to differentiation, individuation, and integration, with their social dimension involving the emergence of true individuality and harmony. The Darwinian biological perspective, aside from

[8] J. W. Burrow, *Evolution and Society*, Cambridge University Press, 1966, p. 104.

its social application as a more scientifically respectable form of evolutionary thinking, could also apply to the individual. Starting out as helpless and dependent, the individual automatically matured to a state of autonomy and rationality. Deviations from this developmental course could be understood as residual adaptations to earlier conditions.

Against the background just sketched out, Freud's metapsychology, and the way in which the theory of unconscious phantasy conflated past and present, can be understood as an internalization of the problems of rationalist theory in positivist form. Libidinal theory was Freud's version of the rationalist assumption of primary autonomy, the fundamental urge toward freedom and self-realization. The conflict between the claims of the autonomous self and the needs of social order and harmony became, in Freud's model of the personality, an inner conflict between the desire of the self to fulfill its own ends immediately and to enforce the moral prohibitions necessary to make the individual fit to be a member of society. But in a parallel to rationalism, the point of these inner prohibitions which enforced repression of instinctual drives was also to guarantee the possibility of safe gratification under the conditions of reality. As Freud explained it metapsychologically, repression was carried out by the ego-instincts on behalf of the reality principle, whose purpose was to safeguard the pleasure principle. Thus, for Freud too, in theory, social harmony and individuality were ultimately, normatively, consistent, even though empirically they came into conflict. Finally, the theory of unconscious phantasy, by interpreting the present neurosis as a repetition of the past, followed the evolutionary model of explaining irrationality by showing that present irrationality was the persistence of a once rational mode of adaptation to reality whose persistence in the present was not further explicable in motivational terms, though the *mode* of persistence, the irrational distortion of present reality in the interests of repetition, was explicable in mechanical terms as primary process functioning.

184

The bearing of this interpretation is clearer when it is compared with the standard interpretation of Freud as having
demonstrated that hierarchical authoritarian relations existed
not only external to the individual but within him—that, in
other words, the individual was the agent of his own subordination and submission.[9] A historically sophisticated extension
of this thesis is that Freud represented the culmination of a
line of evolutionary thinking opposed to the optimistic version of evolution as a theory of progress. He showed both
that the past, in the form of the primitive (irrational and dependent) behavior, lived on into the present and that regression to the past was more typical than progress.[10]

These interpretations are undeniably accurate in regard to
Freud's clinical achievement. What they omit, however, is
that his psychological discoveries were made in the context
of an explanatory theory that was in important ways inconsistent with them. This led to two results, which we will
analyze in more detail. The first was that Freud was unable
to explain the irrationality he perceived because his premises
did not allow for it. In a paradoxical sense, the irrationality
of the behavior was elided in Freud's very description. The
second was that in dealing with neurotic thought processes
that deviated from the norm of rational belief—what Freud
called secondary process—he was forced to treat them theoretically, not as psychological processes at all, but as mechanical, quasi-physical processes involving random displacements
of psychic energy among ideas independent of their meaning.
That is to say, for all Freud's deciphering of the personal historical meaning of neurotic symbolism, he had no theory or
concept of symbolic *thought* as a unique mental, ideational,
or meaningful process.

The first thesis can be illustrated by an example from
Freud's case studies before we go on to a more general dis-

[9] See, for example, F. Weinstein and G. M. Platt, *The Wish to be
Free*, Berkeley, 1969, p. 150.
[10] P. Rieff, *The Mind of of the Moralist*, New York, 1959, pp. 206-207.

cussion. The "Rat Man" suffered from obsessional ideas about terrible punishments being inflicted on his father. These fears masked powerful feelings of hatred for his father, awakened when his family indicated its desire that he marry a cousin they had picked out for him, instead of the woman he was in love with. According to Freud's interpretation, this had created a conflict in the Rat Man between obeying his father and following his own impulses. His father had not only been vehemently opposed to the woman his son had chosen, but had in his own youth followed the course now being demanded of his son: he had also given up the woman of his choice to marry a relative picked out by the family. Thus the Rat Man was faced with a conflict he could not resolve; he was tormented by obsessions and compulsions that made him unable to work and thus complete his education so that he could marry. In this way, the neurotic illness helped him avoid resolving the conflict through the choice of one of the alternatives.

Only in the course of therapy did the Rat Man become aware of his murderous anger against his father. Freud traced it back to a childhood episode in which the Rat Man had received a severe beating for some sexual play with his sister. He had responded with a violent outburst against his father that had left them both shaken and that had turned the child into a coward in fear of the violence of his own anger and the retribution it could bring.

Freud's interpretation rested on the notion that the adult conflict of the Rat Man was caused by the infantile one,[11] or rather that it was a repetition of that conflict, made possible by the boy's repression of his infantile hatred toward his father. To marry his lady meant, for the Rat Man, to destroy his father. In answer to the Rat Man's question as to why, as an adult, he had not simply decided not to let his father's interference with his love for his lady weigh against his love for his father, Freud replied that the destructive wish against

---

[11] Freud, *S.E.*, Vol. x, p. 238.

the father did not date from the later occasion but was a long-repressed wish dating from a time in childhood when such a mature decision was not possible. Thus the Rat Man's adult conflict was a re-activation of childhood events; its proper description was possible only in terms of those events as a living out of the earlier infantile conflict.

At the time the Rat Man had come for treatment, however, his father had been dead for a number of years. He had died even before the plan for his son to marry his wife's cousin had been suggested. Thus the Rat Man's obedience, fears, and repressed fury were directed at a dead man; his father's opposition to his love no longer existed as a real force. Freud's interpretation of the Rat Man's conflict as being basically one between his love for his father and his love for his lady raised the question of what that love for, and fear of, his dead father, both of which inhibited him, could mean in the altered circumstances of adult reality.

To understand why the genetic reduction of the conflict posed a theoretical problem for Freud's metapsychology, we must see how he conceived the original childhood situation in terms of instinct and developmental theories. In the situation of childhood, the child's reaction to his father's opposition to his sexual activities was perfectly intelligible as a biologically rational response to a threatening situation. The child loved his father as the source of security and protection in a world in which he was still weak and helpless, unable to fend for himself. He also needed his father's love as the guarantee of that continued protection, just as he feared the father's superior strength if turned against him in anger. Under these circumstances, it was necessary to suppress those impulses which aroused his father's ire and to suppress the destructive rage that followed their frustration. This situation, however, was, in Freud's biological and rationalist framework, phase specific. Once the adult could fend for himself, he was his father's equal and had no longer any need for his father's protection, and therefore no need to bow to his will, with its consequences of resentful fury and fear of retribution.

187

What, then, could account for his inability as an adult to act on his own desires and his consequent destructive hostility to his father? *That* the Rat Man was both submissive and angry Freud established quite clearly—to the satisfaction of the patient himself. *Why* he was so was inexplicable on the assumptions of Freud's rationalist theory of motivation and development, and indeed inconsistent with it. To characterize the adult behavior as a repetition of an infantile situation was to point to the fundamental irrationality of the Rat Man's conduct in the adult context, when the real environmental obstacles no longer existed, without explaining how it was possible. It was simply to substitute an account of a rational response to an earlier situation for behavior that was not rational under the altered circumstances of adulthood.

The persistence of the infantile situation was a riddle that puzzled Freud himself. Years later, even after he made important innovations clinically and in his metapsychology which brought him closer to an answer, he felt that the ultimate problem of the neuroses, the problem of fixation, had not been solved:

"A great many people remain infantile in their behavior in regard to danger and do not overcome determinants of anxiety which have grown out of date. . . . But how is this possible? Why are not all neuroses episodes in the development of the individual which come to a close when the next phase is reached? Whence comes the element of persistence in these reactions to danger . . . whence does neurosis come —what is its ultimate, its own peculiar *raison d'etre*? After tens of years of psychoanalytic labors, we are as much in the dark about this problem as we were at the start."[12]

This difficulty, we can now see, was the consequence of the presuppositions built into Freud's theory of meaning. The interpretation of neurotic behavior as the repetition of infantile scenes, impulses, and conflicts displayed the unquestionable similarity between adult patterns and infantile conduct.

[12] Freud, *S.E.*, Vol. xx, p. 149.

But by describing adult behavior as nothing more than this, it begged the fundamental question: why did behavior whose original point was supposedly its rationality from a self-interest point of view persist into adulthood when it was un-necessary and self-defeating? It was in this sense that the theory of unconscious phantasy, in purporting to explain ir-rationality, actually redescribed it in such a way as to leave the irrationality unexplained.

We can now explore in more general terms how the posi-tivistic framework of psychoanalysis maintained a basic ratio-nalist perspective that transformed Freud's empirical psycho-logical discoveries about motivation into their opposite. Rationalist presuppositions were built into his theory of moti-vation via instinct theory. Psychic conflict was conceptualized as the struggle between the two basic kinds of instinct, sexual and ego-instincts. The aim of the sexual instincts was pleasure or gratification—ultimately physical pleasure rooted in the erotogenic zones. The self-preservative instincts seated in the ego were to protect pleasure-possibilities against threats from the external world by taking into account the needs of social existence and imposing restraints on the self. Thus Freud ex-plained the existence of the incest taboo, to which the desire for oedipal gratification must surrender, as the result of so-ciety's need to "defend itself against the danger that the in-terests which it needs for the establishment of higher social units may be swallowed up by the family."[13]

But the implied defense of social norms inherent in this explanation was a defense of individual pleasure and free-dom, for the establishment of higher social units was neces-sary to make the procurement of the needs of self-preserva-tion easier and more efficient. This was made explicit by Freud in the complementary characterization of psychic con-flict drawn from the economic sphere of metapsychology, as conflict between the pleasure and the reality principles. "The substitution of the reality principle for the pleasure princi-

[13] *Ibid.*, Vol. vii, p. 225.

ple implies no deposing of the pleasure principle," Freud wrote, "but only a safeguarding of it. A momentary pleasure, uncertain in its results, is given up, but only in order to gain along the new path an assured pleasure at a later time."[14]

In the outline of the rationalist concept of freedom we saw the complex nature of the rationalist utilitarian dualism, which was concerned to affirm both individual autonomy and objective social obligation on a basis that still preserved individual freedom. This was also the basis of Freud's instinctual dualism. That the sexual instinct meant authentic selfhood for him, and that his persistent dualism was basically one of authenticity and social obligation, were clearly revealed at a moment in the history of psychoanalytic theory when the dual instinct theory appeared to be threatened. About 1911, Freud's researches into schizophrenia and his discovery of narcissism led him to the hypothesis of an original libidinal cathexis of the ego, schizophrenia being a regression to this condition. On the basis of his work, Jung challenged the validity of distinction between sexual and ego-instincts and suggested instead the hypothesis of a single neutral primal libido that could be either sexualized or desexualized.

Freud was embarrassed by Jung's proposal, because he recognized that his own hypothesis cast doubt on the necessity of differentiating a specifically sexual libido from the nonsexual energy of the ego-instincts. Nevertheless, he was unwilling to surrender the dualistic theory; his reasons for this are significant. The individual, he argued, "does actually carry on a double existence; *one designed to serve his own purposes* and another as a link in a chain, in which he serves against, or at any rate without, any volition of his own. *The individual himself regards sexuality as one of his own ends*; while from another point of view he is only an appendage to his germ plasm, to which he lends his energies, taking in return his toll of pleasure."[15]

This reasoning did not accomplish the purpose of defend-

[14] *Ibid.*, Vol. XII, p. 23.
[15] *Ibid.*, Vol. XIV, p. 78. Italics added.

ing a dual instinct theory since in fact only one instinct, sexuality, was discussed, though from two perspectives—as it served, or did not serve, the individual's purposes. It is clear that the basic dualism that Freud saw conceptualized in instinct theory was not that of two qualitatively different instinctual purposes but of human energy, epitomized by sexuality, as, on the one hand, free, autonomous, and self-motivated, and, on the other, as constrained and at the service of alien forces external to the self. Freud's language here is crucial; insofar as a person's sexuality was alienated, it was "against, or at any rate without, any volition of his own."

Freud's complex attitude to this dualism was strikingly articulated in two remarks he made a propos of the incest taboo, the symbol of the repressive forces. On the one hand, he wrote that "the catastrophe of the Oedipus complex (the abandonment of incest and the institution of conscience and morality) may be regarded as a victory of the race over the individual,"[16] because desire was subordinated to the needs of procreation; the free expression of sexuality was alienated by an external principle. He saw this victory as tragic but necessary. On the other hand, Freud bluntly asserted that "anyone who is to be really free and happy in love must have surmounted his respect for women and have come to terms with the idea of incest with mother or sister."[17] Individuation and freedom thus depended on the individual's ability to conceive of the possibility of sexual relations with precisely those figures to whom he was prepared to sacrifice his autonomy, of asserting himself with those who incarnated authority, self-abnegation, and the forbidden. The exercise of sexuality was the equivalent of being a free self.

Freud's position here was not really contradictory. Society demanded abnegation, but not on the basis of miracle, mystery, and authority; the incest taboo was to be obeyed because of its social, and thus ultimately its individual, utility.

Freud's fundamental theory of motivation was thus a

[16] *Ibid.*, Vol. XIX, p. 257.   [17] *Ibid.*, Vol. XI, p. 186.

theory of authenticity—in acting instinctually, human beings acted in order to assert themselves, to serve their own purposes; they did not willingly obey alien commands. Clinically, however, he had made a number of important psychological discoveries that were completely at odds with the values and preconceptions embodied in his theory.

The most general one was the discovery of human bisexuality, the existence in all human beings of both masculine and feminine, or less tendentiously, active and passive, drives. The thesis of a fundamental passivity suggested the existence of an original inclination of the self for submission and subordination, an active desire for self-abnegation and surrender to the will of others. Concretely, passivity manifested itself in such psychological phenomena as overvaluation of the love object—the tendency to attribute all perfection to the love object and consequently to defer completely to his judgment;[18] masochism, the desire to be passive sexually or to be hurt, humiliated, and punished, either physically or psychologically; the desire to be loved, i.e., the need of others; infantilism itself, the persistence of childhood dependency into adulthood; and, finally, repression, the suppression of instinctual desires through shame and morality.[19]

Freud's attempts to explain these phenomena in instinctual terms resulted in a theoretical and descriptive transformation that made them phenomenologically unrecognizable. On the most general level, the very definition of instinct was incompatible with bisexuality. In the *Three Essays* Freud had asserted that "libido is invariably and necessarily of a masculine nature whether it occurs in men or in women and irrespective of whether its object is a man or woman."[20] This definition left no theoretical space for the concept of femininity or passivity as an autonomous end of action. The consequences of this position were evident in concrete psychological terms in Freud's analysis of such clinical phenomena as masochism and the need for love.

[18] *Ibid.*, Vol. VII, p. 150.   [19] *Ibid.*, p. 219.
[20] *Ibid.*

Before the 1920's Freud denied the existence of a "primary" masochism—an activity in which the agent's purpose was the infliction of pain or humiliating dependency upon himself.[21] Masochism was a defense against sadism—itself an activity whose original aim was not the infliction of pain in others but aggressive mastery of the object of sexual desire.[22] In masochistic activity the subject identified himself in phantasy with the object, thus continuing his sadistic activity, but in disguised form. After this defensive transformation had taken place, the masochist might pursue pain itself, but only incidentally to the accompanying sexual excitation.[23] Thus, masochism, as a form of passivity, was either repressed activity, or an indirect method of sexual gratification. Explained this way, the ordinary language notion of masochism simply disappeared as a human purpose.

The outcome of Freud's treatment of the desire to be loved was the same. First, however, his analysis of love must be examined. He had defined love as the expression of the whole sexual current of feeling, i.e., the feeling as directed at the object of satisfaction or pleasure. In earliest infancy, in the narcissistic stage, love was directed at oneself. Thus love was "derived from the capacity of the ego to satisfy some of its instinctual impulses auto-erotically by obtaining organ pleasure"; when turned outwards, toward objects, it "expresses the motor efforts of the ego towards these objects as sources of pleasure."[24] Object-love, therefore, retained its original narcissistic character of aiming at the ego's pleasure, with the external object serving as a means to that end. This theoretical analysis of object-love, it should be noted, was not compatible with Freud's clinical observations about the subject's relation to his love object. In the *Three Essays*, he had pointed to the credulity of love, based on the idealization of the love object, which made it an important, if not the most fundamental, source of authority.[25] Later, in the essay "On

21 *Ibid.*, Vol. XIV, p. 128.   22 *Ibid.*, also Vol. VII, p. 158.
23 *Ibid.*, Vol. XIV, p. 129.   24 *Ibid.*, Vol. XIV, p. 138.
25 *Ibid.*, Vol. VII, p. 150.

Narcissism," he described the basis of object-choice as need of an other that compromised one's autonomy: "A person who loves has, so to speak, forfeited a part of his narcissism and it can only be replaced by his being loved."[26] Whereas the theoretical analysis of loving as an instinctual expression made the object a mere instrument of an active desire for one's own pleasure, clinical observation disclosed the erotic foundations of submission to the object, i.e., the fact that submission was willed, actively desired, not coerced.

In "Instincts and their Vicissitudes," Freud applied the same form of explanation to the desire to be loved. It simply represented a return to the original narcissistic state of loving oneself.[27] Elsewhere, however, he recognized the dependent nature of the desire to be loved, the inherent recognition in it of the superior value and significance of the parents. But this dependency and recognition were then explained as *de facto* accommodations to the situation of infantile helplessness and parental power. The desire to be loved was not an original instinctual disposition but a response developed because of its utility for survival. "We learn to value being loved," Freud wrote, "as an advantage for which we are willing to sacrifice other advantages."[28] Strictly speaking, in other words, there was no desire to be loved for its own sake. The need to be loved was the result of a realistic assessment of the child's biological dependency on powerful figures who could not be coerced or controlled by the child; his only hold on them was their love of him. Though Freud classified the desire to be loved as an internal factor in repression—in contrast to the external factor of the force exercised by upbringing—he made it clear that the two were not qualitatively different: "In the last resort, it may be assumed that every internal compulsion which makes itself felt in the development of human beings was originally . . . only an external one."[29]

26 *Ibid.*, Vol. xiv, p. 98.
28 *Ibid.*, p. 282.
27 *Ibid.*, Vol. xiv, p. 98.
29 *Ibid.*

The "other advantages" that were sacrificed in the interests of biological protection were those of instinctual gratification epitomized in the Oedipus complex. There was another even more basic reason for the sacrifice—the threat and fear of castration, which represented the threat to the boy's possibilities of pleasure and self-assertion. It was Wilhelm Reich who best characterized Freud's initial interpretation of the meaning of the boy's submission to the castration threat through impulse control. He phrased the child's implicit reasoning in these terms: "I must preserve my pleasure possibilities and therefore become indifferent to my father."[30] The purposes of self-control were really to free oneself from the suppression of the external environment and guard the possibilities of self-assertion. Freud himself, as we have seen, gave expression to his equation of the incestuous sexual desire with freedom and self-assertion in the provocative statement about the need for the individual to come to terms with the possibility of incest, i.e., to recognize the prohibition not as absolute but as biologically instrumental.

Thus, on the level of basic motivational theory, passivity as an innate disposition of the individual disappeared and was replaced by the rationalist assumption of a desire for freedom modified or constrained only by the needs of survival and threats to the exercise of that freedom. Passivity in all its forms turned out to be, in Freud's theoretical interpretation, an opportunistic concession to reality and not an end in itself. Man was born instinctually free and if he alienated that freedom it was out of utilitarian calculation. It has been noted by one interpreter of Freud that he "had little feeling for the autonomy of childhood."[31] It is possible to see one of the major reasons why this was so. Indeed, one can say that in terms of Freud's theoretical constructs, the remark is an understatement. Narrowly construed, his image of the child was the model of the shrewd egotist surrendering to environ-

[30] W. Reich, *Character Analysis*, trans. T. P. Wolfe, 3rd ed., New York, 1949, p. 147.

[31] Rieff, *Mind of the Moralist*, p. 45.

mental demands neither out of desire nor duty but out of a realistic assessment of the consequences of self-assertion against superior force—the very picture Freud drew of social man at the outbreak of the First World War.[32] From the perspective of the rationalist tradition as we have outlined it, it can be said more generously that Freud's view of the child was the model of the authentic self who was self-motivated rather than other-directed. The Oedipus complex, the core for Freud of adult neurotic disorder, was a microcosm of the rationalist theory of freedom and coercion; the child desired his mother as an object of his own gratification, but surrendered his aim out of rational assessment of the dangers facing him in its pursuit. It is not surprising that he could give no explanation of the persistence of the Oedipus complex into adulthood when he recognized no basic *internal* inclination to dependence, other than situational, even in the child.

Freud's instinct theory was the equivalent of the rationalist view of man in the state of nature. Indeed, in his anthropological work, he advanced his own state of nature theory. It has been argued that Freud's adoption of the primal horde theory marked his divergence from the individualism of rationalist social theory, for it began with a model of society based on authority, with society as equivalent to the family, in which the sons were subordinate to the father. Freud's anthropology, however, rooted freedom in human nature as firmly as any of the earlier rationalist myths. The structure of the primal horde was externally authoritarian; its justification rested on the father's ability to organize the efforts needed for survival and on the *ultima ratio* of force, his brute repressive strength—a mixture, then, of utility and terror. The sons' submission was based on need and fear, and therefore recognized and felt as submission; it was precisely this recognition which made rebellion possible and desirable. Freud's suggestion that the rebellion may have followed some technological breakthrough that gave the sons some new weapons to overcome the superior strength of the father in-

[32] "Thoughts For the Times on War and Death," *S.E.*, Vol. xiv, p. 272.

dicates very clearly that the basis of their original submission was not a belief in the transcendental legitimacy of the father's authority. The hypothesis of a group mind preceding individual autonomy and based on loving submission to a leader was one that Freud broached later, after the First World War, as one of a series of changes that, as we shall see, altered somewhat the perspectives of his metapsychology. His initial theoretical categories entailed the proposition that submission was always *de facto*, not *de jure*. It was for this reason that his attempt in *Totem and Taboo* to derive a concept of guilt from the remorse at the slaying of the primal father was conceptually inadequate. Guilt is an emotion based on a belief in the objective legitimacy of authorities or norms; it cannot be derived from a feeling of regret based on nostalgia for the lost benefits of a situation. Utilitarian constraints and categorical prohibitions are logically different.

The inner tension between Freud's empirical discoveries and his explanatory categories was nowhere more sharply evident than in the concept of the ego-ideal, which he introduced in the 1914 essay "On Narcissism." The introduction of the ego-ideal was significant in that it represented his first explicit clinical-theoretical recognition before the 1920's that repression was carried out in the name of or at the behest of ideal values, rather than utilitarian (ego-interest) considerations. Of course, such an awareness had always been implicit in Freud's reference to shame and morality as the basic repressive forces of the ego, but it had been effectively negated in his metapsychological explanation of repression. However, the crucial break with rationalist utilitarian theory represented by the notion of an ego-ideal was not followed through consistently, for it was based on a theoretical definition of narcissism that made the genesis of an ego-ideal as a transcendental value logically contradictory.

The inconsistency in Freud's analysis of the ego-ideal paralleled the inconsistencies in the rationalist attempt to reconcile autonomy and objective universality. On the one hand, the ego-ideal represented developmentally the internalization of a set of objective norms by which the child judged himself. Through parental prohibitions and structures, through the frustrations of reality, the child was aware that he was not perfect, not automatically good or acceptable; the ego-ideal was the image of the transcendental norm he would have to live up to in order to be of value.

On the other hand, Freud described the impulse to fulfill the ego-ideal as the individual's attempt to recapture the state of original narcissism in which the child was, as he so significantly put it, "his own ideal"[33]—that is, self-sufficient and without need of justification by anything beyond himself. Thus the paradoxical purpose of the child's surrender to alien norms was to restore a situation in which he had no need of them because he was perfect, complete unto himself. This was, in fact, contradictory. If an original state of self-sufficiency had ever existed in the terms described by Freud, there was no way to explain why the child ever came to accept parental norms as legitimate, how he could surrender his original "aseity," his original self-valuation, into the hands of others. And, in fact, in his essay "Instincts and their Vicissitudes," Freud did suggest that the narcissistic ego was *not* primary but rather a defensive development from an original reality-ego that was aware of its finitude and reacted by incorporating what was pleasurable in the external world into itself and projecting outside itself internal sources of unpleasure.[34] Nevertheless, Freud retained a theoretical definition of narcissism as self-sufficiency and unproblematic self-acceptance, a definition consistent with the rationalist premises of libido theory, in its preservation of the notion of an original human autonomy.

This definition thus led to paradoxes in the application of the term "narcisssim." For example, Freud used it to classify someone who was "self-contented" and in love with himself. Yet such a person was also described as above all needing to

---

[33] S.E., Vol. XIV, p. 94. [34] *Ibid.*, pp. 135-136.

be loved. Empirically, it was obvious that the narcissistic form of love, in which the subject was apparently concerned only with himself, was no less a dependent form than what Freud called "anaclitic" object-love, in which the love object was idealized and deferred to. Here narcissism and primary autonomy were opposites, not equivalents; the self-contentment Freud spoke of was defensive. Yet he did not see it that way, did not see the contradiction in his descriptions, because of the bias built into the meaning of narcissism.

Though ego-ideals were supposedly substitutes for original narcissism, Freud himself pointed out that homage to a high ego-ideal represented an impoverishment of the ego's self-sufficiency.[35] Yet at the same time he asserted that "to be their own ideal once more . . . this is what people strive to attain as their happiness."[36] To explain self-alienation, through self-abnegation to an ideal other than the self, as a striving for an original self-sufficiency was, however, precisely to evade the mystery of alienation. In the same way, the rationalists had tried to fuse obligation and objectivity with freedom in their moral and social concepts. The Freudian idea that repression stemmed from the "*self*-respect of the ego"[37] reproduced the contradiction between empirical observation and explanatory theory in all rationalistic accounts of unfreedom, and for the same reason—to assert the existence of autonomy while recognizing the psychic reality that the self maintained a passive attitude to absolute ideals that were other than, greater than, the self.

In the case of psychoanalysis, the contradiction was of crucial significance for the possibility of therapy. Freud's chastened rationalist therapeutic optimism was the result of his basic categories, which made it plausible that the patient could overcome his resistance and gain insight primarily through cognition, because in a fundamental sense the self he really was did not differ from the self he consciously thought

[35] *Ibid.*, p. 100.   [36] *Ibid.*   [37] *Ibid.*, p. 93.

he was and ideally wished to be. As paradoxical as this sounds in view of the clinical discoveries of psychoanalysis, it was the notion of a solid core of autonomous selfhood that underlay Freud's pre-1920 ideas about therapy. Essentially, he believed that the therapeutic process tended to unfold by itself and that the analyst was not an agent of change but a catalyst of internal events. The patient did the real work of changing himself; the analyst provided the rational insights which the patient integrated on his own—a situation that encouraged autonomy and growth in the patient by building on the core which already existed. This set of assumptions was strengthened by the genetic model whose relevant features were discussed in chapter one. Since developmental maturation proceeded automatically, according to the theory the availability of an autonomous self could be counted on to counteract the infantile self. Freud's developmental model incorporated the evolutionary guarantee of freedom as the destined end-result.

Up to this point we have discussed how the theories of unconscious phantasy and instinct preserved the rationalist view of human motivation in psychoanalytic theory. We may now look briefly at the second thesis involved in the proposition that Freud's metapsychology preserved a rationalist view of human functioning: the thesis that his conception of unconscious processes preserved the idea of rationality of belief by treating neurotic ideation not as a psychic process but as a quasi-physical one.

The issue may be put this way. Insofar as neurotic behavior was meaningful, it consisted of desires and emotions of the same order as ordinary wishes and feelings. Neither the desires of the neurotic, however, nor the objects of those desires, were available to his consciousness. Instead, he experienced his impulses and emotions in alien and inexplicable situational contexts. The phobic, for example, had unaccountable fears of animals, of open spaces, of heights; the impotent man was unaccountably incapable of sexual performance with women. What was the relationship, for Freud, between the object of desire or emotion on the conscious level and the real object on the unconscious level?

Once again we can begin by focusing on a concrete example drawn from Freud's clinical work. "Little Hans," the five-year-old son of a former patient of Freud's, developed a fear of horses so intense that he was unable to go out into the street. Analysis revealed that the child was experiencing a powerful surge of longing for his mother, coupled with hostile feelings toward his father. One of Freud's interpretations of the overdetermined fear of horses was that the horse represented Hans's father,[38] whose retaliation Hans feared for his erotic and aggressive impulses. In what sense, however, did Freud understand the idea that the horse "represented" the father? It was certainly not the conscious symbolic representation of literary art, i.e., simile or even metaphor. Did he think that on some level Hans believed that the horse *was* his father? There can be no question that Freud spoke as if he attributed just such an illogical belief to Hans. "The horse," Freud wrote, "must be his father."[39] Hans had played horse with his father on more than one occasion. But this kind of ordinary language paraphrase of unconscious processes was for Freud largely a *façon de parler*, a theoretically imprecise way of rendering the workings of the unconscious clearer for patients and readers, an "as if" formulation.

As early as the article on *The Neuropsychoses of Defence*, Freud had stated explicitly that defense mechanisms, such as displacement, were not psychic but physical processes, "the psychical consequences of which are so represented *as if* what is expressed by the words 'detachment of the idea from its affect and false connection of the latter' had really happened." Displacement *"cannot be proved by any clinical-psychological analysis."*[40] This was to concede that it was not possible to bring the patient to an avowal that he believed the displacement object to be identical with the real object of the

---

[38] *S.E.*, Vol. x, p. 126.   [39] *Ibid.*, p. 123.
[40] *Ibid.*, Vol. iii, p. 53. Italics added.

emotion. A passage in *The Interpretation of Dreams* confirms the view that Freud did not conceptualize defense as a thought process involving beliefs of any kind, rational or irrational: *"These processes which are described as irrational are not in fact falsifications of normal processes—intellectual errors—but are modes of activity of the psychological apparatus that have been freed from an inhibition."*[41] Thus R. S. Peters is correct in arguing that "in so far as unconscious processes are involved in the thinking about getting to the goal [of an unconscious wish or defense], they cannot be described as either correct or incorrect, efficient or inefficient, intelligent or unintelligent. It just happens according to mechanical principles."[42]

While secondary process thinking also had its own quasi-mechanical transcription, the point was precisely that this was a transcription of intellectual processes describable in other terms—in the language of contexts of action and beliefs about that context. Descriptions of primary process functioning were not similarly transcriptions of belief language but explanations of lapses from rationality.

This conclusion is unavoidable on the basis of theory and indicates how Freud preserved the norm of rationality as the very definition of thought. Nevertheless it must be qualified by pointing to the great flexibility of psychoanalysis which for therapeutic as well as expository purposes did speak in terms that would at least suggest the notion of unconscious beliefs.[43] The relationship between ordinary language and theoretical explanation was such as to permit Freud to shuttle back and forth between them without any feeling of inconsistency.

The introduction of the death instinct was a crucial turning point in Freud's thought. It represented a new orientation apparent in major clinical and psychological insights, and, from the point of view of this book, it represented a reversal

[41] *Ibid.*, Vol. v, p. 605. Italics added.

[42] R. S. Peters, *The Concept of Motivation*, London, 1958, p. 64.

[43] The issue is whether its own theoretical premises permit it to do so with consistency.

of Freud's position on freedom. The dethronement of the pleasure principle as the sole motivating force of human behavior meant recognition on the theoretical level of the dimension of behavior pre-war metapsychology had excluded— passivity, a positive desire for self-alienation for its own sake.

It is difficult to know, at least without further extensive research, what brought about this change. The clinical material presented under the general rubric of the repetition compulsion at the beginning of *Beyond the Pleasure Principle* does not furnish adequate explanation, for the earlier metapsychological framework had encompassed a good deal of anomalous clinical phenomena.

It seems very likely that Freud's experience of the war played a large role in the genesis of his new position. His own initial enthusiasm at its outbreak seems totally out of character because of both his analytically disciplined skepticism about human nature and his ironic distance from the conservative, hierarchical, and anti-Semitic Austro-Hungarian empire. The unforeseen length of the war, its carnage and brutality incommensurable with any reasonable purpose, must have made his ultimate reaction to his enthusiasm even sharper than it might otherwise have been. Freud's poignant "Thoughts for the Times on War and Death" seem at any rate to have been written as much for himself as for others. The disillusionment of the pre-war cultivated cosmopolitan European that he described was his own; when he wrote to Lou Andreas-Salomé that "it has come out just as from our psychoanalytical expectations we should have imagined man and his behavior"[44] he was speaking with the wisdom of hindsight. For whatever the clinical implications of psychoanalysis, the theory itself did not present so dark a view of human nature. Before the war, for example, Freud had explicitly rejected the notion of an aggressive instinct.[45]

The war, then, revealed to Freud dimensions of human be-

[44] E. Jones, *The Life and Work of Sigmund Freud*, Vol. II, New York, 1955, p. 199.
[45] See Freud's quarrel with Adler over the existence of a special instinct of aggression, *S.E.*, Vol. X, p. 128.

havior, in himself as in others, that he had known yet in some sense not truly acknowledged. Whether the war's cumulative impact itself brought about the revision of metapsychology, whether it catalyzed changes already underway or helped put clinical phenomena in a new light cannot be readily decided here. What is clear is that the war period was a watershed in the development of Freud's thought, and that after it the appreciation of irrationality was more direct and theoretically better integrated than before.

It is particularly noteworthy that though Freud's increasingly pessimistic mood about human nature developed in reaction to his perception of aggression towards others, its theoretical outcome was a concept of a basic destructive tendency directed towards the self. Aside from the clinical evidence of repetition compulsion phenomena—which Freud himself thought admitted of other explanations—it is possible that he was reflecting on his own wartime surrender to the Fatherland. At the outbreak of the war he had suddenly become an ardent patriot ("All my libido," he wrote on August 23, 1914, "is given to Austro-Hungary"),[46] and was severely disappointed with and contemptuous of Austrian incompetence in the battle against Serbia, which revealed "the hopelessness of such a fatherland, to whom it was not worth belonging."[47] Only late in the war did he begin to feel that the Central Powers had been deceptive and unworthy, as well as inept, finally conceding to Jones that "a German victory might have proved a harder blow to the interests of mankind in general."[48] Thus Freud came to realize that his own reason and judgment (he had long been an Anglophile) had been inhibited by his passive and regressive love for the Empire.

Whatever personal influences were at work, however, the form that the reversal in psychoanalytic theory took was determined by its original direction. Original instinct theory was a theory of activity, of authenticity in the sense of serv-

46 Jones, *Freud*, II, p. 192.   47 *Ibid.*, p. 193.
48 *Ibid.*, p. 231.

ing one's own purposes rather than serving an alien will. The death-instinct was a theory of self-alienation for its own sake.

This was apparent from the psychological meaning of the death-instinct. Freud had conceptualized the drive for passivity as biological instinct in order to show its fundamental nature, its irreducibility to an instrumentality in the service of a more basic end. But as a biological construct, the death-instinct was a phantasy, based on a conceptual confusion between the idea of death as the inevitable outcome of life and death as the aim of life. It can indeed be argued that the very concept of a death-instinct exploded the biological framework of psychoanalytic theory. It could not be fitted into a theory based on survival and procreation, and, because it covered phenomena basic to human psychology, it revealed the inadequacy of a biological framework to encompass a truly human psychology.

The real meaning, then, of the death-instinct was in the psychological facts for which it was meant to account. Positing it did not give an explanation for these facts, but recognized them as facts. Freud's acknowledgment of passivity as an ultimate datum of motivation manifested itself in three basic areas in post-1920 psychoanalytic theory—the theory of masochism, the concepts of identification and superego formation, and the theory of anxiety.

The most important pieces of clinical evidence presented in *Beyond the Pleasure Principle* were the dreams of war neurotics, which insistently repeated the unpleasurable traumas responsible for the outbreak of the neurosis, and the behavior of patients in analysis, who repeated the unhappy situations and painful emotions of the past with the therapist, contriving, as Freud put it, to feel themselves scorned. Both of these were manifestations of masochism, and, along with other manifestations, they demanded revision in theory.

Freud bluntly acknowledged the inability of the original metapsychology to explain masochism. "If mental processes are governed by the pleasure principle in such a way that

205

their first aim is avoidance of pain and obtaining pleasure, masochism is incomprehensible."[49] It was because of this that masochism could not be admitted earlier even as an empirical phenomenon. Now, however, Freud was able to classify and describe different forms of masochism as ends in themselves —the desire to be treated like a small, helpless, and naughty child; the desire to be placed in a characteristically female, i.e., passive, sexual position; the desire for humiliation or punishment. These phenomena were in fact collectively equivalent to the death instinct; "the death instinct which is operative in the organism—primal sadism—is identical with masochism."[50] This confirms the assertion that self-abnegation, the surrender of purpose and will, were the essence of Freud's new conception. Sadism directed outwards was a defensive maneuver on the part of the libido, which tried to render the death instinct innocuous by directing it towards objects in the external world.[51]

Masochistic passivity played a predominant role in Freud's explanation of identification and the genesis of the superego. These concepts were crucial to psychoanalytic theory because they supplied part of the missing links in the theory of repression, the connection between infantile conflict and adult neurosis. Adult dependency on the parental prohibitions and norms of childhood, and the accompanying ambivalence of feeling toward parent figures, were not simply inexplicable "returns of the repressed"; they were the results of the child's identification with his parents that made their norms and definitions part of his own personality. Once they were internalized, there was no longer any necessity for a real external threat to enforce self-control; the child adopted the external valuation of and attitude towards certain types of behavior as his own.

Freud's theory of identification was complex and confused; there were a number of different explanations for identifica-

---

[49] Freud, *S.E.*, Vol. XIX, p. 159.
[50] *Ibid.*, p. 164.　　　　　　　　　　[51] *Ibid.*, p. 163.

tion at different points in his work.[52] It was first introduced as an important concept in the 1917 article on "Mourning and Melancholia," where it was used to explain the melancholic's self-reproaches. The melancholic had, according to his interpretation, identified with a lost love object; the reproaches directed against the self were really directed against the object through the ego's identification with it. In *The Ego and the Id* the psychopathological mechanism was extended to explain basic developments in normal psychology. Ego-formation or character was to an important degree determined by the substitution of identification for object cathexes. "The character of the ego," Freud wrote, "is a precipitate of abandoned object-cathexes."[53] So far as ego-formation as the outcome of the Oedipus complex was concerned, however, the boy's primary identification was not with his mother, as it should have been according to the substitution idea, but with his father. To explain this, Freud suggested that a more complete view of the Oedipus complex had to be taken. Because of bisexuality, the Oedipus complex was bipolar; the boy displayed an affectionate feminine attitude to his father as well as desire for his mother. The post-oedipal identification with the father represented "a substitute for a longing for the father"[54]—that is, it was a primary passive trend, a form of masochism that in extreme cases became "resexualized" in the unconscious feelings of guilt of the neurotic as a desire for passive sexual relations with the father.[55] It was Freud's acceptance of passivity as a basic drive that made possible a proper appreciation of the structure of the ego and a partial correction of the anomaly previously noted in the derivation of the ego-ideal from a totally self-sufficient primary narcissism.

The implications of passivity, however, were even more

[52] For a contemporary attempt to sort out and clarify these issues, see R. W. White, *Ego and Reality in Psychoanalytic Theory, Psychological Issues*, Vol. III, No. 3, New York, 1963.

[53] Freud, *S.E.*, Vol. XIX, p. 29.   [54] *Ibid.*, p. 37.

[55] *Ibid.*, Vol. XIX, p. 169.

radical than the explanation of the superego suggested. They involved not only feminine libido but masculine libido as well. For the boy's very masculinity, as expressed in his incestuous libidinal desires, was not merely, or primarily, a desire for gratification, a form of autonomous self-assertion, but a desire for deindividuation, for self-loss through merger with the mother.

Freud developed this idea in *Inhibitions, Symptoms and Anxiety*, in advancing his new theory of anxiety. Anxiety, Freud now concluded, was not the effect but the cause of repression; defense occurred when the ego signaled, through the generation of anxiety, that danger impended. In the adult the anxiety was social or moral and portended punishment from the superego for forbidden wishes and impulses. But such punishment was an extension of the punishment of castration. This equation was possible because both situations represented danger, and insofar as they were recognized in anxiety as doing so they must represent previous situations already familiar as dangerous from the past. The original danger situation that generated anxiety in the infant was the absence of or separation from the mother. It was this separation anxiety which was revived in the threat of castration. "The high degree of narcissistic value which the penis possesses," wrote Freud, "can appeal to the fact that he can once more be united to his mother—i.e., to a substitute for her—in the act of copulation. Being deprived of it amounts to a renewed separation from her."[56]

This was a striking re-orientation in the interpretation of the castration threat from the earlier metapsychology. Then the emphasis had been on the threat to possibilities that meant pleasure and autonomy; now the impulses involved were those of dependency and fusion, a desire to dissolve the self altogether and reunite it with a greater whole.

However, the post-1920 reversal in Freud's metapsychological premises was far from complete. This was apparent

[56] *Ibid.*, Vol. XIX, p. 37.

in his interpretation of separation anxiety. The child's desire to unite with its mother was the result of its biological helplessness, which made it dependent on external objects for need satisfaction, or, in Freud's economic terms, for mastery of the quantities of excitation built up because of biological needs. "The biological factor, then," Freud asserted, "establishes the earliest situations of danger which will accompany the child through the rest of its life."[57] But this posed a problem that Freud himself underlined. Why should the need to be loved, expressed in the fear of loss of the superego's love, continue through life, if it was biologically phase specific? As Freud put it: "This study of the determinants of anxiety has, as it were, shown the defensive behavior of the ego *transfigured in a rational light*. Each situation of danger corresponds to a particular period of life . . . and appears to be justifiable for it."[58]

In childhood, the individual was dependent on the loving care of parents and was justifiably afraid of parental punishment; separation and castration anxieties were realistic, or at least not irrational, given the observations and theories of the child. This was no longer the case in adulthood, yet the neurotic behaved as if it were: "Although all the agencies for mastering stimuli have long ago been developed within wide limits in his mental apparatus, and although he is sufficiently grown-up to satisfy most of his needs for himself and has long ago learned that castration is no longer practised as a punishment, he nevertheless behaves as though the old danger-situations still existed, and keeps hold of all the earlier determinants of anxiety." This remained for Freud the central riddle of neurosis, the riddle of fixation, which psychoanalysis had not solved. It was at this point that he wrote the words quoted earlier, about the mystery of the persistence of sources of anxiety long since grown out of date: "Why are not all neuroses episodes in the development of the individual which come to a close when the next phase is reached? . . . Whence

<hr>

[57] *Ibid.*, p. 155. [58] *Ibid.*, p. 146. Italics added.

does neurosis come—what is its ultimate, its own peculiar *raison d'etre?* After tens of years of psychoanalytic labors, we are as much in the dark about this problem as we were at the start."[59]

It is against the background of this admission of failure, a failure based, as has been argued, on the rationalistic presuppositions of Freud's metapsychology, that the theoretical innovation and historical significance of contemporary existentialism can be appreciated. Freud had, in his last period, recognized a drive to passivity even if he had not fully developed its meaning and even if, by retaining the biological viewpoint, he had undercut it in positivist fashion by removing it from the realm of motivation and turning it into a biologically deterministic force.

Existentialism, however, had advanced a theory of motivation that explained the human point of self-alienation. Working within the neo-idealist and phenomenological traditions, with their emphasis on the subjective constitution of meaning and the objectivity and universality of meanings and values, Heidegger discovered that the deepest meaning of "objectivity" was its meaning as not-self. That which was ideal and objective, i.e., not merely subjective, had characteristics lacking to and desired by the self. Concepts, values and rules of action had the appearance of timelessness, uncontestability, and prescriptivity. The conferring of an absolute determinateness on the roles and norms of one's social environment gave one a sense of solidity, of sameness through time and of legitimate belonging. At the same time, it involved a surrender of authenticity, an abnegation of the responsibility for choice that was passed off to the facticity of the environment.

Here, then, was a theory of motivation that could account for the passivity Freud had noted but not explained. Here was a way of understanding the continuing power of the past in the life of the present, the meaning of submission to authority

[59] *Ibid.*, pp. 147-149.

figures and identification with them, masochism and the prescriptive form of morality that *was* the experience of guilt.
The quest for Being as stability of selfhood through stability
of meaning structures made Freud's "drive to inorganic stability," as he defined the death instinct, intelligible in human
terms as a will to a changeless state of rest that, while decidedly not death in the physical sense, meant an end to un-
certainty and open-endedness, the fulfillment of life in
"being" instead of perpetual becoming. Indeed, Sartre's version of the human project as the attempt of the for-itself to
become a thing-like entity, an in-itself, was even linguis-
tically similar to Freud's formulation, despite Freud's attempt
to make it a universal biological principle.

In the next chapter we shall discuss how the concept of
motivation inherent in Heidegger's work was used by the philosophers and psychiatrists influenced by him to develop a
concept of selfhood different from that of Freud. Heidegger
himself was not at this time directly concerned with psychology or psychoanalysis, though there is evidence in *Being and
Time* of at least a rudimentary acquaintance with some of
Freud's ideas.[60] Our purpose at this point is to focus, rather,
on the place of Heidegger's early work in the context of the
post-1890 attack on rationalism. If we take Freud as representative of the first stage in the critique of rationalism, Heidegger can be seen as climaxing the second.

In the first stage, there were a number of different approaches. One group of thinkers acknowledged the data of
irrationality—passivity in action and irrationality of belief—
while trying to explain them in positivist or rationalist terms.
It included figures of predominantly positivist orientation
such as Freud, Durkheim, Pareto, Mosca, and Wallas, though
a number of them were critical of aspects of the positivism
of Comte, Taine, Spencer, and Darwinian thinking in social
theory.

[60] See his remarks on wishing and wish-fulfillment in *Being and Time*,
pp. 239-240, and on the biologizing of conscience, p. 320. (This may also
have been a reference to Nietzsche.)

For each of these figures a fascinating analysis of the inter-play of the elements of rationality and irrationality can be carried out that shows contradictions parallel to the ones we have analyzed in Freud. Another group, including both social theorists and imaginative writers, described data of irrational-ity—in the form, for example, of *Gemeinschaft* relationships, charisma, crowd phenomena, and myth—without further explaining them and sometimes even with overt sympathy for them as manifestations of true human spontaneity. The sym-pathy was always tempered by a rationalist orientation that, as in the case of Weber and Tönnies, ultimately refused to ac-cept the equation of spontaneous submission with freedom or, as in the case of Sorel, was able to judge myth as myth, i.e., according to the standards of rational belief. A third group of thinkers, predominantly philosophers, tried to affirm the compatibility of human freedom, conceived in terms of human subjectivity as constitutive of meaning, with the objec-tive existence of universal concepts and values that were nec-essary forms of human thought and existence and thus neces-sary constraints on autonomy. All of these different groups, with their widely varying individual concerns, can be shown to have been concerned with one or both of the issues in the rationalist tradition discussed in this chapter in connection with Freud.

After the First World War, however, the syntheses proved much more difficult to sustain, and frequently fell apart. The facts of irrationality had to be faced without the equivoca-tions still possible in the pre-war period; they had to be un-derstood for what they were, and either explained in their own terms or defined as inexplicable, either embraced or re-jected as values. Many of the characteristic intellectual and literary expressions of the war and post-war periods reflect the dissolution of the complex and tortuous earlier syntheses of rationalism and irrationalism, or at least an exacerbation of the tensions within them.

Thus the 1920's saw on the one hand the birth of surreal-ism, with its open embrace of the irrational and its claim to a method for exploring its meaning, and on the other the development of severely ascetic forms of linguistic and analytic philosophy that restricted the scope of legitimate discourse to the rationally knowable—though, in the case of Wittgenstein, with the open acknowledgment of a sphere of existence for which there were no concepts. The period witnessed the develoment of fascist ideology and calls on the part of intellectuals not to betray their humane and rationalist vocations by flirting with the irrational. It saw in the art of Pirandello and Hesse and in Mannheim's sociology of knowledge the collapse of the belief in an integrated social consensus of objectively knowable norms, and with it the radical isolation of the individual, thrust back on his own truth. But it also saw the Bauhaus attempts to reintegrate society and individualism through the reconciliation of art and technology in architecture and crafts *via* a belief in individual creativity exploiting the objective possibilities of new materials. All of these tendencies had their antecedents before the war, but it was only during and after it that they emerged in an extreme, sharpened form.

In *Being and Time* it was the neo-idealist synthesis that fell apart. The reconciliation of autonomy and the objectivity and universality of concepts and values was argued by Heidegger to be impossible because one was the negation of the other. The temporal understanding of human existence made the atemporal structure of concepts untenable except as a form of illusion. The interpretation of understanding as the projection of possibilities by Dasein made the notion of objective meaning deriving from sources beyond the self equally untenable.

Nowhere in *Being and Time* was this kind of demystification more significant than in Heidegger's analysis of conscience, the Neo-Kantian and phenomenological bastion of ideal values. Traditional idealist interpretations of conscience, wrote Heidegger, pass themselves off as "recognizing the call [of conscience] in the sense of a voice which is universally binding and which speaks in a way that is 'not just subjective.' Furthermore, the 'universal' conscience becomes exalted to a 'world-conscience' which still has the phenomenal character of an 'it' and 'nobody,' yet which speaks—there in the individual 'subject'—as this indefinite something."[61] Such an interpretation—whether on the part of the ordinary subject or the philosopher—was in error. "But this 'public conscience'—what else is it than the voice of the 'they'? A 'world-conscience' is a dubious fabrication and Dasein can come to this only *because* conscience, in its basis and its essence, is in each case mine . . . the call comes from that entity which in each case I myself am."[62] The self hid behind the anonymous mask of universality, to disguise its own responsibility from itself. Norms carried weight only because Dasein lent them their weight by recognizing their legitimacy.

Though Heidegger's analysis proceeded at a level of generality high enough to be applicable to other times and other cultures, it is impossible to miss the mark of his own time and place on his ontology. It is evident in the language in which he couched his basic categories, as well as in certain inconsistencies in the argument. For example, he described the inauthenticity of everyday life as bringing to Dasein a tranquillity "in which all the possibilities of its Being will be secure, genuine, and full" through "the self-certainty and decidedness of the 'they,' " which Dasein adopts for itself.[63] Yet the very problem of the connectedness of experience, the sameness of the self through time, i.e., the problem of identity, Heidegger saw as being generated by the fact that in modern life, "Everyday Dasein has been dispersed into the many kinds of things which daily 'come to pass' . . . it is driven about by its affairs. So if it wants to come to itself, it must first *pull itself together* from the *dispersion* and *disconnectedness* of the very things that have 'come to pass.' "[64] The source of identity fragmentation was the absence of any internal unifying framework, which left the self prey to the pressures and happenings

[61] Heidegger, *Being and Time*, p. 323.
[62] *Ibid.*   [63] *Ibid.*, p. 222.   [64] *Ibid.*, pp. 441-442.

214

of the moment and the environment. This was manifest in the inauthentic understanding of time as a sequence of "nows" that approached one from the future and receded into the past. It was this constant changing of experiences which created the problem of self-constancy: "[It] is only then that there at last arises from the horizon of understanding which belongs to inauthentic historicality, the question of how one is to establish a 'connectedness' of Dasein if one does so in the sense of 'Experiences' of a subject—Experiences which are 'also' 'present-at-hand.' "[65]

Thus it was the breakdown of cohesion in modernity, of a coherent tradition linking the individual's past and future in a subjectively meaningful totality embracing the whole of society, that created the need for unity. Contrary to Heidegger's argument elsewhere in *Being and Time*, modernity did not furnish a unity but a new form of inauthenticity resulting from the breakdown of an old one. It was the fragmentation of modern life and the multiplicity of possible determinants of behavior, changing with every change in public taste as mediated by the organs of "publicness," the media and public opinion generally, that made possible the awareness of the inauthenticity of so much behavior.

There seems little doubt that Heidegger's castigation of urban mass culture reflected the views of a conservative German of lower-middle class small-town origins. It can also be suggested—though direct evidence is lacking—that Heidegger's abstract categories reflected the reaction of a conservative German academic to the collapse of the Wilhelmian Empire and the phenomenon of Weimar. After the revolution of 1918, all the negative features of modernism—materialism, mass society, social conflict and division, competition—were no longer contained and seemingly mastered by the unified ideology of a hierarchical and nationalist authoritarianism but were made nakedly evident by the extension of the same principles from society to the very form of the state. Now,

[65] *Ibid.*, p. 442.

215

indeed, public opinion ruled, and there were no consensual guidelines for behavior but the events of the moment which demanded a response.

Seen in this light, Heidegger's critique of *"das Man"* was not much different from the more overtly cultural and political attacks of academic conservatives, such as Eduard Meyer, who complained about the Republic: "Everything which is independent, unique, national . . . everything which is specifically German is to be eradicated and replaced with the dreadful monotony of colorless homogeneity and dead numbers."[66] This impression is strengthened when one examines further Heidegger's call for Dasein to abandon the "endless multiplicity of possibilities which offer themselves as closest to one—those of comfortableness, shirking and taking things lightly"[67]—and to seize in an authentic manner, and along with its generation, the possibilities given in one's tradition, making them one's fateful destiny. This could easily be read —especially in hindsight—as a call for the spiritual revolution necessary to reawaken Germany's sense of nationalist destiny, broken by the war and buried under the material concerns of everyday life.

Nevertheless, whatever the particularity of Heidegger's angle of vision, it must not be forgotten that the perception of chaos and the collapse of social consensus in the 1920's transcended any one particular social group or even any one country. The specifics of Heidegger's response were unique, but not the dilemma. One need only read such expressions of despair as that of Valéry to realize how widespread the malaise was:

"One can say that all the fundamentals of our world have been affected by the war, or more exactly, by the circumstances of the war; something deeper has been worn away than the renewable parts of the machine. You know how greatly the general economic situation has been disturbed, and the polity of states, and the very life of the individual;

66 Quoted in Ringer, *Decline of the German Mandarins*, p. 214.
67 Heidegger, *Being and Time*, p. 435.

you are familiar with the universal discomfort, hesitation, apprehension. But among all these injured things is the mind; the mind has indeed been cruelly wounded; its complaint is heard in the hearts of intellectual men; it passes a mournful judgement on itself. It doubts itself profoundly."[68]

More than anyone else, it was Heidegger in this period who showed how the mind had come to doubt itself in the most fundamental things, its own quest for freedom and rationality. Whatever its causes, Heidegger's analysis of inauthenticity is not reducible to the social and historical circumstances of its birth. His work brought the critique of rationalism to a climax by making explicit what had been implicit in the earlier criticisms, but not conceptually articulated. That even its specific concerns were not confined to Heidegger's social caste or national situation is evidenced by their adoption by Sartre and others with political views far different from those later held by the German philosopher.

[68] Quoted by H. Kohn, "The Crisis in European Thought and Culture," in J. J. Roth, ed., *World War I: A Turning Point in Modern History*, New York, 1967, p. 29.

CHAPTER FIVE

The Existentialist Concept of the Self

IN THE last chapter it was argued that the existential critique of Freud could not be adequately characterized as a philosophical debate about the proper foundations of a science of human behavior. The attacks on mechanism and biologism, which were explored in detail in chapter three, were part of a more fundamental difference with Freud about the nature of human motivation and selfhood. This difference emerged in the historical setting of crumbling faith in the premises of European rationalism. If Heidegger laid the foundations for the new view of human motivation, however, it was left to others to apply it to psychology and psychopathology. In the chapter that follows, we will examine how Binswanger, Boss, and Sartre elaborated views of selfhood and its problems different from those of Freud, in the process advancing suggestions for dealing with some of the problems created by Freud's rationalist premises. In this chapter we will have to deal separately with each of the figures, for, while their specific differences with Freud had much in common, their own positive concerns within the general framework of existentialism varied greatly and even clashed with one another.

LUDWIG BINSWANGER

Taken in isolation, Binswanger's phenomenological-existential approach to meaning was empty of any special content; it was a neutral descriptive method applicable to all of human behavior without prior bias. In practice, the meaning-categories or existential a priori structures Binswanger discovered in his psychological studies all tended to have a specific, similar theme.

This was not surprising. On the one hand, existential phenomenology seemed to offer a key to the irrational that would make it intelligible in its own terms. It did not reduce the irrational to a mere deviation from the rational, nor did it suffer from the constraints of Jasper's "empathy" method, which limited the intelligibility of the irrational to meanings shared by the "normal" human community. On the other hand, the pure descriptive approach, via Heidegger's notion of Dasein as constitutive of meaning, appeared to leave nothing positive in place of the norms of judgment or health inherent in the categories of psychiatric psychopathology. Merleau-Ponty later put the problem this way: "Since we do not allow ourselves to anticipate, in infantile, diseased or primitive experience, the forms of adult, normal and civilized experience, are we not imprisoning each type of subjectivity, and ultimately each consciousness, in its own private life? . . . Are not mere appearance and opinion brought back under the name of the phenomenon? Is not the origin of precise knowledge being identified with a decision as unwarrantable as the one which shuts up the madman in his madness, and is not the last word of this wisdom to lead us back to the anguish of idle and solitary subjectivity?"[1]

Binswanger frequently argued that phenomenology was not psychopathology but complementary to it, and that it could be left to psychiatry to introduce concepts of illness and health. In practice, however, he was not prepared to leave existential analysis as a method without a content. This would make systematic clinical description impossible. There was no point of reference from which human behavior could be thought about. Hence, as a necessary part of his clinical as well as methodological work, Binswanger was driven to establish his own basic categories of human experience. "Only if we conceive and define the sick person 'as' a human being [Mensch]," he declared in his first existential study, "can we recognize and determine in what ways he *deviates* from the

[1] M. Merleau-Ponty, *Phenomenology of Perception*, trans. C. Smith, London, 1962, pp. 291-292.

219

'norm' of being human [Menschseins], just as biology and neurology can describe the degeneration or deficiency of a normal function only if they have conceived and defined the sick person as an organism."[2]

The effort to construct a phenomenologically grounded philosophical anthropology culminated in a large study titled *Basic Forms and Knowledge of Human Existence*,[3] published in 1942. It had an important complement, however, in the organizing themes of his major case studies. The two sources did not overlap very much; the formal categories of the anthropology turned out to be of little use in concrete clinical description, though Binswanger did use them to help structure his case reports. The concerns that informed the two sources were much the same, and it is to them that we must turn to understand the full import of Binswanger's dissent from classical psychoanalysis.

In the early 1930's, Binswanger published a series of articles on manic psychosis, his first existential analytic studies. Broadly speaking, he interpreted the manic-depressive syndrome as an extreme case of a universal human problem, the attempt to achieve a lasting state of self-integration and stability *(dauernden Selbststand)*. This attempt was an escape from the "problematic" finite selfhood of human existence to a state of ultimate security, of justified, harmonious existence in tune with and supported by the real nature of things. Phenomenological investigation of the world of the manic showed it to be a kind of "festive celebration" of the joy of an achieved, founded identity, a state in which all boundaries between self and world were dissolved and all obstacles overcome, a state of temporal "presentness" without reference to past or future. In much less extreme form, it was a state familiar to normal experience in love and other deep emotions. In mania, however, it was exaggerated, desperate, and tenuous, an unstable "flitting" or "springing" from one object to

[2] L. Binswanger, *Über Ideenflucht*, Zurich, 1933, p. 128.

[3] L. Binswanger, *Grundformen und Erkenntnis menschlichen Daseins*, Zurich, 1942.

another, because the achievement of selfhood was not real. It was constantly haunted and threatened by the patient's belief in the nothingness, the worthlessness of his own life, its lack of substance and continuity—hence the manic's quickness to anger when balked and his oscillation between mania and depression. Despite the manic's exaggerated feelings of power, well-being, and happiness, Binswanger rejected Freud's characterization of the manic state as a restoration of infantile freedom, or as a fusion of ego and ego-ideal derived from the festival of the primal horde. Those were in his judgment typical forms of the psychiatric reduction of basic human problems to biological and genetic levels.

The descriptive categories Binswanger used to characterize the polarized life of the manic were drawn from the work of a close friend, the Swiss Neo-Kantian philosopher Paul Häberlin. Häberlin had contrasted problematic moral existence, in which the individual was faced by norms to be fulfilled and hence a sense of imperfection or incompleteness, with unproblematic aesthetic existence, in which the individual achieved a sense of personal fulfillment and joy through the sense of unity with a universal structure. But Binswanger did not ignore the psychological and interpersonal dimensions of the patient's world for philosophical abstractions. Rather, he tried to show that his anthropological categories were the deepest meaning of these psychic conflicts and relationships. The patient's sense of finitude and need for security were embodied in and intensified by his parental milieu, his dependent relationships, his conflicted identifications, and his punitive conscience; the manic triumph was a phantasy flight from the failure to achieve self-integration through any of his relationships.

The key to Binswanger's approach was the reinterpretation of basic psychoanalytic themes in what might be called depth-anthropology. The biological terms were all replaced by identity terms.

One of his cases was a young man whose father had abandoned the family when the patient was an infant. The patient was deeply ambivalent towards the father he had never known, identifying with his mother's bitterness towards him but also idealizing him to the extreme. His continuing dependent attachment to his mother had made it impossible for him to resolve his ambivalence to his father and hence achieve a stable sense of identity. Thus the collapse of an affair with a married woman, an "oedipal" attempt to resolve the conflicting loyalties to mother and father that was ended when the husband threatened the young man, precipitated a crisis that took on religious form. The patient spoke of his father as God and of himself as Christ longing for union with him.

Binswanger made two main points about this case. First, the "oedipal conflict" and the ambivalence were basically desperate struggles for self-definition, not the playing out of instinctual impulses struggling for gratification. Secondly, the illness itself had to be understood as an attempt to use the father to achieve both independence and a stable selfhood. Writing about the patient's divinization of his father, Binswanger criticized the notion that the idea of God arises out of the father-complex as one of the most "naive theoretical infringements of the psychoanalytic school. It could be asserted with greater justification that the 'father-complex' (in the sense of loving recognition of the authority of the father) derives from the essential 'consciousness of God' immanent to man."[4]

Binswanger here suggested what Sartre later spelled out more clearly. Absolutizing or idealizing the parent was not the result of a biological need for nurture or protection on the part of the helpless child, though the biological situation furnished the object. If it were only biological, utilitarian emotions and attitudes—need and obedience—would have sufficed. It was impossible to derive religious categories from biological ones. Willing filial reverence was the result of a quest for an absolute or God-principle—father was a God-figure, rather than the reverse. Thus the "father-complex"

4 Binswanger, *Ideenflucht*, p. 122.

was one stage in the attempt of the patient to achieve a *Selbst-stand*, a stage "born out of the longing of the son for the unknown father, borne by the religious longing of the creature for support in existence and by the aesthetic longing of man for relief from the burden of problematic reality and for repose in an experience of beauty."[5]

Heidegger's influence was particularly evident in Binswanger's analysis of the world of the manic as a form of inauthentic temporality. It was a world characterized by "curiosity," a superficial springing from one novelty to the next without real commitment or interest, a way of keeping frantically busy. But Binswanger, in a significant dissent from Heidegger, refused to see in this mode of temporality nothing but an evasion of authenticity. However tenuous, it represented the principle of pure joy in existence, the ability to live in the present without longing for an ideal past or looking forward to a future in which self-fulfillment was always out of reach, ahead of one. What was pathological about the state of "presentness" in the manic was not the temporal mode itself, but its ephemerality and brittleness. The causal task of psychiatry was to explain the origins of this kind of instability. This difference with Heidegger was to furnish the basis of Binswanger's philosophical anthropology.

After the case studies of mania, Binswanger published no clinical work until 1944. Indeed, with the exception of the two papers written for the occasion of Freud's eightieth birthday in 1936, he published virtually nothing between 1935 and the *Grundformen* of 1942. After the initial presentation of the existential point of view, Binswanger found it necessary to develop the kind of anthropology he had declared was a prerequisite for a humanistic psychology. In one of his pieces on Freud, he had stated that the natural scientific approach to man as embodied by Freud—the approach that viewed man only in terms of mechanism and organism—"brackets

[5] *Ibid.*, p. 181.

out . . . self and meaning . . . it can never enlighten us as to why a man takes upon himself the divine mission to be productive in the search for scientific truth, why he makes this mission into the guiding light and meaning of his existence."[6] Freudian science saw man as a bundle of separate instincts and mechanisms and ignored the problem of selfhood as a whole. It could not deal with the central issue of man's assuming and living his existence as a self—the problem of self-definition. With the publication of the *Grundformen* Binswanger indicated just what he meant with his talk about the whole man.

Like all of his work, *Grundformen* was heavily dependent on the ideas of others. It drew upon the ideas of Karl Löwith and Karl Jaspers, but above all of Martin Buber and his circle, who were concerned with the nature of community, love, and the relationship of selfhood to them, dimensions of existence largely omitted in Heidegger's work. *Grundformen* was among other things an argument with *Being and Time*. Two decades later, Binswanger was to acknowledge that his work was based upon a misunderstanding, although, he hoped, a creative one, of Heidegger.[7] This admission, however, did a disservice to his unerring instinct for the key issue in Heidegger's work. It was true that *Being and Time* presented itself not as a set of descriptive categories of basic human attributes, which could conceivably be supplemented by others, but as the framework within which *any* future anthropology would have to operate. Binswanger's categories, however, while ostensibly supplementary, were in fact based on a principle that denied the all-inclusiveness of Heidegger's analysis and challenged his view of man.

In *Grundformen* the key opposition of authenticity and inauthenticity was submerged, or rather transformed so radically as to mean virtually the opposite of what it had meant

6 L. Binswanger, *Being-in-the-World*, trans. J. Needleman, New York, 1963, pp. 170-171.

7 L. Binswanger, "Daseinsanalyse und Psychotherapie," in *Acta Psychotherapeutica et Psychosomatica*, Vol. 8, No. 4, 1960, p. 258.

in *Being and Time*. Where Heidegger had characterized as inauthentic the pre-reflective stratagems by which man, to escape his finitude, elevated his particular, concrete values and determinations to the level of universal and objective necessity, Binswanger applied the label of inauthenticity to finitude itself, to the whole realm of determinate relationships between men and things and between men and men. For Binswanger *all* social and economic relationships necessarily involved what he called role-playing, and role-playing constituted the essence of personality. In all of men's concrete purposive relationships with the non-human environment (*Umwelt*), with his fellow-men (*Mitwelt*), and with himself (*Eigenwelt*), he always appeared as a determinate *something*, defining, addressing and exploiting things and men in terms of some particular aspect or quality. This was for Binswanger the core meaning of Heidegger's notion of human reality as "care" or being-in-the-world, and of the world as a reference context of meanings. All activity, whether theoretical or practical, involved grasping an initially undefined essentially indeterminate totality *as* something or relating to a potentially infinite subject *as* someone, characterized by a determinate description. All activity, therefore, assumed a position, a standpoint of one's own from which such grasping and relating took place; these definitions and positions were necessary limitations of human intercourse.

That in the course of things, whether in life or science, the specific ways of defining others or oneself became absolutized and taken for the "whole man" was an alienation of degree, not of kind. To move from an inauthentic situation to authentic self-being, the crux of authenticity for Heidegger, Binswanger saw as merely a deepening of the finite self, not as a qualitative change. Man might change roles; he could not escape the necessity of playing some role, and hence of falsifying the truth of his own potentially limitless nature.

With his penchant for drawing upon colloquial speech and idioms for his categories, Binswanger named this structural aspect of human existence "*das Nehmen-bei-Etwas*"—taking

225

someone or something by something—i.e., taking the part for the whole. The section in the *Grundformen* dealing with relations was in fact a fascinating catalogue, almost a manual of forms of depersonalization and manipulation. All of them depended on seizing upon those modes of being of man which were thing-like in their stability and inertia and hence more or less predictable and controllable—character traits, passions, social roles. In these relationships man was reduced to a ready-to-hand tool, in Heidegger's locution, a pure rationally calculable instrumentality for exploitation for a purpose. Even his moral freedom, the vaunted Kantian trait that supposedly elevated man above unfree nature, could be so used, as in "taking a man at his word," where his own moral probity was a method of binding him. This exploitation was a matter not only of practice but of theory. Binswanger acutely recognized the connection between actual social manipulation and those theoretical disciplines which approached the study of man from a static structural and functional point of view. In every "objective" psychology, Binswanger wrote, "The someone disappears completely behind the sum of somethings by which he can be taken; he is completely objectified, that is, construed as a calculable mechanical-dynamic system of grips and handholds. The subject pole, the 'who,' is forgotten or itself objectified. We fail to see that it is *we* who in grasping make the other into a tool."[8]

But with neither the notion of exploitation nor that of role-playing did Binswanger wish to contrast *Nehmen-bei-Etwas* with a form of social life in which men would not exploit or play roles; *Nehmen-bei-Etwas* was not a critique of bourgeois society but a description of the essential conditions of all social, economic, and political relationships. Even in a perfect Marxist society, with mutual recognition and no class exploitation, the other was affirmed in his being only insofar as his activities contributed to one's own welfare. "The mutual taking-by-something and letting-oneself-be-taken constitutes the

[8] Binswanger, *Grundformen*, pp. 318-319.

whole of human social life; it is not bound to any historical epoch, to any private or public economic or political life form, to any social class, to any special goals . . . or ideals."[9] Men were always "sizing one another up," "getting one another's number." All the modes of classifying or dealing with men were ways of making people accessible; without such determinations and definitions both perception and conceptualization—i.e., knowledge and an orderly social existence—would be impossible.

Nehmen-bei-Etwas therefore had an anthropological, not a historical, meaning, what Binswanger called discursivity (*Diskursivität*), the necessity for man always to exist as a finite being conditioned by a particular situation. "As long as Dasein is finite, there is no *absolute* standpoint."[10] Discursivity defined man as a being always on the way, goal-seeking and future-oriented, a being for whom experience (time and space) was necessarily sequential, with a past always out of reach and a future always ahead. But, while this was an unchanging truth about man, it was not the whole truth. There existed a mode of being in which man could overcome his particularity and ceaseless wandering and reach a state in which time and movement were suspended, in which he was in touch not with a limited aspect of reality but with its totality, not with a limited part of himself but with his whole centered self. This state was the "homeland and eternity" of love, the being together of I and Thou. Only in love could man be whole and know or treat (inappropriate words, since knowledge and activity were discursive) his fellow man as a totality, a subject who was more than any one or even the sum of his roles. Almost a third of *Grundformen* was taken up with phenomenological descriptions of expressions of love in Western literature that contrasted their experiences of time, space, particularity, and relationships with the world and with others, with those of discursive experience.

Binswanger did not hesitate to place himself in the theolog-

9 *Ibid.*, pp. 335-336.   10 *Ibid.*, p. 351.

ical-anthropological tradition of Augustine, Boehme, and Baader, though with the clear, if reluctant, realization that his own anthropology was post-Christian and secular. If it was necessary to return to the traditional concerns of cosmology and theology for a true psychology, it was with the chastened awareness that what had in them been self-evident starting points—God, the cosmos, ethical norms—had to be abandoned in favor of a restatement of the problem of man to which they had been the answer in previous ages. Hence the interpretation of the Christian problem of love was itself necessarily post-Christian and secular. The basic insight of Christian anthropology was the fragmented nature of human existence, its dispersal into a multitude of partial concerns without any inner unity or real continuity. The quest for love was a search for a way of integrating all the disparate and often conflicting roles into a stable, consistent, harmonious being. In love, the potential limitlessness of the self, its not being bound to any given—hence negatable—role was actually realized for another person; the self escaped the fate of being a mere something, and hence nothing, by being everything for the lover and hence someone, a unique individual with objective value.

Binswanger was conscious of the kind of charge that could be leveled against his description of love and the role he assigned it (a charge, ironically enough, being made almost at the same time and within the same anthropological framework by Sartre, who was as yet unknown to him). Love, he insisted, was not "an illusion or phantasmagoria deriving from care [. . .] Heidegger's *Sorge* [. . .] there merely to help man 'bear the burden of the earth.' "[11] Love and care were two co-existing principles of human existence, each independently valid though mutually exclusive.

Nevertheless, the present concern is only to define what was at stake for Binswanger in his concept of love and how he felt it related to the psychoanalytic doctrine. All that they had in common, he claimed, was their effort to tear down the

11 *Ibid.*, p. 266.

distinctions between the various forms of love—i.e., sacred and profane, sexual and spiritual, that had been erected especially through the efforts of Christianity—as for the rest they were so far apart that they could not even be compared. Binswanger reiterated and clarified his charge that psychoanalysis confused the historical with the essential: historically it was true that the mother or sister were the first and basic images of femininity, but this was not to be confused with the fact that the motif of eternity belonged necessarily to the structural whole of love, independently of the particular historical model. He had summarized the difference best, however, in general terms at the end of *Über Ideenflucht*: "If Nietzsche and psychoanalysis have shown that instinctuality, particularly in the form of sexuality, reaches up to the highest peak of a man's spirituality, we have tried to show that—and to what extent—spirituality reaches down into the deepest grounds of vitality."[12]

Binswanger's anthropology was to have a certain impact on German philosophy and particularly on German literary criticism;[13] it proved to be of less use for psychology and psychiatry than he might have hoped. Though he was to organize the case studies published after 1944 according to various sets of headings derived from his anthropology, the framework thus provided contributed little and proved to be largely formal. This resulted mainly from the fact that the basic categories were derived not from the living unities of personal histories but from diverse and isolated poetic—hence idealized—expressions. Personal and philosophical predilections of Binswanger's own had caused him to identify the more general theme and problem of identity with a particular form of it—the "dual mode" of love; the quest for an anthropology caused him to turn these results of phenomenological description into essential structures functioning as

[12] Binswanger, *Ideenflucht*, p. 196.

[13] Emil Staiger, the famous Germanicist, used it in his interpretation of Kleist.

human norms and thus to revert to the judgmental formulations he had attacked as incompatible with a purely descriptive approach. In the body of the case studies, however, his acute powers of observation and description expanded the constricting restraints of the a priori organization to reveal new depths to the problem he had opened up in his previous work.

The basic theme that Binswanger discovered in all his cases was the fanatic, desperate pursuit of some one ideal or life goal on the part of patients. It was in relation to this ideal that they felt inadequate, exposed to and penetrated by the accusations and contempt of others and themselves; it was this ideal that made their whole being one of suffering. In a number of cases, the particular content of the ideal went back to identifications with the mother as well as with other figures. Here, however, Binswanger registered his sharpest difference with psychoanalytic explanation. The basic psychoanalytic concept of identification did not, he affirmed, help in the slightest to understand the formation of ideals. "We understand such a formation only in existential analytic ways, that is, if we can show that, and how, the ideals grow out of the total ways of existence of the individual concerned, and if we can show what role in them they are called upon to play. After all that we now know, this role can be only that of setting up a dam against existential anxiety."[14] In each case the striving for the ideal was related to the most profound feelings of emptiness, worthlessness, lack of solidity, and continuity.

Binswanger described the dynamics of the formation of these ideals as the attempt of the individual in question to be himself but as a different self from what he was, or the attempt not to be himself while simultaneously holding fast to the identity of his person.[15] With these formulations Binswanger was pointing up the elements of *internal* conflict at the

[14] L. Binswanger, *Schizophrenie*, Pfullingen, 1957, p. 282.
[15] L. Binswanger, "The Case of Ellen West," in *Existence: A New Dimension in Psychology and Psychiatry*, ed. R. May et al., New York, 1958, p. 297.

root of the identity problem, the inner dynamics that the anthropology had imposed from the outside as a conflict between two metaphysical states. By "not being oneself" he meant the rejection by the patients of those conditions and determinations, foisted upon them by their birth, parental milieu, and constitution, which were felt as constricting limitations upon the self, or threats to its integrity and independence—social class, sexual role, even physiognomy. The attempt "to be oneself" was one of adhering to a self-chosen but at the same time "objectively valid" ideal that was the opposite of the condition to be escaped. Thus, for example, "Ellen West" longed to become a thin, ethereal, higher spiritual being instead of a fat Jewish bourgeoise; "Jürg Zünd," whose mother had married below her, longed to achieve a higher social status and avoid "proletarianization." The force of these ideals was that they represented ultimate value in and of itself, as was clear from the imagery associated with them. The feeling of worthlessness and nothingness derived from the sense of identification with negatively valued attributes that the attainment of the ideal was supposed to eradicate.

The specific tragedy of each patient, and the core of the conflict, was that under the given conditions the ideal was unattainable. In the first place, because the patients *had* identified also with the negative attributes, they had accepted those attributes as defining themselves indelibly, as what they were; hence by their own self-definition the ideal lay out of reach. Secondly, the desperate attempts to become something were defeated by the accompanying feeling of lack of selfhood. Ellen West's desire to be thin was countered by an overwhelming compulsion to eat, stemming from her feeling of insubstantiality and emptiness, which was only increased by her striving for "ethereality" through total distancing from the material realm (food, pregnancy). Jürg Zünd was tortured by irrepressible sexual desires for upper-class women, the overt manifestations of which (erections) were, he had been taught, evidence of lower-class behavior and stamped him as proletarian.

Most of the "symptoms" of the "illness" were attempts to

231

escape this debilitating vicious circle, or expressions of the patient's lack of being and the overwhelming oppressive presence of the world and of others. Each had surrendered the power to determine his own life into the hands of others, a process variously described by Binswanger as *Entselbstung* (loss of self) or *Verweltlichung* (becoming worldly, i.e., pressured).[16] Precisely because they were not aware of this, however, they experienced the threat to their selfhood not as coming from this original surrender but from the outside (in the case of Ellen West largely from her body, in the case of Jürg Zünd directly from other people). Their efforts at defense, such as withdrawal and aggression, were thus also directed at the outside. This was the chief way in which the unconscious played a role in these cases.

Other psychoanalytic themes were also present, but similarly interpreted from the existential perspective of the attempt at identity. Binswanger recognized, for example, the connection between Ellen West's dread of eating and her fear of pregnancy, but refused to see the first as the substitute for the repressed second. Ellen West was fully conscious of both, and both meant the same thing: the heavy oppressive world of negative value and hence existential death.[17] Similarly Jürg Zünd's obviously incestuous desires for upper-class women were neither merely sexual nor merely infantile-oedipal, but an attempt to be accepted as a social equal and hence by his definition as a person. The purely Freudian interpretation was another example of the replacement of "anthropological" structures by biological and historical ones.

For all the sensitive detail of his cases, however, Binswanger never outlined a systematic theory on the basis of which his own observations could be unified. The tendency to *Entselbstung* and *Verweltlichung* were related to Heidegger's concept of inauthenticity, but Heidegger had not dealt with inauthenticity in the realm of interpersonal relations, the nec-

---

16 Binswanger, *Schizophrenie*, p. 260.
17 Binswanger, "Ellen West," in *Existence*, p. 321.

essary arena of any psychology. It was another philosopher who sketched the outline of an existential theory of interpersonal motivation.

JEAN-PAUL SARTRE

Sartre's concept of selfhood was more unified and coherent than Binswanger's. He did not separate out the methodological from the substantive concerns of *Being and Time*—they were part of a single enterprise, as they had been for Heidegger. Unlike Heidegger, however, Sartre was deeply interested in psychology from the beginning. He rejected Heidegger's absolute distinction between the empirical or "ontic" realm and the ontological realm; it was *through* men's concrete interests, activities, perceptions, and passions that the quest for being took place. Thus for example, Sartre criticized Heidegger for paying no attention to human sexuality.[18]

Nevertheless, Sartre distinguished sharply between empirical psychology and existentialism. Contemporary psychology remained at too shallow a level. It assumed that the basic functions of mental life—perception, memory, imagination, emotion, impulse, and so on—were understood in their essence and that the task of psychology was to explore their physical conditions and causes. This was to beg basic questions about the meaning of the imagination or of the emotions as a mode of human existence, an attitude towards reality.[19] Because of this question-begging, empirical psychology could at best serve existentialism as a preliminary investigation, collecting the empirical data and establishing the factual connections that only existentialism could interpret properly.

For Sartre, the crisis in psychology was more than a crisis

[18] J.-P. Sartre, *Being and Nothingness*, trans. H. Barnes, New York, 1956, p. 383.

[19] J.-P. Sartre, *The Emotions: Outline of a Theory*, trans. B. Frechtman, New York, 1948.

of foundations; it was a crisis of human self-understanding. What was missing in the "scientific" study of man was man. Psychology had divided him up into different functions and faculties, each of which was studied in isolation. The unity of selfhood, however, could not be arrived at by summing the psychic facts discovered in such investigations. However obscurely, man knew himself to be a unity, and the nature of that unity had to be elucidated as the condition of any psychology that pretended to understand him.[20]

It was not only academic psychology that was bankrupt. The accepted categories for understanding and interpreting social behavior in life and literature were no longer self-evidently sufficient. It was not illuminating to explain a man's actions as caused by ambition, for example. Ambition was one of the inexplicable original givens, the "simple bodies" of psychology. But, Sartre argued, "this ambition is an irreducible fact which by no means satisfies the mind. The irreducibility here has no justification other than the refusal to push the analysis further."[21] What was needed was "a *veritable* irreducible" that *would* be self-evident and satisfactory.

Self-evidence and "satisfaction" are not universal objective criteria. The loss of the transparent obviousness of long-accepted categories and ways of understanding human nature that underlay Sartre's criticisms of both formal and literary psychology can be correlated with his awareness of fundamental changes in French society.

Two contrasting images of the French bourgeoisie were presented in his early novel *Nausea*. The first was suggested through the descriptions of the portraits of the founders of the town of Bouville, men of the generation of 1815-1910— the austere, competent, morally self-righteous elite of merchants, shipowners, professionals, and officers who embodied the self-confident and triumphant middle bourgeoisie of the pre-war Third Republic. They were the "men of right," men

20 *Ibid.*, p. 14.
21 Sartre, *Being and Nothingness*, p. 560.

who did not question their existence or their right to rule, and whose self-certainty set the tone for society. The second image was that of the Self-Taught Man, the decaying sentimental bourgeois intellectual humanist, whose love of humanity masked hatred and homosexuality. He represented the utter bankruptcy, the hypocrisy of the bourgeois illusions of knowledge, culture, progress, and community after the First World War—which for the Self-Taught Man personally had also been the occasion of his self-discovery. The certainties, beliefs, and values of the pre-war period no longer suited the reality of the inter-war years.

It is hardly surprising in these circumstances that Sartre should have been somewhat attracted to psychoanalysis. Unlike contemporary empirical psychology, it was guided by an anthropology, a unified view of man; it could view the different manifestations of psychic life as symbols of the fundamental total structures that constituted the individual. "Psychoanalytical psychology," he asserted, ". . . was the first to insist upon the fact that every state of consciousness is the equivalent of something other than itself."[22] More particularly, in the case of the emotions, for example, psychoanalysis characterized what was usually regarded as a passive event or accident as an action, the result of human intention. In two ways, then, psychoanalysis was a doctrine of demystification: it showed hidden meanings behind obvious ones, and it made the individual responsible for those meanings.

Sartre found psychoanalysis defective on these same two points, and this sharply limited his interest in it. His criticism of the unconscious has already been commented on; the psychoanalytic theory of the unconscious was incompatible for him with Freud's avowed aim of reclaiming human behavior for purposiveness, since it was a mechanical causal theory. Of equal importance, however, was the fact that Freud's basic theory of motivation was arbitrary, vague, and impoverished. "Empirical psychoanalysis has decided upon its own irreducible instead of allowing this to make itself known in a self-

22 Sartre, *The Emotions*, p. 43.

235

evident intuition. The libido . . . constitutes a psychobiological residue which is not clear in itself and which does not appear to us as *being beforehand* the irreducible limit of investigation."[23] That is to say, the concept of libido was drawn from an a priori biological theory; and the relationship of that theory to human action was not clear. The concept of instinct was essentially teleological and hence theoretically either independent of subjectivity or else causally related to action. In neither case did it describe the meaning or intention of action.

To the extent that it could be considered as doing so, however, it was superficial. Insofar as libido was congruent with physical pleasure, it could not account for the phenomenological reality of even sexual desire, let alone love and interpersonal relationships generally. The refutation of Freud on this point was important to Sartre, because sex and love were as basic to his understanding of human motivation as they were to classical psychoanalysis—they were the foundation of all human relationships.[24]

It was in this area that Sartre made his most original and important contribution to existential thought. There was nothing fundamentally new about Sartre's basic theory of motivation, except for its language; the notion of a quest for being as permanent identity came from Heidegger. Heidegger, however, had presented it in the most general and abstract terms as a preliminary to grappling with the possibility of authentic existence. Sartre, on the other hand, was fascinated by the light that the quest for being could shed as a theory of motivation on the whole range of concrete human endeavors, from psychological reflection to disinterested pursuit of knowledge, aesthetic experience, and interpersonal behavior. In one respect, *Being and Nothingness* was constructed like a drama in which the for-itself made successive attempts to

[23] Sartre, *Being and Nothingness*, p. 571.
[24] ". . . all of men's complex patterns of conduct toward one another are only enrichments of these two original attitudes [love and desire]." *Being and Nothingness*, p. 407.

achieve its goal, each meeting with failure and each leading by the logic of the failure to another, and more sophisticated, attempt. The enterprise culminated in what was really the heart of the book, the attempt to achieve identity through others. If Heidegger's most important achievement was disclosing the ultimate existential meaning of objectivity, Sartre's was in exploiting it to analyze the ultimate meaning of intersubjectivity.

As a creative writer as well as philosopher, Sartre was able to define the ontological quest in more direct and explicitly psychological formulations than Heidegger's. Anxiety was an experience of body and psyche. "The essential thing," Roquentin reflected at the nauseating moment of his self-discovery, "is contingency. I meant that one cannot define existence as necessity. To exist is simply *to be there*."[25] This terrible awareness lay at the heart of every way of life that claimed justification in virtue of a transcendental necessity or some universal and objective value, any way of life that pretended to the inertia of thinghood. For Sartre, the net was cast very wide: all concrete activity, insofar as it explicitly or implicitly excluded the possibility that it was temporally contingent, a matter of changeable human value, was included. There were, of course, necessities of fact: the past was unchangeable, the body was a given; but these facts had not been decreed from on high, they were "precisely the indicative from which no imperative can be deduced."[26]

The force of Sartre's work was its linking of traditional theological and philosophical themes with psychological concerns and ordinary language descriptions. In Freudian fashion, man's image of God was seen to be the projection of what he wanted for himself, but Sartre described the goal in terms far different from Freud's, or, for that matter, from Feuerbach's. "The supreme value toward which consciousness at every instant surpasses itself by its very being is the absolute being of the self with its characteristics of identity,

25 J.-P. Sartre, *Nausea*, trans. L. Alexander, Norfolk, 1949, p. 176.
26 Sartre, *Being and Nothingness*, p. 120.

of purity, of permanence, etc., and as its own foundation."[27] Man wanted to be totally self-sufficient yet totally justified, the author of his own being yet determined in his life by forces transcending his own contingency and ephemerality. These grandiose ambitions were the stuff of everyday life. In social behavior, for example, the project of "absolute being" was the attempt to identify oneself with, to limit oneself to, the dimensions of one's social role, to define oneself as determined by the a priori set of responses and actions appropriate to the role. In reflection one tried to constitute one's past, what one had been, done, or felt, into a nature that predestined the future. In interpersonal relationships, one tried to identify with the definitions of oneself imposed by others.

The starting point for Sartre's analysis of interpersonal relationships was Scheler's phenomenological observation that our knowledge of other selves was not a hypothesis about observed facts but an immediate experience. There was a serious problem with this proposition. It was true that we responded to others as if they were agents like ourselves, and we interpreted their movements as the actions of agents. But our experience of them as being subjects like ourselves could not be perceptual knowledge, since we could not have direct access to any consciousness but our own. The argument for solipsism was irrefutable. If, then, we experienced the other with certainty as a person, it was because we *conferred* subjectivity on him. In a strict sense we invented the other. The "direct experience" we had of his subjectivity could be only a matter of projection, not of knowledge. The most knowledge could give us was a very high degree of probability, but we did not interact with others on the basis of cool probabilistic calculation as to the reality of their being persons, ready to revise our hypotheses if the facts should warrant. Experiencing the other as a subject through the full range of the emotions was a recognition of the other that was not passive cognition but an active granting of the importance for oneself

[27] *Ibid.*, p. 93.

of the other's subjectivity, values, and meanings. We recognized the other as a subject self because we wanted him to matter to us, because we needed his freedom.

The purpose of this recognition was made clear by the position Sartre gave the problem of relations with others in the analysis of the structures of selfhood. Social roles and psychological traits could not work by themselves as fixed identities to the extent that they depended upon the individual consciousness alone, because they demanded the maintenance by consciousness of an internal contradiction. To identify myself totally with my social role was to deny the possibility of my not being that role; but this denial precisely envisaged the possibility it denied. The problem was that I could not take a point of view on myself as an object, an atemporal closed unity, because, in order to do so, I had to freeze my possibilities, to freeze the future into a static entity; but then, on some level, I would have to be aware that I was doing this, that I remained in some way outside the totality in which I was trying to enclose myself, and that I could change it by becoming something else. A consciousness outside myself, however, could take a point of view on me that would encompass me as a whole without internal splitting. It could do so because for such a consciousness I was enclosed wholly in my body and could therefore be viewed as a material entity like others. Thus the other, seen as an absolute subject, could give me an identity in the strict sense of the word—a fixed meaning that remained the same through time. I could then try to assimilate this identity, to become what I was in the eyes of the other consciousness.

To achieve this identity, however, meant to absolutize the other, that is, to regard his values and imperatives as both true and binding, as the only possible ones. "I experience the Other's infinite freedom. It is for and by means of a freedom and only for and by means of it that my possibles can be limited and fixed."[28] Only if the other was a necessary being

28 *Ibid.*, p. 270.

could his recognition of me endow me with being, with legitimacy.

This explanation of absolutization impinged directly on important psychoanalytic concepts and hypotheses, especially the whole Freudian view of object relations. Freud had derived idealization and the need to be loved from the libido and the ego-instincts, that is, from basically hedonistic and utilitarian needs and desires. Sexual desire and the need for survival were at the base of credulity and the willed submission to authority. But it was impossible to explain in these terms why the love object should be endowed with transcendental legitimacy so that it had to be obeyed even if obedience opposed self-interest. Idealization of the object from whom love was desired was not conceptually derivable from utilitarian calculations about biological pleasures and needs. For this reason, Sartre claimed that "existential psychoanalysis is *moral* description, for it releases to us the ethical meaning of various human projects. It indicates to us the necessity of abandoning the psychology of interest along with any utilitarian interpretation of human conduct—by revealing to us the *ideal* meaning of all human attitudes."[29]

Love and sexual desire were the basic modalities of the project of identity through others. Here Sartre's quarrel was with instinct theories of sexuality that defined it either as a desire for purely physical gratification or as an obscure instinctual urge independent of an object. "Every subjectivist and immanentist theory will fail to explain how we desire particular women and not simply our sexual satisfaction"[30]— i.e., through autoeroticism. Even if this objection could be met by the theory of repression—a possibility Sartre did not discuss but which still has serious theoretical difficulties—an even more basic objection remained. From the standpoint of the pleasure principle, the intentional object of sexual desire was indeed an object, an instrumental means to the end of gratification. This was a phenomenologically inadequate de-

29 *Ibid.*, p. 626. 30 *Ibid.*, p. 383.

scription of desire. "We do not desire the body as a purely material object," he argued; "this organic totality which is immediately present to desire is desirable only insofar as it reveals not only life but also an appropriate consciousness."[31] Sexual desire was not primarily an instrumental relationship to a body but a special kind of relationship with a person, not just the quest for an object but for a free subject.

The difference between love and sexual desire was the difference between passive and active modes of attaining the goal of being. In the case of love, the absolute freedom of the other was recognized explicitly and one's own freedom only covertly. Being in love meant having the desire to be loved, being wholly dependent on being the other's love object. This was dangerous, because by the act of love one was granting the other the power to make one feel one's contingency—through rejection, disapproval, ignoring, and so on. Hence it was also necessary to rouse and hold the other's love. This could not be done with the clear consciousness that one was thereby limiting the other's freedom by trying to constitute oneself as necessary for him, because such a consciousness would destroy the absolute freedom of the lover. It could be done only by seduction, by making oneself into a fascinating, indispensable object. In sexual desire or conquest, the self consciously conceived of itself as the active subject, and of the other as the object; but the freedom of the other, and one's own dependence, were evidenced in the very aim of conquest. That aim was to arouse desire in the other and reduce him to his body, to nothing but physical need and dependence, so that the other's freedom became identical with pure need and thus affirmed one's own power and subjectivity. Then one could safely surrender to physical desire in turn and attempt to become simultaneously the passive body and the active consciousness.

These modalities constituted the existentialist version of psychoanalytic bisexuality—fundamental human activity and

[31] *Ibid.*, p. 386.

passivity. There were interesting parallels between Sartre and Freud on this theme. Despite the generally careful neutrality of his ontological descriptions, which described the doings of abstract consciousnesses, a clear identification of the active mode with masculinity and the passive with femininity was evident in Sartre's work. Occasionally, the identification even appeared to be based on the anatomical differences between the sexes. For example, Sartre wrote that "The obscenity of the feminine sex is that of everything which 'gapes open.' It is an appeal to being as all holes are. In herself woman appeals to a strange flesh which is to transform her into a fullness of being by penetration and dissolution. Conversely, woman senses her condition as an appeal precisely because she is 'in the form of a hole.' "[32]

The differences with Freud were, in fact, much more important. For Freud, activity was at first the only principle recognized theoretically, and then activity and passivity were held to be two equal, basic, and complementary aims, a true duality. For Sartre, empirical activity and passivity were subcategories of the fundamentally submissive orientation to the other as absolute subject. Activity was a defense against the danger inherent in the absolutization of the other; sexual conquest, the "masculine" orientation, was as much a form of submission as the need to be loved.

Sartre's analyses were concerned to prove that the basic attitudes one could take to the other were not only ambivalent but that they rested on contradictory assumptions. One submitted to the absolute freedom of the other while at the same time trying to control him, thus denying the absoluteness of that freedom. Hence all human relationships were inherently unstable and logically unable to fulfill their basic purpose. In life, some stability and happiness in the sense of fulfillment in love were factually possible, but only as long as a certain kind of bad faith was sustained.[33] Sexual pleasure was certainly also possible, but such pleasure was the death and failure of sexual desire as a project to achieve being, for,

32 *Ibid.*, pp. 413-414.   33 *Ibid.*, p. 371.

after the climax, both the other's subjectivity and one's own reasserted themselves.

In terms of its basic considerations, Sartre's conception of human motivation closely resembled that of Binswanger in its stress on the ideal purposes of human emotions and actions. Whereas, however, for Binswanger, the dual mode of love was an achievable reality, for Sartre it was based on an illusion—the illusion that in a couple, each could be both needy and the absolute for the other, without realizing the dual and contradictory roles they were filling in order to sustain the structure.

Of all Sartre's works, only *Baudelaire* conformed more or less strictly to the program for existential psychoanalysis sketched out in *Being and Nothingness*. Even before he had written it, Sartre's thought was shifting in the direction of social analysis and Marxism; later works of psychological analysis, such as *Saint Genet*, were radically affected by the transition.

Sartre's psychobiography of Baudelaire was a running debate with classical psychoanalysis. Nowhere in Sartre's work to that point was the ambivalent affinity to Freud more apparent. It appears as if the book could not have been written without a good working acquaintance with psychoanalytic theory. At every point in the analysis, Freudian themes appeared: oedipal attachments, ambivalence, compromise formations, defense mechanisms, fear of success, self-punishment, over-determination. Many of the detailed causal connections and interpretations would have been appropriate in the most orthodox case study. Like Freud, Sartre had a keen eye for and subtle understanding of the serpentine twisting of the human spirit in its ability to deceive itself, for the multiple but compartmentalized levels on which it operated. Yet the spirit of the two approaches was profoundly different.

The issue between them was not one of facts. The clearest illustration of this was in the analysis of Baudelaire's relationship to his mother. From a psychoanalytic point of view, Baudelaire's conflict and its consequences as described by Sartre were obviously the product of an intense oedipal attachment. Sartre rejected this description because of the instinctual meaning psychoanalysis gave to the attachment. "It matters little," he argued, "whether or not he desired his mother sexually; I should say rather that he refused to liquidate the theological complex which transforms parents into gods; this was because it was necessary, in order to evade the law of solitude and find in other people a remedy against gratuitousness, to confer on other people, or rather on *certain* others, a sacred character."[34]

In essence, Sartre presented an existential version of infantile sexuality and dependence, developing the same criticisms of Freud's understanding of them as Binswanger had earlier in less systematic form. The utilitarian psychology inherent in the biological framework of instinct theory could not explain the aura of sacredness, of transcendental legitimacy, with which the superior power of the parents was endowed, and which made it more than merely superior power:

"The child takes his parents for gods. Their actions like their judgments are absolutes; they incarnate universal reason, the law, the meaning and purpose of the world. When these divine beings cast their gaze upon him, this look justifies him immediately to the very heart of his existence; it confers upon him a definite and sacred character; because they cannot be wrong, he *is* as they *see* him. . . . An eternal essence in the midst of eternal essences, he has *his* place in the world —an absolute place in an absolute world."[35]

What the child did in experiencing pride, shame, and guilt was to appropriate others' valuations of impulses and actions and then of the definitions of himself that followed from

[34] J.-P. Sartre, *Baudelaire*, trans. M. Turnell, London, 1949, p. 54. (Translation slightly modified.)

[35] *Ibid.*, p. 50. (Translation slightly modified.)

wanting or doing certain things. Self-judgment was not only the implicit recognition in oneself of certain impulses but the implicit consent to consider parental standards as universal and objectively binding.

It was because of this vital role which parental figures fulfilled that it was so difficult to supersede them either in their personal form or in the form of the norms and ideals they represented. If, for whatever reason, the child came to feel that he was not the exclusive and positive focus of his parents' attention, he could not easily give up the need for their love and approbation; to do so would require recognition of their lack of necessary being and consequently of his own. However, the continued dependence on parental love would be equally intolerable because it had proved a fickle source of positive recognition.

In Baudelaire's case, his father had died when he was five and his mother had remarried two years later. The shock of this rejection caused him to develop a particular strategy—to affirm his own aloneness as if he had willed it, while simultaneously trying to win approval for the unique and supposedly individuated self he was. To be independent, he rebelled against his mother and her standards, trying to become through his poetry the incarnation of the evil that would offend her moral nature. This rebellion, however, was not designed to free himself from her domination by transcending her values. On the contrary, the rebel took care to keep them intact so as to continue to rebel. Being dependent on his mother, the only way for him to be free was to define himself against her and then to try to secure her approval for his rebellion.

In his relationships with women, Baudelaire chose either ones who were inaccessible and whom he could see as frigid and aloof, or debased prostitutes. The frigidity Baudelaire sought in the first group, Sartre noted, "mimed the glacial severity of the mother who surprises the child in the middle of 'doing something naughty.' "[36] Baudelaire was obviously

[36] *Ibid.*, p. 118.

in this sense repeating the patterns of the past. The women, however, were not primarily objects of desire, but sexual incarnations of the judge-ideal who could both condemn and justify. Moreover, insofar as they were "mother substitutes," they were not his mother. They were ideal figures in a drama first played out with his mother but now independent of her and dependent on Baudelaire's sustained desire for the authority who could grant the benefits of absolute guidance.

The choice of debased women was a part of Baudelaire's choice of evil, and, with it, self-punishment and unhappiness. Contrary to the Freudian view, the choice was not made to gratify sexual desires while avoiding incest; nor were guilt and self-punishment simply the price paid for gratifying wishes. According to Sartre, Baudelaire specifically chose evil for the sake of choosing evil. This was another way of manifesting both his freedom and his allegiance to his mother's moral standards. To choose evil for its own sake, in other words, meant acting contrary to what he continued to affirm as the good.

Baudelaire thus necessarily condemned himself to constant guilt. His complex and contradictory attitudes, painful as they were, provided, however, a number of psychic benefits. The original value of the identification with parental morality was the security provided by norms of objectively valid behavior. Rebelling against it through the imaginative evocation of evil in poetry manifested Baudelaire's freedom, and also punished his mother for her rejection of him, while the guilt feelings that were evoked preserved the moral framework intact. The guilty person also had a role and set of rights within a theocratically and morally structured universe—the right of recognition as a sinner, the right to punishment, repentance and even forgiveness. Nevertheless, insofar as the negative identity of sinner was a threat, Baudelaire could take comfort in the fact that his evil took place on the purely imaginative plane, in poetry, and thus never materially subverted moral values. Thus Baudelaire could preserve a sense of innocence, not by rejecting the system, but by arguing that he had been judged unfairly. Finally, he always had his remorse as evidence that he was not limited to his nature as a sinner but could rise above it.

Thus Sartre wove all the complicated details of Baudelaire's psychic life, with its inconsistencies and contradictions, into a tightly unified picture of a single project. However many ramifications the project had, they all fitted into the logic of the main theme—the loss of self in the sense of freedom in order to find the self as a stable and enduring structure through time. Whatever the empirical similarities with Freudian themes, this made Sartre's concept of the self the opposite of the one embodied in the Freudian polarity of reality and pleasure principle.

Because of this, Sartre was able to deal with a number of issues in his existential psychoanalysis that Freud had wrestled with unsuccessfully. Why should the superego take on an objective, categorical form if it originated as a utilitarian response to a concrete situation of danger? If guilt were the response to an act resulting only in the loss of something wanted or needed, why should the resulting emotion not simply be remorse, regret, fear or anger at oneself? How was it possible to understand a desire for punishment or pain? These questions were illuminated by the existentialist notion of spontaneous self-alienation. The superego existed in categorical form because its purpose was not only defense against impulses but the embodiment of the universal objective truth of a set of norms. The phenomenology of guilt feelings involved the affirmation in the very act of violation of the standards violated. The point of masochism, both sexual and moral, was the attempt to divest oneself of the last vestiges of autonomy so that the absolute power of the other, or of one's moral principles, would be enhanced—and with it their viability as a source for conferring identity.

MEDARD BOSS

Boss's explicit definition of the self was derived from Heidegger's later work and was addressed, as will be seen in the next chapter, to the difficulties within existentialism. Dasein was a "world-openness," a being whose essence was the dis-closure of new meaning and possibility. Clinically, however, Boss was preoccupied with the closure and constrictedness of man's openness, with the fact that he could not become what he essentially was without the aid of his environment. The meaning of his critique of Freud's concept of primary narcissism, of his own existential analysis of the power of the past and of his interpretation of the workings of therapy, was man's primary dependence.

If there was one issue that focused most sharply the differ-ence between Boss and Freud, it was that of the child's rela-tionship to the mother. The center of Freud's psychology was the Oedipus complex, the erotic and competitive relationship to the parents. For Boss the crux was the child's "oral" de-pendent relationship to his mother, which included the con-firmation of his being if his possibilities were to unfold.

In orthodox psychoanalysis, the importance of the pre-oedipal relationship to the mother was explored only after Freud's death, though Freudians could point to the origins of the idea in his writings. One way of looking at Boss's work is as an independent but parallel appreciation of the impor-tance of the earlier stages of child development. For Freudians, however, these were complementary to the oedi-pal stage, and they saw no need to set themselves in opposi-tion to Freud in insisting on them; the picture of infantile development left by Freud was simply being filled out with further discoveries.

Boss did not see things this way. The "Oedipus complex" in adults could not be divorced from their dependent ties to their parents. Otherwise, the persistence of a fixation on the mother, or on mother substitutes—the ideal or the maternal woman—remained mysterious. The attributes of the "oedi-pal" woman or situation desired by the man clearly revealed the nature of his infantilism: it was not simply the repetition of the triadic relationship of childhood, with its attendant repression of genital sexuality, but a continuing situation of dependence vis-à-vis both parents. Hence Boss de-emphasized the importance of the classical Oedipus complex, at least as a determinant of adult psychic disturbances, and stressed, instead, the general structure of childhood dependency. Since dependency was not in essence biological, however, Boss was not faced with the dilemma expressed by Freud in *Inhibition, Symptoms and Anxiety*. The need for confirmation was not phase specific. If it was met early in life, the self-esteem it brought was internalized; but it remained a function of external objects that were carried about within oneself. If it was not met, it persisted as a demand that conditioned every other need and activity. More than the other existentialists', Boss's work pointed to the paradox of freedom: autonomy itself, where it existed, was the gift of the other.

CHAPTER SIX

Authenticity as an Ethic
and a Concept of Health

EXISTENTIALISM, it was argued in chapter four, completed the critique of rationalism begun before World War I by offering a theory of motivation that accounted for the human desire to escape from freedom. This did not put the existentialists into the camp of the irrationalists, however; on the contrary, they insisted on the inescapable reality of human responsibility for human choices and used their theory of motivation to explain the ideological belief systems and everyday self-deceptions by which men tried to escape it. However, the existentialists did not fully appreciate the negative implications of their own conclusions.

In rejecting the objective universal values and meanings of idealism, existentialism had taken the classical rationalist conception of freedom to its logical conclusion, liberating man from the last vestiges of heteronomy. At the same time, however, existentialism subverted the rationalist idea of freedom. For, though freedom, in the sense of choice and of being oneself, was ostensibly the core of existential philosophy, it was only a negative pole that the self revealed in its flight.

Existential authenticity, like a geometrical point, had no dimensions. Given the monistic theory of motivation of existentialism, no motive or action could be specified that would be authentic. The sole motive recognized by existential philosophy was the quest for identity, a quest defined as the negation of an authentic selfhood that was experienced not as a desire but as a curse. Authenticity was only a regulative idea, a limiting case against which could be measured the inauthenticity of all concrete life activities insofar as they reified or absolutized the temporal structure of existence. In

250

showing that the reconciliation between freedom and universality posited by rationalism was impossible because the second was the negation of the first, the existentialists made problematic the very concept of freedom they upheld. The existentialist dialectic worked out by Sartre and Binswanger did incorporate the experience of desires for freedom, but showed them to be contradictory and hence futile rebellions against self-imposed authority in the form of idealizations of others.

The existentialists never explicitly recognized this dilemma in their work. They took authenticity or freedom to be viable as an ethic and as a concept of health. Nevertheless, in the attempt to develop both theoretically and practically the consequences of their original views, they ran up against difficulties and contradictions that ultimately forced them to abandon those positions and turn their work in new directions. This was particularly true of the philosophers; the psychiatrists, less acutely aware of the conceptual problems, maintained an apparent continuity in their work, but within it can be discerned the inconsistencies that marked their efforts to meet the difficulties of the existential concept of authenticity. In this chapter we shall explore the efforts of the existentialists to move beyond the impasse created by their own pessimistic theory of motivation and its consequences for social and personal unfreedom.

Heidegger's purpose in *Being and Time* was to reveal the concrete potentiality for authentic existence in the inauthentic everyday life of man and to describe the general features of authentic being. Authentic existence, he claimed, was "a factical ideal of Dasein";[1] it had a positive content. The challenge to this assertion lay in his own analysis of everydayness. The sole motive force recognized by Heidegger was the need to escape the awareness that one was responsible for one's own being and for the categorical content of one's world. People did what they did precisely because they believed that

[1] Heidegger, *Being and Time*, p. 358.

social norms and conventions were objective and hence binding on them. Their value to Dasein was not their content but their form, expressed in such language as "this is the way things are done," with its crucial ambiguity between descriptive and normative meaning. Such statements could not be challenged in the everyday consciousness by empirical counterexamples, because with their normative weight they functioned as criteria for what was do-able; a counterexample could thus be met with the assertion "But such things are just not done." The language structure of everydayness articulated an irrational, incorrigible set of beliefs whose purpose was to create a stable world of meaning that doubt could not disturb. This being the case, however, Heidegger had to face the question of what the positive contents of authentic existence could involve.

He answered it in an ingenious but highly ambiguous and ultimately dangerous way. He had defined inauthenticity as the rejection of possibility, the acceptance of the merely factual conditions of one's existence as inevitable necessities. Social, religious, and national designations were to the inauthentic consciousness objective givens of the same status as physical structure and characteristics. But, Heidegger argued, these identity designations were in fact equivalent to their histories. The meaning of every atemporally defined identity designation in the present was the sum total of everything it had been in the past, of what people identifying themselves with that designation had done in the past. History and tradition, therefore, determined in the first instance what one was, or rather, what one took oneself to be. The past, because it was beyond choice and change, was characterized by that finality that Dasein ardently sought for itself. To the degree that one attached oneself passively to a historical tradition or destiny, one was no longer rootless.

In what he called Dasein's essential "historicality," man's creation of history through his self-creation, Heidegger saw the possibility of authenticity. If, instead of relating to historical tradition passively, as something that could not be renewed, adapted to changing conditions, or applied as a guideline for future activity but merely copied, if instead Dasein were to view the past as possibilities once realized and capable of being chosen and acted upon again, a totally different attitude was possible. It amounted, at least in the first instance, to a revolution in consciousness rather than in a way of life. Viewed as possibilities, the norms of tradition were repeatable. Repeatability was the key to authenticity because the condition of repeatability was the awareness of choice. The inauthentic man accepted the past as a *fait accompli*; the results of historical events were not seen as consequences of the past actions of men but as impersonal present imperatives in a timeless perspective. Thus, for example, the border between two countries represented to the inauthentically historical existence a set of absolute rules to be followed; it was not understood as the outcome of the territorial desires of ethnic or linguistic units, warfare, negotiation, and compromise, whose results were always potentially modifiable:

"The 'they' evades choice. Blind for possibilities, it cannot repeat what has been, but only retains and receives the 'actual' that is left over, the world-historical that has been, the leavings, and the information about them that is present-at-hand. Lost in the making present of the 'today' it understands the 'past' in terms of the present."[2]

By contrast, the authentic self was aware of rules as conventions and of the historical determination of these rules. It could, therefore, go behind them to the fundamental intentions they served and distinguish between the basic purpose and its current reified expression. Instead of being passively buffeted by historical events, it could then take them over responsibly and act on them. To live authentically, in Heidegger's sense, was to stop letting history merely wash over one and to consciously make what up to now had been passively given as a destiny into one's active goal. "When one's existence is inauthentically historical," Heidegger wrote, "it is loaded down with the legacy of a 'past' which has become

[2] *Ibid.*, p. 443.

253

unrecognizable. But when historicality is authentic, it understands history as the 'recurrence of the possible,' and knows that a possibility will recur only if existence is open for it . . . in resolute repetition."[3]

The only authority a free existing could have was the repeatable possibilities of existence.[4] In advancing this solution to the problem of authenticity, however, Heidegger ignored his own explanation that people accepted the identities made available to them by their historical circumstances only because they believed that these were a permanent part of the necessary structure of the world and objectively valuable. If it were suddenly discovered that value was a subjective creation and that social identities and norms were constituted as permanent only by the beliefs about them, all such identity structures collapsed. They could no longer fulfill their function. There would be no reason for taking up the contents of current historical identities in an active way because they had nothing to offer in themselves, at least within the considerations of existential philosophy; they were just contingent facts about one. Moreover, with the collapse of the beliefs that made the merely contingent seem necessary, a Pandora's box of possibilities appeared to open up. With necessity dead, everything was permitted. What criterion of choice could there be among the manifold possibilities of existence? History itself could offer no principle of positive content by which the self could choose meaningful activity.

Heidegger evaded the implications of these difficulties by defining tradition in a homogeneous, one-dimensional way that converted freedom into necessity. What was revealed to Dasein in the moment of vision that dispelled the illusion of necessity and opened the vista of authentic choice was the reality of its situation, which in fact dictated its choices. The historical situation in which one found oneself was well-defined and pointed in only one direction. "Once one has grasped the finitude of one's existence," Heidegger asserted,

---

[3] *Ibid.*, p. 444. [4] *Ibid.*, p. 443.

"it snatches one back from the endless multiplicity of possibilities which offer themselves as closest to one—those of comfortableness, shirking, and taking things lightly—and brings Dasein into the simplicity of its *fate*. This is how we designate Dasein's primordial historizing . . . in which Dasein hands itself *down* to itself, free for death, in a possibility *which it has inherited and yet has chosen*."[5] Freedom consisted in the self-conscious acceptance of destiny, a destiny, moreover, that was not individual but collective; the individual did not define his own situation. "Dasein's fateful destiny in and with its 'generation' goes to make up the full authentic historizing of Dasein."[6]

Freedom as the acceptance of necessity was a not unfamiliar position in German philosophy, but it contradicted much else in the definition of authenticity, and the arguments Heidegger made for it based on the ideas of facticity and thrownness were bad ones. Heidegger correctly saw that possibilities in a society were not limitless if they were to be real rather than utopian abstractions. He also saw that "being-with-others," i.e., the context of existing social relations, circumscribed the individual's possibilities and that individual choice and identity, to be efficacious, depended upon social confirmation. These restrictions did not amount to the rigid determinism of facticity in which Heidegger imprisoned the liberated consciousness. His own society furnished ample evidence of the existence of conflicting traditions and of views contesting current actuality in the name of as yet unrealized possibilities whose seeds already existed in the present. Moreover, his definition of authenticity did not permit the identification of the individual with the group that his notion of "generational destiny" suggested. The whole thrust of *Being and Time* was the separation of the individual out of the collective consciousness of *"das Man"* and his awareness of his radical subjectivity and individuality.

In retrospect one can see Heidegger's later political activity

[5] *Ibid.*, p. 435. Italics added.   [6] *Ibid.*, p. 436.

foreshadowed in his analysis of historicality. In May 1933, six years after the publication of *Being and Time*, Heidegger was installed by the new Nazi regime as rector of the University of Freiburg and in the same month he joined the Nazi party. He remained in the rectorship less than one year, leaving his post in February of 1934. There has been a good deal of controversy surrounding this episode in Heidegger's life, and it is questionable whether its full significance can be properly evaluated without hitherto unavailable private papers and testimony. Why he joined and why he resigned when he did remain matters of fiercely debated conjecture.[7]

It *is* a matter of public record, however, that during his tenure as rector, Heidegger made a number of speeches defending and extolling the Nazi regime and the Fuehrer.[8] In addition to the standard neo-idealist, anti-modernist and anti-Marxist rhetoric of cultural and political conservatism in Germany, the speeches contain specifically Heideggerian themes and language from *Being and Time*. In his inaugural address as rector, "The Self-Assertion of the German University," Heidegger exhorted the students of Freiburg to fulfill their new duties to the nation through labor and army service. "Knowledge and German destiny must come to power above all in the adherence to tradition, and will do so only when teachers and students alike suspend knowledge as their innermost need, and participate in the destiny of Germany in its most extreme need."[9] Assessing the meaning of the Nazi take-

[7] See on this issue F. Fédier, "Trois attaques contre Heidegger," *Critique*, Nov. 1966, pp. 883-904; R. Minder, J. P. Faye, A. Patri, "A propos de Heidegger," *Critique*, Feb. 1967, pp. 284-297; Fédier, "A propos de Heidegger: une lecture dénoncée," *Critique*, July 1967, pp. 672-686; B. Alleman, "Martin Heidegger und die Politik" in *Heidegger*, ed. O. Pöggeller, Berlin, 1969; "Deux documents sur Heidegger," *Les Temps Modernes*, No. 4-6, 1946, pp. 714-724.

[8] See the collection in G. Schneeberger, *Nachlese zu Heidegger: Dokumenten zu seinem Leben und Denken*, Bern, 1962, and the translations in D. Runes, *German Existentialism*, New York, 1965.

[9] Runes, *German Existentialism*, p. 19.

over, Heidegger proclaimed in a pledge of allegiance to Hitler and the National Socialist state, "The National Socialist Revolution is not simply the taking of power in the state by one party from another, but brings a complete revolution of our German existence [deutsches Dasein]. Henceforth every matter demands decision and every act demands responsibility. . . . Our resolve to be responsible to ourselves alone demands that each people seek and guard the greatness and truth of its own choice. The Fuehrer has awakened this resolve in the whole people and has fused it into a single resolution."[10]

What light does Heidegger's political commitment shed on *Being and Time*? One possible interpretation is that it indicates its "cash value," the real concrete meaning of the philosophical abstractions of that work. According to this view, Heidegger was the intellectual spokesman for the anxiety and desperation about security that characterized those members of the German middle and lower middle classes who after the First World War found their economic security and social and political status severely threatened under Weimar. These groups had identified with the idea of the nation as a buttress of or surrogate for their own social position.[11] The transition from inauthenticity to anxiety to the "authentic resolve" of activist nationalism was not difficult for Heidegger because the lesson he had learned as a result of the war and its aftermath was not that of the false consciousness of group identity per se but that of the disastrous consequences of a merely passive acceptance of it. It was such a passive acceptance that led to one's being a helpless

---

[10] *Ibid.*, pp. 32-33.

[11] The first part of this interpretation was suggested by Günther Anders in an article in *Die Neue Rundschau*, Stockholm, October 1946. quoted in Schneeberger, *Nachlese*, p. 265. For discussions of the nationalism of the German lower middle and intellectual middle classes, see E. Nolte, *Three Faces of Fascism*, trans. L. Vennewitz, New York, 1966, pp. 299, 313; Ringer, *German Mandarins*, passim; F. Stern, *The Politics of Cultural Despair*, Berkeley, 1961.

prey of events, as epitomized in the shock of Germany's defeat. The remedy for this was the abandonment of the traditional apolitical attitude of the intelligentsia and the middle and lower middle classes, and active participation with or support of those pledged to promote national interests. In such acts as withdrawing from the League of Nations, which Heidegger supported in one of his speeches, Hitler represented the individual authentically resolving to take his fate into his own hands and thereby setting an example for others.

This explanation seems in broad outline plausible for the interpretation of Heidegger's concept of historicality; it will not do as an interpretation of authenticity. Given the definition of authenticity as *Jemeinigkeit,* there could be in all consistency no such thing for Heidegger as a "deutsches Dasein," nor could a single man be, as Heidegger proclaimed of Hitler, "the current and future reality of Germany," whose "word is your law."[12] A "national purpose" or "national will" was a contradiction in terms; there were by the criterion of authenticity only free individuals with autonomous wills acting in concert with one another to the degree their interests and circumstances converged, but not bound by an identity of "being." A people as an entity could not will to be responsible for its own future and destiny,[13] since the idea of such an a priori common destiny was a fiction created and sustained by the inauthentic consciousness of individuals.

Moreover, there is evidence that Heidegger's individualistic and libertarian concerns predated the war. Biographically they may be closely related to his move away from Catholicism. Until 1914 he had been a novice in a Jesuit seminary in Freiburg; there is no available information about the circumstances of his leaving. However, in his *Habilitationsschrift* on *Duns Scotus' Doctrine of Categories and Meanings,* published in 1915, Heidegger attacked medieval scholastic philosophy for its want of courage to ask questions independently of authority: "The Middle Ages," he wrote, "lack what

12 Runes, *German Existentialism,* p. 28.
13 Schneeberger, *Nachlese,* p. 150.

makes the characteristic of the modern spirit: *the liberation of the subject from his ties with his environment, the firm establishment of his own life.*"[14]

We are left, then, with the contradiction between the concepts of authenticity and historicality, between Heidegger's libertarian concerns and the surrender of his political commitment. This contradiction can be best explained as a consequence of the unrecognized dilemma posed by the existentialist concept of authenticity. Heidegger had asserted that the resoluteness of the "moment of vision" in which Dasein became free for authentic being-one's-self did not detach Dasein from its world or isolate it so that it became a free-floating "I"; the world did not become another one in its content, nor did the circle of others get exchanged for a new one.[15] This protest pointed to its opposite; it was a whistling past the graveyard, and the only way Heidegger could avoid seeing this was to plunge wholeheartedly into historical commitment, regressively replacing internalized alienated tradition with external historical happening as the new absolute. Existential authenticity could in fact be only a negative moment in which the self suddenly became aware of the irrationality of all "necessary" beliefs and the self-constituted nature of permanent identities. It was a moment of disengagement, of distancing; beyond that, it revealed nothing. For something positive, one had to go beyond the concept of authenticity.

In part the direction Heidegger chose to go can be understood with reference to the special intellectual tradition of the German idea of freedom, with its origins in the weak social and political situation of the German intelligentsia; in part it can be understood in terms of Heidegger's own rural, lower middle class background, with its deep suspicion of diversity and change (already sharply, if abstractly evoked in *Being and Time*) and of the urban technological civilization explic-

14 H. Spiegelberg, *The Phenomenological Movement*, 2nd ed., The Hague, 1965, Vol. I, p. 295.
15 Heidegger, *Being and Time*, p. 344.

itly criticized in the pro-Nazi speeches. But serious attention should also be given to the Nazi rhetoric of regeneration, renewal, and the recapturing of control over the chaos of events that were leaving many Germans helpless. This provided a plausible bridge for someone for whom the urgency of the need to choose something resulted from the abyss opened up by existential self-awareness. This awareness had to be both assimilated and defended against, and National Socialist activism, justified as the return to the self-responsibility and authentic existence of the German people, was a first compromise formation.

Between 1929 and 1936 Heidegger published nothing new except for his inaugural address. Beginning with an essay on Hölderlin in 1936, however, a new phase of his work opened up to which the vast bulk of his writing now belongs. This new phase was marked by tone, language, and concern very different from the period of *Being and Time*. Heidegger himself called the change the *Kehre*, the turning or conversion, in his philosophical viewpoint. Seconded by many of his interpreters, he insisted that the turn was a shift in the priority of two elements present in his work from the very beginning, a reversal brought about by his awareness of the impossibility of interpreting the meaning of Being starting from an analysis of Dasein. A substantial body of critical opinion argued, on the other hand, that the *Kehre* represented a complete reversal of the position of *Being and Time*, and hence a total negation of the original meaning of his philosophy.[16]

16 The literature on the issue is too vast for review here. The *Kehre* was first mentioned by Heidegger himself in his published writings in *Über den Humanismus*, Frankfurt, 1947, p. 17. A statement of Heidegger's insistence on the continuity of his own work can be found in his preface to *Heidegger: Through Phenomenology to Thought*, by W. J. Richardsons, S.J., The Hague, 1963. He had, however, already in 1937 protested in a letter to the French philosopher Jean Wahl (cited in A. de Waelhens, *La Philosophie de Martin Heidegger*, Louvain, 1941) that the "anthropological" interpretation given to his early work misrepresented his own intentions. The best defense of the idea of a radical reversal in Heidegger's work is in K. Löwith, *Heidegger: Denker in dürftiger Zeit*, Frankfurt, 1953.

There is obviously no question that the problem of Being that occupied the center of Heidegger's later philosophy was, verbally at least, the problem to whose solution *Being and Time* was devoted. In that book he thought to explicate the "meaning of Being" by analyzing the existent, man, who raised the question explicitly in philosophy, or implicitly in his pre-reflective interpretation of it. Understanding the meaning of Being meant, in the first instance, articulating and making precise the vague and, as it emerged, erroneous interpretation of Being which men made in their everyday lives and codified in their philosophy. As we have already seen, Heidegger's conclusion was that man's ordinary comprehension of Being was inauthentic, an illusion manufactured to escape temporality. Insofar as the Being of entities and of the meaning-structure of the world was seen as static, it was the projection of an a priori nature on the meaning of phenomena, produced by man's thematizing activity, a fiction, a hypostatization. Meaning was a process, the result of man's temporality, his constant active actualizing of possibilities; to speak of objective meaning or eternal truth outside this framework was meaningless.

In his later work, however, Being as some kind of mysterious source replaced Dasein as the central focus. Instead of understanding Being as a concept of man, philosophy was to understand man from the standpoint of Being. Man's thrownness no longer denoted his ultimate purposelessness; Heidegger now spoke of man as having been thrown into existence by Being to be the guardian and "shepherd" of Being.[17] Being disclosed itself to man by its own grace and will in all the things of heaven and earth. Man was there as the "clearing place" of Being; his task was to answer the "call of Being" by opening himself for its disclosure. This meant opening himself to all the things of the world and "letting them be" what they were, rather than trying to subjugate them to his own arbitrary will and subjective meanings. Au-

[17] Heidegger, *Über den Humanismus*, p. 19, quoted in L. Versenyi, *Heidegger, Being and Truth*, Yale Univ. Press, 1965, p. 128.

thenticity was not individual resolve and the free repeating of possibilities; man was now authentic to the degree that he renounced his will and answered the call of Being. Inauthenticity, however, was not man's failure anyway, for it was Being that either granted or failed to grant itself authentically.

"No one," Karl Löwith has written, "will be able to assert cognitively what this Being, this mystery, is, of which Heidegger speaks. Those who come closest to understanding will be believers, who after all do not even pretend to understand the God of revelation."[18] But if the meaning of Heidegger's mysticism of Being is obscure, it is possible to say something about its significance. It is difficult to see in the hypostatization of Being and meaning and in the redefinition of inauthenticity anything other than a reversal of the call to decision, self-responsibility, and individuation of *Being and Time*. This radical conversion of Heidegger's thought demands explanation. Since the period of his political involvement falls between the published writings of the two phases, it seems plausible to assume that the involvement was in some way connected with the change. Unfortunately for the neatness of this hypothesis, at least one of the documents of the second phase, *The Essence of Truth* (*Vom Wesen der Wahrheit*), was supposedly given as a lecture as early as 1930, though it was not in fact written until 1940 nor published until 1943.[19] In the absence, however, of any other hard evidence to support

18 Löwith, *Heidegger*, p. 19.

19 There seems to be also some question about *Plato's Doctrine of Truth*, which, according to Versenyi, though not according to Richardson's far more exhaustively researched book, was ostensibly given as a lecture in 1930. Heidegger himself admits that he made several revisions in the text of the original *Essence of Truth* lecture, which he claims, however, left the point of departure, fundamental position, and basic structure unchanged. In the preface to Richardson's book, Heidegger states that though the *Kehre* was first mentioned in 1947, it was at work in his thinking "ten years prior to 1947." In fact, if we leave aside the controversial *Essence of Truth*, the first clear statement of the new position was in the lecture series of 1935 "Introduction to Metaphysics," published in 1953.

the earlier date for the essay, at least in its published form, and in view of Heidegger's obvious interest in maintaining the continuity of his own work, an interpretation can be ventured that singles out the Nazi experience as the crucial turning point.

In essays published in the 1950's, Heidegger defined history as a realm of error whose significance man was bound to misinterpret because it was, more than any other, the realm in which Being held itself back.[20] Since, however, this realm was also sent by Being, such a misinterpretation was inevitable, and man could do nothing about it. These sibylline utterances can be seen as both a veiled explanation of, and apologia for, Heidegger's political commitment. There is some evidence that he was dismayed by the reality of Nazi, or rather, Hitlerite, Germany; the idealized national renewal he called for in his speeches apparently revealed itself as the embodiment of the chauvinist barbarism he deplored. In any case, Heidegger abruptly resigned the rectorship of Freiburg after less than a year; he no longer spoke on behalf of the regime and he was attacked as a nihilist by Nazi publicists. He may even have spoken privately against the regime and was, according to one account, toward the end of the war on the point of being sent to the front as punishment.[21] Whether or not these last assertions are true, however, Heidegger's revulsion did not turn him into activist political opposition even on an abstract philosophical plane.[22] What he concluded from the disappointment of his historical hopes was the potential error and danger of all human activity, of all "subjec-

[20] Löwith, *Heidegger*, pp. 51-52.

[21] On the Nazi attack, see Schneeberger, *Nachlese*, p. 262. On the allegations of Heidegger's opposition to the regime, see Fédier, *Critique*, July 1966, pp. 900-904, and A. de Towarnicki, "Visite à Martin Heidegger," in "Deux Documents sur Heidegger," *Les Temps Modernes*, Nos. 4-6, pp. 713-724.

[22] In his 1935 lectures published in 1953 as *An Introduction to Metaphysics* (trans. R. Mannheim, Yale Univ. Press, 1959), Heidegger let stand a reference to "the inner truth and the greatness of this [the Nazi] movement" (p. 199).

tivism." He could no longer trust human resoluteness to achieve authentic self-being, because decision could lead, as it had led him, to false and destructive commitments.

On the other hand, Heidegger could not face the negative implications of *Being and Time* either. A new resolution of the problem of authenticity was called for. And so, instead of absolutizing one current in the flux of history, he hypostatized the abstract absolute, Being, which he himself had shown to be a fiction. Being became a god-term that consecrated meaning as already given in language—as we shall see, language of a specific provenance and with a concrete social bearing. The effect of this intellectual re-orientation was the re-objectification of truth, the removal of man from the field of action and his conversion into pure passivity. Man's freedom consisted not in free willing and repetition of possibilities but in allowing things to reveal themselves as what they were. Meaning was thus no longer relative to the thematizing activity of the self but, in just the sense rejected by *Being and Time*, objective. The locus of meaning in Heidegger's later work was language; a central aspect of the *Kehre* was the substitution of a philosophy of language for the analytic of Dasein. Meaning was disclosed only through language; without language there was neither self nor world.[23]

Now it was not just the plurality of meanings that language revealed; Being itself was disclosed through words. "The essence of saying," Heidegger asserted, "is the saying of Essence."[24] Thus Heidegger's philosophy of language was not anthropocentric in the way in which the analysis of the origin of meaning in *Being and Time* was; man was not the creator of language but its agent. It was not man who spoke but language that spoke through man. "The event and advent of Being in and through language, word and saying 'puts man to use for its own sake.' "[25] At the same time, however, lan-

23 Versenyi, *Heidegger*, p. 132.

24 *Ibid.*, p. 133.   25 *Ibid.*

guage not only revealed Being; it also concealed Being, precisely to the extent that man began to put language to use for his own purposes. The revelation of the objective, the "wholly other," was tainted by man's subjectivity. Absolute truth existed, but man could do nothing by himself to reveal Being in its entirety or hasten its appearance. Everything was in the hands of Being. Perhaps in its own good time it would reveal itself to man. In the meantime, man should wait with *Gelassenheit*, "a higher kind of action that is, however, no activity."[26]

In the essay *Nothing is Without Ground*, Heidegger quoted from a poem by a seventeenth-century mystic and philosopher, Angelus Silesius:

> The rose is without why; it blooms because it blooms.
> It cares not for itself, asks not if it's seen.

This was what Heidegger now proposed for man in place of resoluteness and authentic decision. To ask "why?" was to ask for the justification of existence, a question that assumed the existence of doubt. Instead, man should live like the rose, without seeking, questioning, and demanding grounds, just being in the serene confidence of justification. Heidegger had abandoned the earlier view of authenticity as a reaffirmation of human possibilities in the face of the transcendental homelessness of man. His exhortation to meet the problem of homelessness by denying it is understandable. It was he who most clearly in the twentieth century had seen man as the being who asks for ultimate justification in vain and who, in the process of seeking it or trying to live self-consciously without it, destroys himself or destroys others.

Heidegger's Nazism, I have argued, can in part be linked with the tensions in his existential philosophy. As Sartre was to point out, he himself was proof of the fact that there was no necessary connection between existentialism and Nazism,

[26] *Ibid.*, p. 149.

for he had adopted the first without the second.[27] In this Sartre was of course correct. Yet he escaped the dilemma and the contradictions into which Heidegger had plunged in the latter part of *Being and Time* only by concentrating on the purely demystifying implications of existential analysis. When at the very end of *Being and Nothingness* Sartre discussed the ethical implications of his ontological analysis, he could show only that the desire to live in accord with the truth revealed by existentialism contained a negative imperative; the rejection of the "spirit of seriousness." This spirit consisted in regarding values as objective givens independent of human choice, and of assigning normative value to the qualitative attributes of things without recognizing their origins in a human project.[28] An existentially clarified ethic was debarred from such locutions as "It is necessary to live" or from such moral deductions as "Bread is nourishing; therefore it should be eaten." The first expression concealed the fact that life was a choice being made in the very declaration of its necessity, the second that it was in virtue of this choice that bread could be revealed as nourishing and that its instrumental value was relative to the choice and contained no imperative of its own.

The argument of *Being and Nothingness* was that in fact *all* human projects were suffused with the spirit of seriousness. The purpose of existential psychoanalysis was to reveal the "ideal meaning of *all* human attitudes,"[29] that is to say, their bad faith. In one respect at least, Sartre's treatise was an empirical advance on Heidegger's because rather than an analysis of inauthentic everydayness on a very high level of generality, Sartre presented extremely detailed phenomenological descriptions of a wide range of activities—utilitarian activity, scientific research, art, philosophical reflection and psychological analysis, interpersonal relationships—revealing the spirit of seriousness that characterized all of them. In the

27 J.-P. Sartre, *Critique de la raison dialectique*, Paris, 1960, Vol. I, p. 34.

28 Sartre, *Being and Nothingness*, p. 626.

29 *Ibid.*

face of the rigor and scope of his analyses and in the face of
his definition of freedom as negation, it was impossible to
envisage an existentially pure way of life as ongoing activity.
Sartre expressed his own doubts on the possibility of a lived
existential freedom in the last lines of *Being and Nothingness*,
in which he promised a treatise on ethics: "This freedom
chooses, then, not to recover itself but to flee itself, not to
coincide with itself but to be always at a distance from itself
. . . can one *live* this new aspect of being?"[30]

Put in these terms, the answer might still be yes, but the
affirmation was not one that could inspire an ethic of positive
action. Many people—Sartre himself, according to his own
later evaluation—lived a constant attempt to avoid being
labelled, pigeonholed, turned into things. R. D. Laing was
later to demonstrate the presence of this syndrome as a basic
defense mechanism of the "schizoid" personality, caught between the need to secure the sustaining approval of others by
being what others approved, and the need for autonomy and
self-worth on one's own terms. For that matter, freeing oneself, remaining at a distance from oneself, constituted a moment in Sartre's dialectic of desire in *Being and Nothingness*.
The problem of action, however, existed for Sartre in quite
different terms. The historical realities of war, oppression,
and genocide had caught up with him at the very point that
he was declaring man to be a useless passion. Despite a rou-
tine leftist allegiance during the 1930's, Sartre's energies and
enthusiasm were consumed by the detailed working out of
Heidegger's insight into man's escape from freedom.

That Sartre was concerned with social and political issues
out of leftist sympathies in the 1930's is evident in such writings as the novella *Childhood of a Leader*, the story of the
formation of the identity—the successful bad faith—of a
right-wing anti-Semite out of a conservative entrepreneurial
bourgeois background. The focus of the story, however, was
entirely on the ontological motivation behind Lucien's bad

30 *Ibid.*, pp. 627-628.

faith, not on its social content. No conclusions were drawn about the political menace of anti-Semitism nor were there any implications for political commitment; the sympathies showed only in the choice of example. The convergence of historical events with the dilemma created by the internal logic of his existential philosophy in the early 1940's forced Sartre to face directly the issue of reconciling political action with the pessimistic conclusions of his ontological analysis. The imperatives of his ethical and emotional life had forced him into Resistance activity far in advance of his intellectual readiness to justify that action theoretically.

Indeed, *Being and Nothingness* presented at least two obstacles to the very kind of action that Sartre was engaging in—action on behalf of the liberation of others. In it he had argued that respect for the other's freedom was an empty word, because any attitude that was adopted toward the other would violate his freedom by depriving him of certain possibilities—for example, the possibilities of resisting oppression and of tolerance.[31] He had also argued that unfreedom could not be caused by external circumstances, since the self was necessarily always free; succumbing to coercion was itself a matter of choice. The only limits that freedom came up against were those which it imposed on itself.[32] These arguments were, in fact, incompatible with one another. In making the first, Sartre was involved in precisely the confusion about the issue of freedom that he had warned against, that is, defining freedom as the ability to obtain whatever ends had been chosen instead of as autonomy of, or responsibility for, choice.[33] Moreover, the first objection was spurious even in its own terms; depriving someone of possibilities was not a violation of his freedom unless that person had chosen those possibilities as his own ends. Nevertheless, insofar as Sartre accepted the arguments, his own Resistance activities were not only contradictory but futile. The second argument was really the heart of Sartre's existentialism. Unfreedom was

31 *Ibid.*, p. 409.   32 *Ibid.*, p. 531.   33 *Ibid.*, p. 483.

self-imposed; it was a matter of the false and irrational belief that one had no choice, that one could do no other.

In the same year as the publication of *Being and Nothingness*, Sartre published a play in which he tried to come to grips with these issues. *The Flies* was pivotal in his development and marked the first step in a lengthy and tortuous intellectual journey that was to culminate in the reversal of the original existentialist theory of motivation and freedom. Dealing with the theme of liberation from tyranny, written and produced under the Nazi occupation, the play had apparently obvious political implications. In fact, however, it was an extended reflection on the possibility of action within an existential framework.

The Flies is a play divided against itself. Ostensibly the dramatic crisis comes at the end, in the three-way confrontation of Zeus, Orestes, and Electra on the problem of responsibility. Electra had been dreaming for years of deliverance from the tyranny of Aegisthus and Clytemnestra, nourishing herself on fantasies of revenge and on the small rebellions possible within the compass of servitude. Orestes brought with him both evidence of the possibility of a way of life different from Argos' cycle of guilt and penance, and the instrument for achieving it. The murder of the king and queen, however, exposed Electra to a liberty she could not stand. With their death, the framework of her life collapsed; however much she had been oppressed under them, she had found an identity in her rebellion that depended upon their continuing authority. She therefore escaped the "dark night" of her freedom by preserving that authority even after their death, punishing herself with guilt for her crime. Thus Zeus, the transcendent authority who had ordained the law against matricide and so represented that which made it an "objective" crime, could offer Electra a way out of her torment through penance. Penance served as attitude of excuse for the sinner at the same time as it entrenched Zeus's authority.

Orestes, however, could not be prevailed upon to accept Zeus's offer, because he refused to feel guilty. This refusal was the badge of his freedom. He accepted full responsibility for the act of murder and all its consequences, but refused to see it as a crime against an objective higher law. Murder was painful to him; if he had murdered, it was because the alternative was even more painful. But it was he alone who had established the hierarchy of values by which Aegisthius and Clytemnestra had to die. Zeus could not even bring him to regret or feel guilty about Electra's suffering because, Orestes insisted, "her suffering comes from within and only she can rid herself of it. For she is free."[34]

All of this was consonant with the view of authenticity defined in *Being and Nothingness*. The real problem of the play, however, lay not in its resolution but in its beginning, with the issue of Orestes' reasons for undertaking the liberation of Argos in the first place. Through the fortune of his early history and the guidance of his tutor, Orestes had received a thorough education in existential lucidity; taught the diversity and relativity of men's ideas he was free from all prejudice and superstition, from all family ties, religion or calling. Yet the broad cultivation and "smiling skepticism" of his tutor had left Orestes empty, and he responded bitterly to the tutor's reminder that he need not get involved in Argos:

"You've left me free as the strands torn by the wind from spiders' webs that one sees floating ten feet above the ground. I'm light as gossamer and walk on air . . . some men are born bespoken; a certain path has been assigned to them, and at its end there is something they *must* do, a deed allotted. I suppose that strikes *you* as vulgar—the joy of going somewhere. . . . Whereas I—I'm free as air, thank God. My mind's my own, gloriously aloof."[35]

---

[34] J.-P. Sartre, *No Exit and Three Other Plays*, trans. S. Gilbert and L. Abel, New York, 1959, p. 116.

[35] *Ibid.*, p. 62. Most interpretations of the tutor portray him as an object of ridicule, like the humanist of *Nausea*, and as representing a position that Sartre established only to indicate its distance from his own meaning: the tutor is a symbol of "false freedom," a "negative

This was just the attitude to be expected from the emptiness of existential lucidity and detachment, and here, unlike in *Being and Nothingness*, Sartre expressed it in its full negativity. Orestes was homeless; above all, he wished to belong. He had no great desire to kill, as Electra discovered to her intense disappointment, yet he would if that was what was necessary to achieve solidarity with a community of men. He was not part of Argos because he had left at too early an age to acquire the memories that link men in a common identity, but "if there were something I could do, something to give me the freedom of the city; if even, by a crime, I could acquire their memories, their hopes and fears, and fill with these the void within me, yes, even if I had to kill my own mother. . . . I want my share of memories, my native soil, my place among the men of Argos. . . . I want to be a man who belongs to some place, a man among comrades . . . ."[36] To the extent that these desires motivated Orestes' act, it was an escape from freedom into the spirit of seriousness, an attempt to end his existential aloneness by making a destiny, an identity, out of the accident of his family, his place of birth, and the past he would acquire by acting.

Yet the apparent transparency of this analysis is blurred when Orestes justifies his action to the dying Aegisthus in very different terms. Rejecting Aegisthus' invocation of Zeus's prohibition against murder, Orestes proclaims: "What do I care for Zeus? Justice is a matter between men, and I

---

freedom, but not the freedom of choice and action." (V. Brombert, *The Intellectual Hero*, Philadelphia, 1961, p. 185. See also T. Spörri, "The Structures of Existence: The Flies," in *Sartre, A Collection of Critical Essays*, Englewood Cliffs, 1962, pp. 55-59.) Such interpretations, in addition to displaying a certain insensitivity to the text itself, ignore Sartre's historical development. The image of the tutor they present is consonant neither with the tone and content of the tutor's remarks nor with the seriousness and despair with which Orestes took them. Moreover, they overlook the fact that the tutor represented the end result of *Being and Nothingness* and that the problem of the play was to find a philosophical basis for transcending that position.

[36] *Ibid.*, pp. 63, 91.

need no god to teach me. It's right to stamp you out like the foul brute you are, and to free the people of Argos from your evil influence. It is right to restore to them their sense of human dignity."[37] This claim of Orestes was in bad faith, on two counts. Despite his rejection of divine law, he was invoking objective moral standards of right and justice in the very form Sartre declared existentially illegitimate in *Being and Nothingness*. Moreover, Orestes' assertion that his action could free the people of Argos from Aegisthus' tyranny was contradicted by the repeated insistence in the play that Aegisthus maintained his tyranny only because of the self-imposed guilt of the people of Argos. What Orestes himself said of Electra held also of them: their suffering came from within and only they could rid themselves of it.

Sartre was to recognize the first of these forms of bad faith when he repudiated as an error the ethical position he attempted to take in his essay "Existentialism is a Humanism."[38] There he had argued that existentialism entailed an ethic of responsibility for others because each person in choosing for himself was implicitly choosing on the basis of some general criterion of what man ought to be; what he willed he thus necessarily willed for all men.[39] The implications of Sartre's existentialism, however, were quite the opposite. There were no universal standards to guide the choice; each person made his own choice without confidence that it was objectively right or suitable for anyone but himself.

Thus *The Flies* failed to give an existential foundation for action. After killing Aegisthus and Clytemnestra, Orestes proclaimed the sudden, crushing awareness of real freedom; he had acted with terrible consequences, and the act was his own, for him alone to bear. Yet, from an existential viewpoint, Orestes' freedom was not any greater after his commitment than before, nor his life more real. At the beginning of

37 *Ibid.*, p. 105.

38 F. Jeanson, *Le problème moral et la pensée de Sartre*, Paris, 1965, p. 36.

39 J.-P. Sartre, *L'existentialisme est un humanisme*, Paris, 1946, p. 25.

the play the tutor had argued for the attitude and life of the uncommitted observer. These were consistent and viable alternatives; if Orestes rejected them, it was not on existential grounds. Such obvious contradictions suggest that Sartre was trying to construct a model of authentic action within what he himself perceived on some level to be an inauthentic framework. Commitment came not out of Sartre's definition of freedom, but out of the need for roots expressed in the existential dilemma. Not so paradoxically, the desperate attempt at identification with a community was by its very nature proof of its failure, of the fundamental conviction of being *de trop*, of not really belonging anywhere.

Orestes prefigured those intellectuals of Sartre's drama and fiction who distrusted their own motive for political activism, who were afraid that they were role-playing, but who were also afraid that as bourgeois intellectuals they had no genuine roles to play because they belonged neither by birth nor condition of work to the oppressed class.[40] The guilt and self-punishment inherent in these attitudes cannot be attributed in a sociological manner to the bad conscience of a French intelligentsia caught between its humanistic and revolutionary pretensions and its class allegiances and preferences. The feeling of illegitimacy preceded Sartre's political commitment, and his commitment was indeed suspect from a political point of view, for its aim was partly the solution of the problem of the existential dilemma. Commitment was Sartre's fundamental project and, like all such projects, a venture in bad faith.

Within this project, however, commitment had to satisfy certain requirements in order to maintain a plausible link with the ontology of *Being and Nothingness*. Action was authentic if its aim was liberation and if the actor took sole responsibility for his act and its consequences. *The Flies* did not explain how one could liberate another; it would have been necessary to attribute a role to externality, to coercion

[40] For example, Hugo in *Les mains sales*. See Brombert, *Intellectual Hero*, pp. 199, 202.

in the genesis of bad faith; this, Sartre had specifically denied. In the play Aegisthus suggested that Orestes' dangerousness lay in the fact that he could teach by example: his act would reveal to others the hitherto undisclosed possibility of their own freedom.

The inadequacy of this method seems to have been recognized by Sartre himself; at the end of the play he has Orestes proclaim to the people of Argos that they are free because he has taken away their sins, remorse, and fear. Having dethroned God, Orestes cannot himself take on the role of Christ; the ending must be seen as an ironic gesture on Orestes' part and at the expense of the author. It announced, however, Sartre's next theoretical task: the discovery of the role of the other in unfreedom. Sartre was to pursue this task in two directions. The first was a further exploration of the conditions of bad faith in which he found a role for others at the cost of reversing himself on the issue of the legitimacy of causality in the explanation of behavior. The second involved a double shift: Sartre's concern with freedom changed from the issue of automony of choice to the one he had specifically rejected before: that of the nature of the obstacles to achieving concrete ends. The concrete ends involved in these considerations related to man's needs as a biological creature. The second direction was essentially a return to a traditional rationalist position and over the decades of the 1950's and the 1960's it gradually took the place of the first, until the existential problem had been completely left behind.

Binswanger never faced Sartre's problem of defining a context for a positive ideal of selfhood because he never accepted a purely negative definition of freedom or authenticity. The security of a sense of personal identity based on the belief that one had a rightful permanent place in the objective order of things did not seem to him to be in any way bad faith but a psychological necessity. Yet the notion of grounding the self in a structure with claims to totality was problematic for Binswanger because it also figured in his definition of pathol-

274

ogy. Thus, in working out an ethic that could also be applied to psychopathology as a concept of health, he was forced to mediate between an autonomy that recognized no limits and an identity structure that made total demands on the self.

In his earliest existential work, Binswanger argued for the need to supplement Heidegger's account of mood as either the inauthentic disclosure of a closed world or as the anxious apprehension of nothingness with a description of a mode of being in which man celebrated the joy of a secure existence in contact with the "All."[41] In the *Grundformen*, the experience of totality, of being both a unique individual and the incarnation of universality, of being justified and necessary, of reconciling such opposites as activity and passivity, giving and receiving, was attributed to the loving I-thou relationship. It is ironically appropriate that the *Grundformen* was published in the same year as Sartre's demystification of love in *Being and Nothingness*. Where Sartre analyzed the bad faith of love in absolutizing the other, and the contradictions involved in loving another and wanting to be loved, Binswanger affirmed, through the testimony of the experience of writers and philosophers, that a genuine we-ness was the very condition of real individual autonomy, furnishing the experience of universality and the recognition necessary for the self to exercise its own authentic will. Binwsanger's differences with Sartre, however, emerged even more directly in his attempt to define the content of authentic selfhood through an attack on a figure who in many respects could be seen as a nineteenth-century precursor of Sartre: the Left Hegelian, Max Stirner.

In his book *Der Einzige und sein Eigentum* Stirner defended a radical anarchistic individualism that could flourish only at the expense of society. Binswanger reproduced a number of quotations from Stirner to illustrate the kind of individualism he thought was a false form of authenticity.

"It is said of God, 'Names do not really name you.' This

---

[41] Binswanger, *Ideenflucht*, p. 34.

applies to me as well: no *concept* expresses me, nothing which one declares to be my essence exhausts me; they are only names.

"So long as one institution stands which the individual may not dissolve, my self-being, my belonging to myself are still far off. How can I, for example, be free . . . if I must renounce 'body and soul' to my people? How can I be my own, if I may develop my abilities to the degree that they do not disturb 'the harmony of society'? The destruction (*Untergang*) of 'people' and of 'humanity' will invite me to my self-development (*Aufgang*). . . . The degree of my sinning indicates the extent of my belonging to myself."

"Only Lucifer," Binswanger exclaimed, "could speak this way. . . . Nihilism itself here rears its head."[42] Binswanger was reacting to a rather too literal reading of Stirner's undoubtedly exaggerated rhetoric. Stirner's position was a fetishizing of one element of Hegel's dialectical thought, the power of negation, which constituted man's infinite freedom and made it impossible to define him permanently by a set of fixed social and historical concepts. Stirner called for man to exercise that power of negation against his own allegiance to institutions and norms that he falsely believed he had to obey, in order to free himself for genuine self-realization. His ideas had met furious criticism from his contemporary Left Hegelian social critic Karl Marx, who attacked him for his petty-bourgeois inability to see man as a social being and to realize that emancipation must be a social act.

Binswanger's attack, however, was an index of the radical shift in the problem of the self from the apogee of nineteenth-century rationalism to mid-twentieth-century thought. From Binswanger's vantage point, Stirner's position, originally pregnant with new possibilities and the excitement of vast unlimited horizons, appeared as a terrible threat. Stirner's "I," wrote Binswanger, "is 'creative nothingness,' the freedom to be above determinations, the 'form' of being one's own

[42] Binswanger, *Grundformen*, pp. 460-465.

[*Eigenheit*] without matter."[43] But being oneself without "being-to-ground," i.e., being independent without any need for a ground other than the negative will, was impossible. The very essence of Stirner's form of individualism was a rebellion against the consensual social world; Stirner's free individual was therefore totally dependent on its existence. The destruction of that common world would not be an invitation to the rise of the individual but would spell his own destruction, for, with nothing to rebel against, he would have nothing to define him.[44]

Binswanger believed that he had good psychological and psychiatric reasons for rejecting Stirner's definition. He had had cases in which individuals strove to free themselves from everything, including their bodies, that others could use to get a hold on them, label them, and devalue them. Because Ellen West had identified with values of slimness and spirituality, she defined her "real self" as an ethereal, non-material, infinitely free being. She dismissed all her concrete attributes as not really being her. The result was that her "real" self was only an ideal phantasy self, emptied of all possible content, pure capacity, and intention that would only be limited by action, since action was the dead end of possibility. This vacuum, however, became as intolerable as the negative identity conferred on her by her body and her ethnic identity, because it made her feel unreal and insubstantial; hence she was driven to fill it up by eating, which only intensified her self-loathing. Caught between a reality she would not be and an ideal she could not be, Ellen West chose suicide as the only way out.

Being oneself, then, for Binswanger, was not just a matter of rebellion, for this left the self worldless. Authentic being oneself meant rather that the individual carried out, or strove for, the unification of his particular being with the "ground of Being."[45] Just what the ground was that could furnish the self with an objectively legitimizing criterion of action, Bins-

[43] *Ibid.*, p. 464.   [44] *Ibid.*, p. 468.   [45] *Ibid.*, p. 459.

wanger could not say. It was not love, for in the dual mode of love the individual was not "in-the-world," concerned with choice and action, but "beyond-the-world," in a timeless sphere of being, the "eternity and homeland of love," where everything was realized and perfect and nothing had to be done. The individual, however, was also finite; finitude meant the necessity to choose among possibilities and temporalize existence. The alternatives were, on the one hand, an existence entangled in irrelevant necessities and external claims, in which the self responded to outside stimuli and time consisted of discrete split-up fragments of immediacy, and, on the other, an existence in which a sense of inner unity and purpose gave the time of one's life continuity and coherence. The ground of being was the mysterious something, a "principle of being" giving form and meaning to life by structuring it in terms of an objective value which was at the same time not something alien but a genuine expression of selfhood.

Binswanger was not able to say more about this structuring principle of existence in the *Grundformen*. Some years later, however, he came back to it in the context of a discussion of aesthetic philosophy and artistic creativity. In his book *Henrik Ibsen and the Problem of Self-Realization in Art*,[46] Binswanger examined the nature of the work of art in its relationship to the self of the artist and as a response to the existential problem of authenticity and wholeness he had sketchily raised earlier. He chose an artist, a writer, as his subject because he saw in the problem of artistic creativity an explicit formulation and the only genuine solution of what was implicit as the life-problem of everyman.

The essence of the work of art for Binswanger was its creation of a total world. The problem of form was nothing other than the structuring of such a world, the design of a picture or model that offered a completed view or interpretation of life. "The work of art represents the complete illumination

---

[46] L. Binswanger, *Henrik Ibsen und das Problem der Selbstrealisation in der Kunst*, Heidelberg, 1949.

of the totality of existents [*des Seienden im Ganzen*] in an artistic form which is 'necessarily liberating.' "[47]

The totality created by artistic form was not a matter of quantity or breadth of experience, an arithmetic summing of the artist's life. Experience was in principle infinite, inexhaustible, and hence not containable in a closed form. The "horizontal," quantitative, dimension of existence did have a role to play in the process of artistic self-realization. To discover his true self, the artist had first to ruthlessly reject the givens of his past, which are his merely by accident of birth, and to explore the many different forms of experience in a "full-bloodedly egoistic" quest for what felt necessary and genuinely his. Artistic self-fulfillment did not, however, mean an unending quantitative expansion of experience; it involved rather a *reduction* of the experimental possibilities of existence, and thus of the whole of human existence, to a determinate unique and unified world design in which existence disclosed or made accessible the whole of being in a specific way. This totalizing of experience involved a shift from the horizontal to the "vertical" plane of existence, a shift that made endless multiplicity fall into place, as in a pattern ordered by a higher principle. The work of art was the act of creative imagination whose essence was the discovery/creation of timeless order and structure in the unordered, ceaseless, and oppressive flow of time.

Artistic form thus corresponded to the ideal of individual and social identity by which the personality and its world became something settled and determinate, its activities defined by a closed set of rules and roles. This kind of self-realization, however, was possible, Binswanger argued, only through the act of creative imagination and not in life as lived. Classical German idealism had erred in believing that the personality could be made into a work of art, a harmonious "whole man." Heidegger had shown that man was a temporal and historical being, unfinished as long as he lived.

[47] *Ibid.*, p. 22.

Existence constantly temporalized itself, reaching into the future; it could never make itself into a finished totality. By contrast, the creation of form in art involved a denial of the essentially open-ended structure of existence. The universe of the work of art was closed and complete, informed by a unified interpretation whose unfolding was the form itself. Time in the play or novel was really non-existent. It was only the necessary condition, imposed by human finitude, of laying out a structure. For the artist, however, the elements of that structure co-existed from the very beginning, as the conclusions of a logical or mathematical deduction were entailed in the statement of the initial axioms.

The artist was thus necessarily a *Zwischenwesen*, a being hovering between the two spheres of eternal beauty and temporal existence in the most fragile kind of equilibrium because he partook of both in the most immediate way. On the one hand, the artist experienced the unfolding of the structural form of his work as a kind of "eternal present"; on the other hand, he also presided at its completion and thus experienced the temporal break that called for new initiative and actions and that therefore impressed upon him the temporal structure of existence.

"Poetic creation [*Dichten*] is a constant revolution of existence and a constant breaking up of world project, and at the same time a passionate longing for repose in believing *trust*, in *loving* encounter with the whole of existence in the 'poem.' . . . But the 'poem' can never express the whole; it can only be a (temporary) repose in the eternal wandering, in the eternal oppression of the spirit by the world and from within. Because of this the wandering of the past never reaches its goal; every poem, like every work of art in general, means simultaneously a being at home and a striking of tents."[48]

Binswanger recognized not only the necessary, but the necessarily illusory absolutizing of experience inherent in aesthetic form. Claiming totality but incapable of expressing the

---

[48] Binswanger, *Vorträge*, Bd. II, p. 249.

whole, the artistic venture into the idealizing vertical dimension of life was bound to lead to a fall, a collapse of the ideal structure. This awareness of the fragility of aesthetic form, of the fact that it was essentially a fiction, was implicit in Binswanger's denial of the possibility of wholeness to the person as historical actor. He explicitly defined the artistic imagination as the *"believing* imaginative projection of infinite being into finite being"[49] and spoke of this as the highest form of phantasy.

Instead of stopping with this insight into the inevitable failure of form as identity, Binswanger made a virtue of necessity, turning the fate of the artist into a paradigm of existential health and then a norm of mental health. It was the ability of the artist to be flexible, to change and grow with experience, to survive the relativization and thus the collapse of one point of view and go on to the next, that marked his health. The danger to the artist was that he would cling to an absolute structure or ideal even when it was no longer in line with experience, and thus unfit himself for living in and coping with the world. This danger Binswanger called *Verstiegenheit*, using the word to denote a situation in which one climbed beyond one's reach and was unable to go either forward or backward. *Verstiegenheit* was epitomized in Ibsen's play, *The Master Builder*, whose hero tried to reach God despite his loss of spiritual vocation, and, literally building a church too high for its narrow base, fell to his death when it collapsed. Thus the emphasis in Binswanger's work shifted subtly from an analysis of the necessary false consciousness and inevitable collapse of any absolute to the false consciousness and fall that resulted from the failure to harmonize ideal values with one's real resources—the failure, that is, to keep the vertical and horizontal dimensions of life in proper balance.

In these terms, *Verstiegenheit* could be applied to the understanding of mental illness; it could become a category of

49 Binswanger, *Ibsen*, p. 38: "gläubiges Sicheinbilden des Seins als Unendliches in das endliche Sein."

psychopathology and a prescription for therapeutic intervention. Binswanger used it to characterize the dilemma of the psychotic individual. The victim of *verstiegene*—absolutized and exaggerated—ideals lived in a phantasy world whose goals could never be realized because they denied basic conditions of the individual's real existence. Ellen West's ideal of ethereality, for example, was so extreme that it was incompatible with bodily existence. In such a case it was necessary to get the patient to accept the inescapable facticity of his existence, and to realize that any choice he made, even to transcend that facticity, had to begin by recognizing it as a given. "The goal of psychotherapy," wrote Binswanger, "is to bring the patient back 'down to earth' from his *Verstiegenheit*. Only from this point is any new *departure* or ascent possible."[50] The therapist's job was thus to counter the patient's false and destructive absolutes and free him from their tyranny.

In dealing with the *Verstiegenheit* of mental illness, Binswanger also ventured an explanation of why the individual clung so desperately to his particular ideal. The Dasein characterized by *Verstiegenheit* was " 'despairingly' exiled from the home and eternity of love and friendship, where, therefore, it no longer knows or senses the 'relativity' of the 'above' [i.e., of the vertical dimension] and 'below' seen against the background of an unquestioning trust in Being, an unproblematic ontological security."[51] In speaking about the "relativity" of the vertical dimension, Binswanger was introducing yet a further modification into his original version of the function of form in giving existence a determinate structure. Here too the effect was to change a situation marked by ontological fatality to one in which the negative outcome could be seen as the effect of a possibly reversible cause, and hence open to therapy. Thus the inflexibility of the mentally ill person's relationship to his self-destructive ideal derived from the fact that it had to provide the basic ontological security that could

50 Binswanger, *Being-in-the-World*, p. 347.
51 *Ibid.*

be furnished only by love and that was missing in his life. Presumably, the "artist" in Binswanger's paradigm of health had a sufficient core of basic security so that the collapse of his belief in the absoluteness of his ideal did not destroy him but enabled him to go on to a new project. Binswanger elided the original insight that the totalizing project of aesthetic form—or any set of forms, for that matter, that give existence a fixed character—was an illusion based on a contradiction.

Yet, though Binswanger's implied "solution" to the identity problem rested from a Sartrean standpoint on bad faith, its bad faith was of the most lucid kind, for it took into account the insights of existentialism to the degree compatible with the needs of identity. Binswanger's solution was the ideal of the Protean individual not inextricably committed to one way of life but able to commit himself wholly to one thing and then move on with its completion. Nietzsche at one point had described the characteristic structure of this way of life as a temporary over-evaluation and idealization of the present combined with the simultaneous but compartmentalized knowledge that one's present project would be relativized in the future and replaced by another that would appear to be of ultimate significance.[52] In *Steppenwolf*, Herman Hesse had described the lucid life as a constant reorganization of the personality in ever-changing structures without ultimate commitment to any one, since none could legitimately claim wholeness.[53] To these descriptions Binswanger added the requirement of a basic ontological security that alone could make the abandoning of old absolutes possible without a disintegration of the person. This split form of existence came closest to meeting the requirements of both identity and authenticity, and hence psychic equilibrium or health. It made possible genuine freedom, the ability to assimilate and explore new possibilities, without either the total collapse of

[52] F. W. Nietzsche, *The Use and Abuse of History*, trans. A. Collins, New York, 1957, pp. 8-9.

[53] H. Hesse, *Steppenwolf*, trans. by B. Creighton, revised J. Mileck, New York, 1963, p. 192.

one's world and one's self-concept in anxiety as the beliefs and values that sustained them gave way, or the need to ward them off and maintain a rigidly closed world in order to sustain one's sense of self.

Like Binswanger, Boss never faced the problem of trying to give a purely negative concept of freedom a positive content. There was potential in his work for this kind of difficulty precisely because of the opposition between his existential understanding of the nature of neurotic imprisonment in the past and of the working of therapy, on the one hand, and the goal of psychotherapeutic liberation, on the other. But Boss was able to avoid this problem because he adopted the viewpoint of Heidegger's later philosophy with its rejuvenated objectivism. It is in the context of the conflict between freedom and identity and the need to reconcile them for a working ethic that Boss's attack on subjectivist misinterpretations of existentialism must be understood.

Binswanger's conceptualization of existential health, psychopathology, and the goals of therapy had been worked out in abstract philosophical and aesthetic terms, apart from the immediate concerns of clinical therapy. It is significant that his major case studies were not reports of therapies he had conducted himself but cases from the files he had worked over, trying to unify and explain the different phenomena in the patient's life by the existential a priori categories which informed them. Though Boss was only partly right in arguing that little new initiative for therapy came from this sort of work, his own approach was rooted much more directly in therapeutic necessities.

Above all, as he saw it, it was necessary to break through the absolutes that dominated the patient's life and made it impossible for him not only to be other than he was but even to be able to recognize the imperatives and prohibitions governing his behavior and judgment. These absolutes resulted from the patient's total identification with restrictive parental beliefs and values, to the point where they became the very condition of experience, blocking out all other possibilities; the notion that there could be alternatives could not even be envisaged. The dissolution of these schemata derived from the past took place through the therapeutic relationship; both by passive acceptance and active encouragement the therapist taught the patient that his old belief and value scheme was not universally valid, and that the suppressed parts of his personality had their own legitimacy.[54] The teaching, however, depended on the success of the therapist in replacing the authority of the internalized absolutes and of the parents who were their forerunners with his own.

This raised all kinds of serious problems. Boss recognized that the "mitigation of the harshness of the superego," which Freud had seen as therapeutically necessary, called for a value change—something Freud had not recognized. What was the therapist's authority for questioning the patient's old value structure, and what was the source of the new values that were to replace it? Boss's interpretation of neurosis and cure was based on his awareness of the human need for absolutes. What was to replace them in the life of the patient? Indeed, was not the idea of psychotherapeutic liberation through authority paradoxical, if not actually contradictory?

In this connection, it is interesting to note the remarks of Philip Rieff, no friend of what he regards as religiously oriented existential therapies, on psychoanalytic therapy:

"The aim of psychoanalysis is the aim of science—power, in this case a transformative technology of the inner life. This final technology aims to increase the range of choice. Yet, without a parallel range of god-terms from which choices may be derived and ordered, choice itself may become a matter of indifference and man becomes a glutton choosing everything. There is no feeling more desperate than that of being free to choose, and yet without the specific compulsion of being chosen. Finally, one does not choose; one is chosen. What men lose when they become free as gods is that sense

54 Boss, *Psychoanalysis and Daseinsanalysis*, p. 198.

of being chosen which encourages them, in their gratitude, to take their subsequent choices seriously. Another way of saying this is: freedom does not exist without authority."[55]

The concern expressed here is distinctly post-Freudian and existentialist; it could never have occurred to Freud, for whom the purpose of life was furnished by the pleasure principle as a universal mechanical-biological principle.[56]

It is against the background of these issues that the force of Boss's adoption of Heidegger's later version of man's relationship to Being can be appreciated. Heidegger himself had seen that the only way to escape the relativistic and purely negative consequences of *Being and Time* was to abolish altogether the concept of person or subject, of the Dasein as a being projecting possibilities and disclosing meanings in relation to them, and to replace it with the concept of man as a "world-openness" or "luminating realm" in whose light all particular beings appear and shine forth, revealing their Being. Superficially, there was no contradiction between Heidegger's earlier and later positions so far as the objectivity of meaning was concerned. He had been at great pains in *Being and Time* to argue that what Dasein disclosed was a facet of the real world and not an idealist figment. But, in the later work, man was represented as being on a mission to disclose and to revere objectively existing meaning, instead of being concerned with becoming authentic and realizing that he was the source of meaning.

Using this definition, Boss criticized the position he attributed to Binswanger and Sartre, according to which man as a subject cast a net of meaning over a previously formless existent; such an interpretation made meaning purely subjective, and, though Boss did not say so explicitly, left him once again without objective guidelines. Boss's criticism failed to make the necessary distinctions between the other two thinkers, nor did it free him from the necessity of accounting for the prin-

---

[55] P. Rieff, Introduction to S. Freud, *The History of the Psychoanalytic Movement*, Collier Books, New York, 1963, p. 21.

[56] Freud, *S.E.*, Vol. XXI, p. 76.

ciple of selection by which certain things and not others were available to any given individual. His use of the idea of individual "attunement" was as subjective as anything in Sartre or Binswanger. But the significance of the criticism was clear; it was an attempt to furnish man with a sense of objective purpose:

"To understand man . . . as servant and guardian of the truth inherent in things as they are permitted to come into being is to free him from the egocentric self-glorification, the autonomy and autarchy, of subjectivist world views. *The Daseinsanalytic point of view gives back man's dignity*: he is the emissary of the ground of everything that is; an emissary who is sent into his life history entrusted with the task of letting the truth of particular beings become apparent to the extent that this is possible at a given time and place. *On the basis of this fundamental feature of man's existence all so-called ethical values become self-evident*."[57]

The utility of this belief in meeting the problems raised earlier is obvious. It could be used by the therapist to justify his direct attempts to counteract resistance and repression; the higher obligation of the individual to admit everything into his sphere of existence could be pitted against the loyalty of the patient to certain "absolutes" really deriving from arbitrary, subjective human wills. Since shame, guilt, and anxiety were reactions to absolute prohibitions that had been contravened or absolutized parents who had been disobeyed, the invocation of the requirements of Being was helpful in counteracting the emotions by relativizing the absolutes through the establishment of a moral counterweight not dependent upon the personality of the analyst and the vicissitudes of transference. "The analysand," wrote Boss, "is called upon completely to relinquish his conceit, in particular his vainglorious conviction that either he or the pseudo-moralistic traditions of his environment have a right to determine who he is and how things should disclose themselves to him."[58]

[57] Boss, *Psychoanalysis and Daseinsanalysis*, p. 70. Italics added.
[58] *Ibid.*, p. 71.

The same injunction applied to the therapist as well. The therapist had no right to impose his own values on the patient; he had to accept the patient fully as he was and allow all of his possibilities to emerge spontaneously from his own being. These possibilities—sexual expression, artistic inclinations, religious feelings—the fundaments of the patient's new life and the source of his new sense of value, were virtually consecrated for the patient as well as the therapist by the concept of Being. They were not merely human activities, subjective preferences, but solemn obligations to Being to cherish the things and creatures of the world, to be open to new experience and to develop one's own capacities, whatever they might show themselves to be. In this sense of being justified and sustained by Being, the patient now had a positive identity to put in the place of the old world of compulsion and restriction, to which he had clung despite its costs, because of its absolute nature; the therapist had a buttress for his authority, which transcended his own person and thus enabled the patient ultimately to free himself from dependency without losing security.

Since the invocation of Being has been seen as a barely disguised turn to religion, it is interesting to examine Boss's own attitude to religion in the life of his patients. Many of them came from pious backgrounds with restrictive sexual ethics grounded in religion. In his analysis of dreams and in therapy generally, Boss gave full credence and sanction to emergent religious strivings, so long as they did not make claims to exclusivity and particularly as long as they did not oppose sexual gratification. Though he called religious dreams "numinous" experiences, direct appearances of the Divine,[59] Boss subordinated the Divine to Being; it was one sphere or aspect of Being, and while it could not legitimately be reduced to anything else, it had no claim to reduce the earthly realm either. Being, then, was the wider term that sanctioned all experience that was not restrictive or destructive.

[59] Boss, *Interpretation of Dreams*, p. 49.

In Boss, then, as in Binswanger, the process of therapy consisted in replacing one form of inauthenticity with another. The imperative of this authority was self-realization in the context of a productive relationship with the objective world in all its manifestations. This was a most paradoxical form of authority, since what it commanded was eternal openness and flexibility; but precisely because it was a command, openness did not threaten an abyss. In this most ironic way existentialism had come full circle.

CHAPTER SEVEN

Ideology and Social Theory
in Psychoanalysis and Existentialism

PSYCHOANALYSIS, it was argued in chapter four, represented the internalization of rationalist social theory and its central problem. In the guise of biological instincts, the conflict between individual interest (autonomy) and social harmony was fought out on the level of the individual rather than on that of society. The same difficulties of reconciliation that in social theory were manifest as interpersonal conflict and social and political disequilibrium were manifest within the personality as internal conflict and symptom formation.

At this point, however, it is necessary to make distinctions within rationalist social theory that were initially glossed over in the emphasis on the concept of freedom common to the whole tradition. The same theory of human autonomy could be allied with very different explanations of unfreedom and thus have different consequences for the practice of liberation, depending on the other beliefs associated with it—as the political theories of nineteenth-century liberalism, idealism, and Marxism show. This can best be seen for our purposes in the differences among the Marxist, psychoanalytic, and existential conceptions of alienation. As existentialism changed character under the pressure of internal contradictions, historical events, and therapeutic necessity, these distinctions evolved into even more clearly differentiated ideological positions.

THREE TYPES OF ALIENATION

Alienation may be defined broadly as the loss of freedom and selfhood involved in seeing human acts and capacities as alien forces, as attributes of things other than the self and in opposition to it. For Marx, alienated consciousness was not wholly irrational but a function of alienated personal and social existence. The belief that the social and economic world was governed by objective laws similar to those of the natural world was the consequence of a social world in which the individual was in fact the helpless victim of forces and events. In the case of the worker, his activity was turned to ends other than his own by the capitalists' monopoly of the means of production. But, though the exploited suffered most both materially and in the scope of freedom possible in their activity, the consciousness of both exploited and exploiters was alienated by the anarchy of private property production, in which a myriad of individual decisions produced consequences neither intended nor desired by any individual.

It followed that the "cure" for alienated consciousness was necessarily a social one. Consciousness could not be liberated without a restructuring of the reality it reflected. "All forms and products of consciousness," ran one of Marx's most famous statements, "cannot be dissolved by mental criticism, by resolution into 'self-consciousness' . . . but only by the practical overthrow of the actual social relations which gave rise to them."[1] This argument, however, posed a serious dilemma. If false consciousness were the necessary consequence of specific social circumstances, it would be impossible for anyone in those circumstances to transcend them and picture any alternative to them.[2] Liberation would thus be impossible. Marx escaped this dilemma only because he retained the rationalist belief in an a priori human freedom, which had been articulated in the philosophical anthropology of the *Economic and Philosophical Manuscripts* (man as essentially free sensuous activity), and the belief in a pre-existing desire for freedom, which he held to be congruent with the class in-

[1] K. Marx, *The German Ideology*, Pts. I and III, New York, 1947, pp. 28-29.

[2] G. Lichtheim, "The Concept of Ideology," *History and Theory*, IV, 2, 1965, p. 177.

terest of the historical proletariat. This belief, however, was incompatible with the causal theory of ideology, which made alienated social practice the necessary and sufficient condition of alienated consciousness. With the historical failure of the assumption of the revolutionary proletariat, this inconsistency was exposed and Marxism was seen to be without an adequate theory of consciousness.

In psychoanalytic theory the term "alienation" was applicable to those portions of behavior experienced as foreign intruders by the "official" self or not fully under its control because their real meaning was not understood. Alienation had been explicitly defined by Freud as the alienation of libido under the pressure of the ego. The self was the agent of its own repression; since the self was also simultaneously in the alien behavior, the cure involved achieving self-consciousness, recognizing selfhood in otherness. Because the alienation of the self in unconscious phantasy was interpreted as the joint product of desire and of anxiety, impulse and defense, the help of an outsider was necessary in reaching this goal. Yet for the very same reason there was no way within psychoanalytic theory of accounting for the efficacy of the analyst's role.

The ambiguous position of the analyst in the cure was a reflection of the totally internal causal analysis of the genesis of neurosis. Alienation occurred because the individual could not bear too much reality—primarily internal reality. The external environment hardly played any active role in the process; it was a neutral constant. "Perverse" impulses, oedipal desires, castration anxiety, repression, and regression were automatic consequences of man's biological make-up and of the excessive length of human childhood; such frustration as did play a role in the genesis of neurosis was largely the necessary consequence of an unchanging reality. Individual differences in coping with the impulses were accounted for in terms of the hereditary strength of instinctual components. In the end the problem of neurosis came down to the individual's capacity, or lack of it, for tolerating psychic reality and frustration without resorting to repression and unconscious phantasy. Given this conceptual framework, it was not at all clear just what role the analyst played in increasing this capacity. As we have already seen, it was Freud himself who first pointed out that an analyst's interpretations were no better than the patient's acceptance of them, and he relied on the authority granted by patient to analyst in the transference for this receptivity. But since external authority was not seen as a factor in primal repression—in the *Three Essays* Freud had argued that it took place even without education—there was no way to understand how external authority could overcome repression.

To the degree that social institutions played a frustrating role above and beyond the demands of "reality," psychoanalysis did at least license a critical approach; in his criticism of the Victorian sexual ethic Freud adumbrated what Marcuse later called "surplus repression."[3] Freud was certainly outspoken in his attack against the irrational repressive force of institutionalized religion, even though religion too was ultimately seen not as an external coercive agency but as the product of unconscious phantasy created out of the inability to face reality. Precisely because what was repressed was seen in theoretical terms as individual gratification, however, and what was doing the repression was seen theoretically as the agent of social utility, there could be no major implication for social change in psychoanalysis.

In the original existential positions of Heidegger and Sartre alienation meant the abdication of choice to others and even to inert things that seemed to contain their own imperatives. The description of the inauthentic consciousness was in important respects strikingly similar to the Marxist false consciousness. The inauthentic consciousness converted the contingent facts of social structure and behavior into natural processes and was thus unable to see them as human choices. But where Marxism saw this process as the consequence of unfree conditions, existentialism argued that alienation was

[3] H. Marcuse, *Eros and Civilization*, Boston, 1955.

a matter of interpretation and belief. Between the facticity of social structures, even such coercive ones as slavery, and the set of beliefs that accepted them as the inviolable order of things, there was a logical gap into which subjective interpretation had to be inserted. From the fact that something was a certain way, it did not follow that it had to be that way. If the beliefs about the eternal nature of social order were rationally derived, they would be open to challenge and criticism on the basis of its inconsistencies or of alternative possibilities. For the most part, however, the norms of the social order were the criteria of the admissibility of possibilities, and thus excluded disconfirming counter-examples.

The function of these irrational beliefs in existentialism has already been discussed in detail. The desire to escape the anxiety of existence through alienation or "falling" was for Heidegger a permanent feature of Dasein. "We would . . . misunderstand the ontologico-existential structure of falling," he wrote, "if we were to ascribe to it the sense of a bad and deplorable ontical property of which, perhaps, more advanced stages of human culture might be able to rid themselves."[4] From the language it seems as if this statement was a refutation of a position that asserted the opposite, and, though there are no direct clues in the text, it is possible that Heidegger was here taking issue with the Marxism of Georg Lukács.[5]

In *History and Class Consciousness*, published four years before *Being and Time*, Lukács had recovered the original Hegelian impulse in Marx's work, restoring the concepts of alienation and reification as the center of Marx's liberating concern and correspondingly relativizing contemporary forms of alienation as the historical and hence alterable product of specific forms of social organization. Heidegger agreed that fallenness had "various possibilities of becoming concrete as something characteristic of Dasein" and that "the extent to which its dominion becomes something compelling and ex-

4 Heidegger, *Being and Time*, p. 220.
5 See above, pp. 102, 407 fn. 44.

plicit may change in the course of history."[6] But if for Heidegger the concrete historical form of social organization provided the content of reified consciousness, its form, the absolutization of the historical and the reification of the human, was the expression of the desire to confer Being on the contingent and changeable. These features of inauthentic consciousness could not be explained in terms of interest psychology as the ideological products of class interest, for such an explanation would fail to distinguish between "sincere" false consciousness, i.e., belief, and hypocrisy; nor could it account for the inauthentic beliefs of those to whose interests the prevailing order was presumably opposed.

Like psychoanalysis, then, existential liberation was an internal process of achieving true self-consciousness. There was no room even for a therapist except insofar as the existential philosophers could be considered to have shown by example the way to the kind of "purifying reflection" necessary to arrive at authenticity or lucidity. Yet insofar as existentialism was concerned with freeing man for the realization of his own, rather than of alienated, possibilities, Heidegger's insistence that in authentic disclosedness the world remained unchanged,[7] and that only one's relationship to it was different, created serious problems.

Heidegger's work certainly supplied an important element missing in the Marxist account of ideology, with its idea that the self was imprisoned by its own structure of belief as well as by objective conditions. To become free one had first to free oneself by an act of self-awareness of the irrational beliefs that were the initial obstacle to transcending one's situation. To actualize freedom, however, it was necessary to have the objective means at hand to choose among possibilities. Here it is necessary to go outside Heidegger's frame of reference to make the point clear. Someone might have chosen an occupation or vocation because it was a family tradition and then have come to realize that he need not be bound by that

[6] Heidegger, *Being and Time*, p. 167.
[7] *Ibid.*, p. 344.

tradition. Such a person might continue in his profession for his own reason, if he actually liked it, or he might try something else. But his ability to realize himself elsewhere depended crucially on whether or not he had the resources and whether social rules allowed him to do so. Heidegger completely ignored the question of concrete social possibility. As we have seen, he short-circuited the whole question with a one-dimensional conception of historical possibility that turned it into determinism. It was in part the absence of a category of alienated labor, and of a critical approach to reality that envisioned the possibility of changing factual conditions, that forced Heidegger to make of facticity a leaden destiny.

In addition to this problem, there was a curious paradox in the very enterprise of existential philosophy itself. Somehow the existentialists had managed to surmount the anxieties and defenses that were the existential condition of all to analyze the condition instead of escaping from it. This suggested the plausibility of some sort of explanation to account for the differences between those who were able to do this and those who were not. Such an explanation might to a degree relativize the supposedly universal characteristics of the existential situation by pointing out the causes for the differing degrees of intensity or explicitness of anxiety among different people or historical periods. Yet the existentialists rejected the possibility of any causal explanation of inauthenticity or bad faith; it was a free choice of the self in the face of unchanging ontological anxiety.

Thus all three versions of alienation and liberation suffered from internal contradiction and incoherency. In psychoanalysis these stemmed from the basic legitimization granted the repressive forces insofar as they were seen as instances of self-preservative instincts. Since those forces were therefore justified in their goals, the responsibility for neuroses lay with the impulsivity of the individual, his insistence on immediate gratification, to the extent of abandoning reality for phantasy. What made psychoanalysis more than mere moral exhortation was the fact that the impulses could not be controlled if they were not recognized. Psychoanalysis was concerned with recognition; control was presumed to come more or less automatically along with it. Because the repressive forces were theoretically the agents of legitimate purposes, Freud was not able to appreciate on the level of theory what he observed clinically: that for recognition to take place, the harshness of the superego had to be mitigated. The theoretical implication of this was that the form of the superego itself represented "surplus repression." Mitigating its harshness to permit acknowledgment of concealed impulses meant changing the form of control from irrational categorical prohibition to reasoned control. This was a form of social engineering and it presumed previous faulty social construction. The authority of the superego was the embodiment of an arbitrary hierarchical authority whose commands were to be obeyed without reasons being given or asked. But if Freud was not prepared to recognize this aspect of social influence on symptom formation, he was certainly not prepared to recognize the effect of the social environment on the instincts themselves, the degree to which infantile fixation might itself be a social phenomenon.

It was just this which Boss's existential therapy explicitly insisted on. Existential therapy, however, in turn demanded a reversal of the existentialist position on causality. The possibility of therapy implied the necessity for a causal explanation of the loss of the sense of ontological security that drove men to the fanatic idealization of goals beyond their reach and the crushing sense of nothingness and lack of value that underlay it. Only with such an explanation could there be meaningful therapeutic intervention. To relegate ontological insecurity to a "human condition," moreover, was not only to destroy the foundations of psychotherapy but to fail to distinguish *degrees* of anxiety, conflict-free existence, liberation, and even happiness. As Sartre soon saw, it also made impossible any kind of social commitment and political judgment, for social and political arrangements were irrelevant to ontological conditions. Thus as existentialism faced the problems of individual and social therapy it was forced to modify its own initial ahistorical universalism as well as its concept of authenticity. In this modification, however, different existentialists took different directions, and the results were sharply differing diagnoses of the ills of modernity.

BOSS, HEIDEGGER, AND THE TECHNOLOGICAL CRITIQUE OF MODERNITY

The most obvious approach to a social theoretical understanding of the genesis of acute identity anxiety in existential analysis seemed to lie in Boss's conception of transference. The role of the analyst in changing the patient's beliefs and values and thus the way he related to other people pointed backwards to the roles of parents and other authority figures in first producing his fearful and constricted mode of existence. Boss insisted that change in the patient's structure of relationships was in fact effected through the creation of a new pattern of relationship between analyst and patient, and in this the analyst took the initiative. By accepting the patient as he was, by permitting and indulging dependent behavior, by constant questioning of the patient's harsh and self-punitive value schemes, by stressing the patient's right and obligation to be himself, the analyst helped to give the patient the sense of value, of positive identity, that he had hitherto lacked.

Boss frequently indicated that it was this kind of loving acceptance of the individual's intrinsic value on the part of parents, and of the opportunity for free and confident self-development through rational permissiveness, that had been missing in the patient's early life. The therapist's job was to restore them and reverse the negative process. This task was more difficult than the original one of child-raising because the patient had long since internalized the values of his milieu and had come to believe fully in the "pseudo-absolutes," as Boss called them, to which he had sacrificed his freedom

298

and self-esteem. Insofar as the patient felt the desires that his absolutes opposed, he had to see the analyst as an unalterably critical and hostile other, for by his own definitions his impulses made his whole being condemnable. Boss did not believe that remembering the first occasion of that impulse and condemnation would by itself effect change. Indeed, such remembering would not be possible until the patient felt safe in remembering. In asserting that it was the analyst who provided this safety, Boss was in fact taking a position similar to Marx's: dissolving products of consciousness came about only through changing the actual social relations that had produced them. Certainly the patient had to be willing to change. But the proper role of the other was as much a necessary factor.

Boss was thus proposing an interactional theory of the genesis of ontological insecurity and alienation of being. He even made the blunt and sweeping statement that *"all psychiatric diagnoses are basically only sociological statements."*[8] However, in the end he proposed a detailed social theory neither on the nuclear family level, where he might have systematically analyzed the ways in which specific actions of family figures affected identity, nor on the socio-historical level, showing the effect of wider social institutions and norms on the family. There were many descriptive statements in Boss's case studies of his patient's oppressive social and family environments. Thus he described one patient as growing up "in the rigorously ascetic atmosphere of a sectarian community characterized by its inordinate zeal for mortification of the flesh and all that appertains thereto. An inexorable self-image, drilled into her since childhood, demanded unremitting self-denial and sacrifice to duty."[9] Without any rigorous attempt to build a theory, Boss simply assumed that these environments had a deleterious effect on the personality development of his patients, and, though he apparently took for granted that the degree of repressiveness was unnecessary

[8] Boss, *Psychoanalysis and Daseinsanalysis*, p. 56. Italics added.
[9] *Ibid.*, p. 5.

as well as destructive, he proposed no theory of "surplus repression" from which consequences for social change might be derived.

More interesting in its social implications than his scattered remarks about the ascetic Protestant traditional rural backgrounds from which many of his patients came was his lucid description of the family structures of India and Indonesia, where he had spent some time teaching. Boss's account of his visit was a pioneer venture in comparative psychiatry. He tried to correlate similarities and differences in the types and in the severity of mental illness in the East and West with their respective family structures and values. He argued, for example, that in some key ways the traditional Indian family resembled the patriarchal, authoritarian, prudish, and work-oriented family of Freud's Vienna and thus produced in its members many of the same classical neurotic symptoms as Freud had observed; meanwhile, these symptoms were decreasing in the West as a result of social changes. Just what these changes were, however, and how they affected character structure and symptomatology Boss did not say in any detail.

The reasons for this were that Boss did in fact have a social theory of sorts that he thought explained these developments and that did not depend on detailed observations of economic and social change and structure. It was part of the whole intellectual position he had taken over from the later Heidegger.

One aspect of Heidegger's conversion from the analysis of Dasein to the preoccupation with Being was his concern with the question of how and why man had come to be forgetful of Being and of his own nature as the realm in which Being revealed itself. This concern was a modified extension of the issue that Heidegger had raised in *Being and Time*: the need to reopen the question of the meaning of Being because it had been so long ignored or taken for granted by Western philosophy. In the later work, however, the critique of philosophy was amplified into a critique of modernity.

In *Being and Time* Heidegger paid special attention to the ontology of Cartesian philosophy, contrasting the Cartesian notion of the world as *res extensa* with the ontological approach that concerned itself not with the structure of some given world but with the condition of worldhood in general. Heidegger singled out Cartesianism because he believed it particularly relevant to modern man's difficulty in understanding the nature of existence as being-in-the-world. This was because the dominant intellectual structure of modern times, natural science, with its basic concept of the world and of man as objective nature and measurable thinghood, was based on Cartesian reification; more precisely, the Cartesian ontology had made explicit the assumptions on which modern science in its origins had been based. Insofar as *Being and Time* offered an explanation of man's misconception of the nature of meaning and his own relationship to the world, it was a critique of modern science by way of an attack on Descartes. The all-pervasive conceptual universe of mathematical science had affected even the average man's everyday pre-theoretical perception of the world, which gave priority to "thinghood," the present-at-hand, even when he was in fact more directly concerned with tools.

In his later work, Heidegger saw in the Cartesian reification of the world the epitomization of false subjectivism and the ultimate cause of man's distance from Being. According to this interpretation, it was through Cartesian philosophy that man had liberated himself from subservience to churchly authority and made himself the measure of all things. The self-certainty of the *cogito* was the expression of the new principle of truth; the criterion of truth was the clear and distinct cognition of the subject. Since the prototype of self-evidently clear and distinct ideas was mathematics, mathematical-physical calculation became the only method of approach to the world. Man thus became an autonomous lawgiver who prescribed to the world the conditions on which it could become an object of human cognition. Such an approach no longer let beings show themselves as what they were but, by prescribing the manner in which they could be apprehended, reducing them to their mathematical descriptions, it violated the phenomenological essence of things.[10]

The spirit of modern science, therefore, was, contrary to its own conception of itself, not one of humble, passive reception of the disclosure of what was simply there; i.e., it was not truly objective. The "passivity" of objective knowing was indeed not primary at all; it was at the service of something else, an active goal. The real point of science was what Heidegger called *Technik*, the technological spirit, the exploitive approach to the world embodied in modern Western machine technology. Even though, Heidegger conceded, modern technology did not really begin until almost two centuries after the rise of modern science, science was really in the service of *Technik*.[11] What Heidegger had in mind was the spirit embodied at the birth of modern science in Bacon's famous phrase about men's new-found power to become "the lords and masters of nature." The scientific representation of nature as a calculable relationship of forces was a function of the basic technological approach to nature as the chief reservoir of supplies of energy to be drawn upon and forcefully extracted.

Heidegger's attitude to *Technik* was not unambiguously condemnatory. As a mode of disclosure of the world, it was a destiny (*Geschick*) of man ordained by Being, and of equal value with any other mode. If it ran the danger of exclusivity, of shutting out other aspects of the world, it was no different in this respect from any other form of disclosure. But the degree of danger from *Technik* was greater. Precisely because it appeared to give men mastery over nature, it tended to displace all other possible relationships to the world. The illu-

---

[10] Versenyi, *Heidegger*, pp. 60-62.

[11] M. Heidegger, *Die Technik und die Kehre*, Pfullingen, 1962.

sion of mastery concealed the tyranny that *Technik* exercised and made man forget that as a creature claimed by Being to be a realm of disclosure, he ought not to foreclose other dimensions of the world. Moreover, *Technik* threatened man more directly with the loss of his essence as freedom, potentially available for all experience, because, as part of nature himself, he too could be approached in the technological spirit and be exploited as a mere supply of energy. Finally, the exploitative attitude of the technological spirit drove men to a constant, restless forcing of nature and themselves and prevented an attitude of *Gelassenheit*, the calm give-and-take with the world, a letting-things-be in the peace and acceptance of harmony with nature.

Heidegger's critique of *Technik* was one voice in a broad chorus of attack on technology that arose in Europe in the second third of the twentieth century.[12] The opposition to soulless mechanization, of course, goes back to the Romantic protest against rationalism and the Industrial Revolution; in the German context it is possible to go back to Novalis' complaint against the rationalist picture of the world as a cold, heartless, calculable mechanism.[13] But the phenomenon that Heidegger represented was distinctly modern and post-Marxist in its refusal to make any distinction between different possible social organizations of technology. Capitalism and socialism were irrelevant because the technological *spirit* dominated both.

The significance of this position can best be pointed up by comparing Heidegger's discussion with the critique of advanced industrial society made by an important representative of the Frankfurt School, Herbert Marcuse. What makes the comparison interesting is that both positions show the

[12] See, among many others, the work of Jacques Ellul and Claude Lévi-Strauss.

[13] Novalis, "Christianity or Europe" in *Hymns to the Night and Other Selected Writings*, Library of Liberal Arts, 1960, trans. C. E. Passage, pp. 53-54: "reduced the infinite creative music of the universe to the monotonous clatter of a monstrous mill."

303

enormous influence of the traditional Germanic critique of modernity, which in many ways cut across the ideological lines dividing conservatives and radicals. Marcuse's work, for example, expressed sharp antagonism to the compulsiveness of man's effort to dominate nature and himself, to man's need to prove himself by constantly testing the value of his existence against some external object or person and proving it by conquest. His critique of the contemporary norms of performance and productivity, which made human value depend upon the individual's ability to produce and thus augment the quantity of useful objects, paralleled Heidegger's critical characterization of *Technik* as the drive to extract ever greater amounts of usable energy from nature. Marcuse's utopian vision was also strikingly similar to Heidegger's in its goal of overcoming man's constant Promethean struggle to become and allowing him simply to be, liberated from time and united with god, man, and nature.[14] Marcuse's image, derived from Schiller, of "unproductive" and "useless" play that did not attack and overwhelm reality but toyed with it in an easy give-and-take, was the counterpart of Heidegger's concept of *Gelassenheit*.

The differences, however, were as significant as the similarities. Like many cultural conservatives, Heidegger attributed the evils of technological modernity to a set of ideas largely independent of any context of economic and social conditions. In the last analysis, *Technik* symbolized a state of mind, a set of norms and beliefs that, as an autonomous intellectual structure, was determinative of social reality. So, while Heidegger asserted that man could not save himself from the increasing threat of *Technik* by his own efforts, since it was only in the power of Being to accomplish this, man could help the process of salvation along by reflecting on the essence of *Technik* as a mode of disclosure—i.e., as only one among many possible modes—and thereby undermine its grip on the modern consciousness. By contrast, Marcuse's neo-

14 Marcuse, *Eros and Civilization*, p. 147.

Marxist analysis linked the ethic of technological mastery, however loosely, to a repressively organized society and argued, however bleak the empirical prospect, that social reorganization could alter that ethic.

It is perhaps even going too far to suggest that Heidegger considered the various possible social organizations of technology as irrelevant to the issue of the domination of *Technik*; his whole treatment of the subject was too abstract to consider such problems. Unlike other critics of technology who held positions not far different from his, he did not produce arguments to the effect that, for example, existing socialism was as concerned with modernizing and maximizing production as capitalism, or that modern industrial society had imperatives built into it that transcended the differences between forms of property ownership. His theory of *Technik* was a kind of "vulgar idealism" in its virtually exclusive focus on technique as global spirit. Nevertheless, it was not without its own specific, though unwitting, social bearing.

A nostalgia for the pre-industrial life of the peasantry and artisanate permeated Heidegger's work. It was present, however muted, even in *Being and Time*, many of whose examples of everyday activity were taken from the crafts of premodern town life. It broke through to the surface in his 1936 essay on "Hölderlin and the Essence of Poetry," with its lovingly painstaking description of the peasant boot painted by Van Gogh. In Heidegger's second phase, examples of authenticity were drawn from the homely life of village, farm, and forest, his own native environment of the Black Forest. In *Die Technik*, for example, Heidegger contrasted the attitude of violation inherent in the extraction of coal and minerals from the land with the peasant's reverent activity of sowing, in which he left the seed to the earth's powers of growth and carefully watched over its development. While left-wing critics differentiated between a neutral technology, on the one hand, and its uses, purposes, and controlling agents, on the other, including in their vision of utopia a technology subservient to the collectivity and to human purposes, while even other non-Marxist critics did not believe it possible or desirable to turn the clock back, Heidegger's concrete imagery was almost wholly reactionary.

In adopting Heidegger's conception of the technological spirit, Boss in effect undercut the real social bearing of his ideas about the causes and therapy of mental illness. Boss obviously put far more weight than Freud's biological theory allowed on the role of environmental factors in repression and the development of positive identity and self-esteem. The sources of repression were social beliefs mediated by the family. Family and society had a far greater role than Freud had seen in creating (or perpetuating) needs by the frustration of other needs. Any existential theory would stress the role of the individual's willing acquiescence to external authority out of the need for the ontological security of identity that that authority conferred. But for Boss the active critical role of the external authority was an equal contributing agent. From the Heideggerian conception of man's duty as the "primary world-openness," which "granted everything that is the possibility of appearing," Boss derived a simple ethical theory of social relationships that demanded the same receptive, reverent attitude toward other human beings and the free development of their possibilities. However, instead of analyzing the reasons for the absence or failure of such relationships, he attributed them simply to the egocentric and exploitative attitudes of modern science and technology, which left individuals isolated without either communal or transcendent support.

Unlike Heidegger, Boss did not seek his counter-model to modern technological society in the past. He turned to Indian philosophy as an example of the spiritual attitude that by combatting material striving and egotism could lead to the calm, anxiety-free equilibrium of the wise men he had come to admire during his stay in India. In so doing, Boss was part of a long-standing European tradition, one that received new impetus in the twentieth century, of seeking in the East what was lacking in the West. He believed that he had discovered in Hindu philosophy a living tradition that incorporated the truths that Heidegger had only recently begun to reveal in the West.

But his preference for Eastern thought was very far from absolute; his reflections on his trips to India and Indonesia revealed a strong ambivalence. On the one hand, his idealization of Hindu philosophy and his critique of the dislocation of established ways of life caused by industrialization led him to statements of regret about the modernization of India; he even pointed out approvingly that the caste-system preserved men from the metaphysical anxiety created by the open-ended indeterminateness of a highly mobile society.[15] On the other hand, as a cultured humanitarian and a true exemplar of the European bourgeoisie, he was horrified at India's poverty and shocked by its inefficiency. Furthermore, he was too good an analyst not to see how traditional Indian social forms and values contributed to the development of various neuroses and psychoses, and he underlined sharply the difference between a neurotic escape into meditation, which left intact and unresolved unconscious impulses, and a mode of life built on genuine self-knowledge, emotional maturity, and choice. Without fully intending it, therefore, Boss not infrequently took very reactionary positions and then felt constrained to defend himself against charges of being an anti-scientific and anti-modern obscurantist. Caught in the assumptions of German idealism, he did not have the tools to make his thinking consistent, to begin thinking about a process of modernization that might at the same time preserve modernizing countries from the worst spiritual horrors of the Western industrial revolution.

SOCIAL CAUSATION AND ANXIETY IN BINSWANGER

There was nothing in Binswanger's work that seemed to have any implications for a theory of the social causation of mental illness. In an article on the conditions of successful

15 M. Boss, *Indienfahrt eines Psychiaters*, Pfullingen, p. 92.

psychoanalytic psychotherapy (whose goal he described in a more or less orthodox fashion as bringing the patient to take over his concealed wishes and feelings in a conscious, responsible manner), Binswanger did insist that the ability of the patient to overcome his resistances depended on whether a relationship of trust could be established between therapist and patient, and that this in turn depended in part on whether the therapist acted in such a manner that the patient could believe that he wished to help him as person, and not repair him with his knowledge and skill as if he were an object.[16] This meant that the personality and behavior of the analyst were necessary conditions of therapeutic success. But Binswanger did not elaborate on what "being helped as a person" meant even to the extent that Boss did later; nor did he draw any inferences about the causation of neurosis from his beliefs about the social prerequisites of its cure. In one of his early cases, a young girl suffering from hysterical aphonia precipitated by her mother's refusal to permit her engagement to a young man for what Binswanger called "no valid reason," he intervened by persuading the parents to permit the engagement. Here also, however, Binswanger did not even comment on the role of external frustration in precipitating a neurotic episode, though it was apparently important enough to warrant an act of what he referred to as "social psychotherapy." In fact, the farther away Binswanger moved from clinical considerations towards theoretical analysis and existential redescriptions of old case material, the more conservative his conclusions became. The reason for this lay in the nature of Heidegger's original ontological analysis, which furnished the basis of Binswanger's work.

In the case studies of *Schizophrenia*, Binswanger described his patients' inner problem as a fierce unwillingess to accept the life situations into which they had been thrown and their recourse instead to phantasy modes of ideal existence. For example,

[16] Binswanger, *Vorträge*, Bd. ii, p. 139.

"Ellen West's desperate defiance in wishing to be herself but as a different being from the one into which she had actually been thrown from the ground of her existence, shows itself not only in revolt and battle against her fate (her being a woman, her home, her social class, her desire for sweets, her tendency to get fat, finally her illness) but also in revolt against time. Insofar as she refused to become old, dull, ugly, in a word fat, she wants to stop time. . . . In her stubborn adherence to her separate self . . . which is however not her real self but a 'timeless' ethereal wish-self, she does not run away from the ground of her existence . . . but runs into it."[17]

The implication of his assertion that Ellen West was trying to escape her real self was that this self was in fact inescapable, and that her conflict was the result of her unwillingness to accept the human condition. The therapeutic goal of making her free for being authentically herself necessitated the patient's recognition and acceptance of herself as she was. "Freedom consists in the commitment of the Dasein to its own thrownness as such, non-freedom in denying it autocratically and violating it on the basis of an extravagant [*verstiegene*] ideal."[18]

This conclusion was the inevitable result of Binswanger's application of the concept of "thrownness," Heidegger's term for the givens of human existence over which Dasein had no control, the contingent necessities that Dasein in its anxiety tried to convert into metaphysical necessity. Because he did not limit the sphere of thrownness to historical situations, Binswanger's position was somewhat stronger than Heidegger's. Certain features of human existence, such as embodiment, were inescapable and unalterable, not subject to human determination. It was in this framework that Binswanger saw Freud as the theorist of the sphere of "thrownness," the one who had pointed out to men the ineradicable claims of their own bodies, their biological constitutions. If someone's ideal

[17] Binswanger, "Ellen West" in *Existence*, p. 299.
[18] Binswanger, *Being-in-the-World*, p. 321.

of spirituality precluded bodily existence, it was indeed, in Binswanger's terms, a *verstiegene* ideal. But Binswanger made no distinctions between changeable and unchangeable conditions. In the case of Ellen West he never tried to ascertain why she had come to loathe her identity and to regard it as an impediment. The result was a kind of moralizing psychiatry that, while containing some truth in its prescriptions, undercut its own effectiveness by its inability to show how its goals might be achieved.

Similar difficulties existed with Binswanger's prescription for the attainment of authentic selfhood and wholeness in the *Grundformen*. The loving mode of relationship, though the opposite of the fragmented role-determined relationships of social intercourse, was compatible with any set of social forms, since both represented fundamental dimensions of human existence. The mutual recognition of love and friendship did not supersede the exploitative and manipulative attitudes of *Nehmen-bei-Etwas* but co-existed with them. Since such mutual recognition was possible under all conditions, it had no critical implications for the forms of social organization.

This conservative social fatalism represented a contradiction in personal ideals that had consequences for psychopathology. Love was able to furnish the desired positive identity because it fulfilled two necessary conditions: in love, the beloved was recognized unconditionally "for himself," and not in virtue of some extraneous quality or some condition that had to be met to make him worthy; at the same time he was also recognized as "everything that I called good" for the lover. For the lover, then, the beloved represented the indissoluble concrete unity of the unique and the universal: the universal qualities were so fused with the individual person that he became their sole possible embodiment. But as a social actor the individual did not occupy this exalted position. As interchangeable embodiments of social roles, social individuals had neither uniqueness—since role designations were general categories that could be occupied by many—nor universality—since roles were determinate and limited.

Thus the two identities—that of beloved and that of "person"—were contradictory. In Binswanger's case studies the contradiction, in somewhat different form, emerged as the condition of pathology. Occasionally he remarked in his discussion of his patients that there was little if any sign of the dual mode of love in their relationship to others. He did not connect this, however, to the fact that the patients had internalized self-images that made it impossible for them to think of themselves either as good in themselves or as embodying some objective, let alone ultimate, value. In cases where sufficient background information was supplied, these self-images were closely related to negative religious and socio-economic group designations; the designations were mediated and reinforced by identifications and conflicts within the family. Thus Ellen West defined herself negatively as a "fat Jewish bourgeoise" longing for, but by definition unable to attain, "Aryan spirituality." Jürg Zünd's sexual desires stamped him in the eyes of those who mattered and in his own eyes as a "proletarian type" who longed to be a member of the upper classes but who was constantly threatened by the "dirty" impulses of his own body with being declassed. These identifications with socially low-valued groups were the very roots of the patient's aspirations toward universal value embodied in their respective ideals, but also the obstacles to their attainment.

At the very least, the cases indicated that certain types of role-classifications and identifications connected with traditional ethnic and religious divisions and functional and status-groupings were not compatible with the positive self-acceptance necessary for the lover and friend. This alone ought to have been sufficient to make Binswanger realize that "thrownness" was not a monolithic concept, that distinctions had to be made between the limitations of human finitude per se and the extra limitations imposed by some individuals on others in different historical and social conditions. From there it might have been possible to generalize further about the nature of the external factors contributing to the formation

311

of destructive self-identifications and feelings of contingency and about their interrelationship with internal feelings. With his thinking circumscribed by the original Heideggerian perspective, however, Binswanger was unable to take even the first step in this direction. It was necessary to transcend Heidegger's polarity between an inert, determining factical situation and a self with fixed unitary desire to escape itself, in order to make room for the observed data of environmental forces. Of the figures discussed in this work, only Sartre was prepared to do this.

SARTRE: THE MARXIST APPROACH TO THE EXISTENTIAL DILEMMA

In order to found the possibility of social commitment, Sartre had to modify the original existential explanation of bad faith by introducing the other as a causal factor in alienation. In the biography of Baudelaire, Sartre's main theme had been that the poet, rather than being a victim, had exactly the life he deserved because he freely created his own disabilities and conflicts. At the very same time that he was carrying out an existential psychoanalysis on the lines of his original conception, however, he was exploring a different approach to understanding the role of the environment in the fundamental project. *Reflections on the Jewish Question*,[19] published even before *Baudelaire*, introduced new considerations into the existential problem that already showed the effects of his initiation into Marxist thinking.

Reflections presented a concrete example of a position that Sartre only later generalized and made explicit: the feeling of contingency was never experienced in a vacuum as an abstract "metaphysical" emotion but always "in situation," that is, within a specific environment pressing against the individual. The idea of the "situation" was nothing new for Sartre; it was to be found in *Being and Nothingness* as an expression

[19] Published in English as *Anti-Semite and Jew*, trans. G. J. Becker, New York, 1948.

for the individual's particular being-in-the-world. In *Reflections*, however, its use represented a radical shift in perspective. Causal responsibility was placed on the external factors in the situation for the individual's bad faith, in this case for the inauthenticity of both the Jew and the anti-Semite. The popular, polemical style of the essay precluded systematic analysis but only sharpened the new point of view: "It is the Christians," Sartre proclaimed, "who have created the Jew."[20]

Such a statement would have been inconceivable on the basis of the philosophy of *Being and Nothingness*. In attempting to relate that philosophy to his political and social observations, however, Sartre saw that the sense of contingency of individuals in society was obviously related to their exclusion from and/or their negative valuation by the majority or by the holders of power in that society. Certainly such individuals collaborated in their own alienation by identifying with the image of them held by the majority, i.e., by accepting the truth and legitimacy of the majority's authority and judgment. Nevertheless, the *initiative* was in the hands of the others, the powerholders, either to accept Jews as equals, as free persons, or to treat them as devalued objects with defined, inescapable natures.

Indeed Sartre went too far in this direction. There was a basic circularity in his argument because he defined as Jews only those who responded to the anti-Semites' negative picture of them with some sort of defense, whether of shame or defiant pride, both of which implied at the very least a tacit recognition of the moral authority of the other. For Sartre there could be no internal or rational reason for being a Jew. He did include in his sketch the portrait of the "authentic Jew," but, consistent with the dilemma of *Being and Nothingness*, the authentic Jew was a purely negative character who did nothing specifically Jewish. His authenticity lay in his ability to live his life without being swayed from an independently chosen course by the labels and motives that anti-Semites attributed to him. Nevertheless, his description of the

20 *Ibid.*, p. 68.

defensive reactions of many Jews was acute and insightful; among other things, he convincingly demonstrated how the character structure of the defensive Jew often parodied the stereotype of the anti-Semite as a consequence of the stereotyping.

More interesting from a theoretical point of view was Sartre's explanation of anti-Semitism. Not only the victims but the victimizers, the supposed subjects, were themselves objects, or victims, "in situation." His psychological description of them was couched in the language of *Being and Nothingness*, somewhat simplified. "There are people," Sartre wrote of anti-Semites, "who are attracted by the durability of a stone. They wish to be massive and impenetrable, they wish not to change. . . ."[21] This desire, however, was not interpreted as an ontological category, a universal given of human nature. In the case of French anti-Semites, the anxiety that gave rise to this desire stemmed from their precarious relationship to what in France was the supreme value and the source of value: the possession of real property.

"Many anti-Semites—the majority, perhaps—belong to the lower middle class of the towns; they are functionaries, office workers, small businessmen, who possess nothing. It is in opposing themselves to the Jew that they suddenly become conscious of being proprietors: in representing the Jew as a robber, they put themselves in the enviable position of people who could be robbed. Since the Jew wishes to take France from them it follows that France must belong to them. Thus they have chosen anti-Semitism as a means of establishing their status as possessors. . . . They own less than the gentleman-farmer of Périgord or the large-scale farmer of the Beauce? That doesn't matter. All they have to do is nourish a vengeful anger against the robbers of Israel and they feel at once in possession of the entire country. . . .

"The anti-Semite chooses the irremediable out of fear of being free; he chooses mediocrity out of fear of being alone,

21 *Ibid.*, p. 19.

and out of pride he makes of this irremediable mediocrity a rigid aristocracy. To this end he finds the existence of the Jew absolutely necessary. Otherwise to whom would he be superior? Indeed it is vis-à-vis the Jew and the Jew alone that the anti-Semite realizes that he has rights. If by some miracle all the Jews were exterminated as he wishes, he would find himself nothing but a concierge or a shopkeeper in a strongly hierarchical society in which the quality of 'true Frenchman' would be at a low valuation because everyone would possess it."[22]

This analysis had clear historical limitations: it omitted upper middle class and aristocratic anti-Semitism, aspects of which Sartre had himself explored in *Childhood of a Leader*. However incomplete, it nonetheless suggested a model of explanation that historicized existential categories, and provided a foundation for a social theory of contingency. While it was reasonable on Sartre's assumptions to call for the inauthentic Jew to become authentic by refusing to define himself by the labels of others, it followed also that the social and political situation made even the "authentic" Jew's choices turn against him. It was no use being subjectively authentic if objective circumstances made the realization of one's choices impossible. The only way to liberate the Jew, therefore, was to end anti-Semitism, not utter existential exhortations to the Jew.

To do this it was necessary to destroy the conditions that produced the anti-Semite. According to Sartre, anti-Semitism was an attempt by the low in status to realize national unity in the face of the hierarchical division of society by raising passions against a common enemy to a heat that would melt the barriers between the classes and end the self-hatred of the non-possessors. Such a solution was doomed to failure because the economic and social divisions persisted; their abolition took place only in phantasy. The only effective cure was the real abolition of class society and the institution of an

22 *Ibid.*, pp. 25-28.

egalitarianism in which the possession of property would no longer be available to encourage the mystical symbiosis of man with his "goods" that generated the sense of being and non-being in contemporary French life.

Reflections bore the marks of Sartre's transitional dilemma. On the one hand, he could not, in the wake of the horrors of Fascism, interpret Jewish anxiety in terms of the absolute freedom of *Being and Nothingness*. On the other hand, he was not yet prepared to abandon his belief in the reality of the ontological problem, in which the anxiety that caused inauthenticity was the "pure" anguish of metaphysical nothingness. The curious result was a distinction between two types of anxiety-experience according to social origins: the uneasiness of the Jew or the anti-Semite was social, not metaphysical, while metaphysical anxiety was the "special privilege" of the "Aryan" governing classes who were sure of their rights and firmly rooted in the world.

This was something of a false distinction because it ignored the fact that "social" anxiety was still concerned with the "metaphysical" problem of identity, while "metaphysical" anxiety was always experienced in a *social* situation, since the individual always existed in a social structure governed by a hierarchy of norms that defined for him what wholeness, acceptability, and self-esteem depended on. The real distinction Sartre was pointing to was between an internally and an externally directed form of anxiety, the external form involving the belief that concrete others actually incarnated the value whose attainment would confer the sense of being. Ontological anxiety as such was primarily a philosophical construct rather than a real experience, a limiting concept portrayable only in a fictional form such as *Nausea* or in a work like *Being and Nothingness*. Sartre's awkward and inaccurate distinction served to dismiss a problem he was not then able to solve but that he could not allow to block the urgent need to enter the political arena.

The problem is not difficult to state. Sartre did not believe at this time that social reconstruction would eliminate the ontological quest, the quest for Being. Even under oppression it was the victim's genuine belief—not simply his coerced assent—that validated the oppressor's authority. This represented a free choice, a will to believe, on the part of the victim. On the other hand, it was absurd to equate the situation of oppressed and oppressor; it was impossible to believe that the Jew's particular sense of contingency and his flight from himself could exist without anti-Semitism. Sartre might have moved towards a theory that, taking the ontological need as a universal tendency, would point out how the dominant social groups internalized ideals that their social position gave them the means to strive for realistically, while hierarchical or ethnic exclusion or devaluation prevented other groups from fulfilling such ideals and thus created in them psychological feelings of nothingness. He did not do this. Instead, in postponing the problem of metaphysical anxiety to a period when all men were liberated and as socially secure as the present ruling classes, Sartre was really serving notice that it was one-sidedly false to look at the problem ahistorically and from the point of view of the isolated individual alone, as he had done in *Being and Nothingness*.

However, because Sartre resorted to the artificial expedient of splitting in order to rid himself of his former overemphasis on individual responsibility, he came to equate the problem of contingency and its overcoming exclusively with that of individuals and groups excluded from the mainstream of bourgeois society. It was not solely the result of his political position and identification with oppressed groups, but also the consequence of the theoretical re-orientation his moral stance had produced, that the existential psychoanalyses in the work of Sartre's second phase were of excluded or marginal types—members of minorities, orphans, and writers. All of them, including the writers of bourgeois origins, had in common the fact that they had been prevented in one way or another from integrating smoothly into the ruling class and its values. The only member of the "governing class" to figure as the subject of an existential analysis appeared in a story written before Sartre's theoretical shift. Afterwards, the psychology of the ruling bourgeoisie lay outside his explanatory scheme, which required agents external to the self to generate by oppression the victim's sense of contingency. The external agents could not themselves be victims.

The idea of a social contribution to the ontological problem raised yet another issue. Economic, social, and political factors were now seen by Sartre to be related to the absolutization of figures as the ideal Other who could confer identity. There was, in other words, a connection between social status and power over the material conditions of life, and the metaphysical attributes of absolute freedom and necessity with which the ideal Other was endowed. Conversely there appeared to be a relationship between material dependence and social insecurity, and the sense of contingency or precariousness of the sense of objective worth. Just what these connections were was obviously a crucial matter for the existentialist social theory that could succeed *Being and Nothingness*. Instead of turning to such issues in a systematic way, however, Sartre approached them through yet another existential psychoanalysis of a writer, Jean Genet.

Saint Genet, Actor and Martyr, was Sartre's longest and most ambitious work since *Being and Nothingness*. Compared with his *Baudelaire*, it showed how far he had gone in the direction of social theory. Like *Baudelaire, Saint Genet* was concerned with the writer's self-conscious choice of what he himself regarded as evil. In both cases Sartre explained the choice as serving the dual and contradictory purpose of declaring independence while simultaneously affirming dependence upon authority for setting standards and conferring recognition. The difference was that Baudelaire had excluded himself from the Good because of his jealous resentment at his mother's remarriage, while Genet was excluded from the Good by the peremptory judgment of society. Yet Sartre was at this point still concerned to preserve the balance between inner and outer in his explanation of Genet's fate, suggesting a pithy formula that summarized the essence of his position: "What is important is not what people make of us but what we ourselves make of what they have made of us."[23] Genet's acceptance of society's verdict was as much responsible for his fate as the verdict itself.

A good deal of emphasis, however, was placed on that verdict. It was the objective circumstances of his birth and early life, within the context of the social values of his rural traditional French surroundings, that created for Genet a specific, and negative, being-for-others that he believed in and adopted for himself. Without a mother, he belonged to no one and was therefore nothing, the ward of the National Foundling Society to whom he was merely a number. Being no one, he possessed nothing in a society in which having was the criterion for a sense of the solidity and permanence of one's being. Forced by his anxiety to steal in order to possess without being dependent on the bounty of others, he was branded a thief, and he accepted that definition of himself, despite the innocence of his motives, because he had, by his activity, fulfilled the criteria for the role of thief in a society whose norms he accepted.

More than before in his writings, Sartre put great weight on the helplessness of the child, though not so much a biological as a moral and intellectual helplessness. The young Genet could not defend himself with the perception of the hypocrisy and weakness of his elders, which he could not yet discern. Needing orientation in an alien world, he took their words for absolute law. Adults had the initiative in the world of the child and never lost it.[24] If Genet later turned against this world, it was only to affirm as his will a criminal identity that others had conferred on him.

As psychology, Sartre's analyses of Genet's writings were obsessively brilliant. As a set of clues for a middle-range socio-historical theory of identity anxiety, his explanations

23 J.-P. Sartre, *Saint Genet, Actor and Martyr*, trans. B. Frechtman. New York, 1963, p. 49.

24 *Ibid.*, p. 21.

were at once too particular and too general. On the one hand, he convincingly evoked the narrow piety and traditionalism and the almost symbiotic relationship to the soil of the Morvan peasant society in which Genet spent his early years. In such a society the accidental circumstances of Genet's birth necessarily made him appear as an outsider and hence as illegitimate in a fundamental existential sense. On the other hand, he explained the readiness of the people to attribute an unchangeable thief's nature to Genet as a product of their Manichean attitude towards Good and Evil; Manicheism served as a defense against their own potentially anti-social impulses by projecting them as a permanently evil nature on others. Sartre tried to connect his Manicheism to *les justes*, the "good folk" of traditional bourgeois society, but there was no reason to assume that this defense mechanism was peculiar to any particular socio-historical group. As a general theory of bourgeois society, *Saint Genet* was, if full of sharp aperçus, impressionistic and inadequate. But if Sartre did not prove himself a social theorist in this work, he had once again pointed in the direction in which the sociological determinants of the identity problem were to be sought.

When, however, toward the end of the 1950's Sartre did turn to systematic social theory, it was on a new basis that abandoned the original existential concerns. The *Critique of Dialectical Reason* made no mention of the ontological problem even in the sociologically modified context of his post-World War Two writings. The change was all the more striking in that Sartre preserved some of the basic terminology of *Being and Nothingness*. Thus he spoke of man as a being of need, suffering from a lack that forced him into activity in order to overcome it. This similarity of language has misled some commentators into believing that the essential line of approach had not changed from the early work. The similarity, however, was purely superficial; it could not conceal the fact that Sartre had completely reversed his theory of motivation from exclusively spiritual to crudely biological. The need to survive physically was the fundamental project of man toward the surrounding world, and the fact of material scarcity defined his relationships to other men, which were predominantly those of conflict over available resources. In contrast to the way he stated his concern about freedom in *Being and Nothingness*, Sartre was now interested, not with how men related to their own purposes and values, whether authentically or inauthentically, but with their ability to realize one very concrete, specific desire, an ability limited or enhanced by external circumstances.

The consequence of production in conditions of scarcity was inevitably, in Sartre's view, class differentiation, as the needed products turned against their producers and divided them into rich and poor, haves and have-nots. Once such differentiations were established, they became determining features of the lives of the individuals who were born into them, for though they were human actions, the forms of productive activities brought about unintended effects that as part of a system could not be altered in isolation. Men might try to break out of the system, and collective action for change was possible, but individual alternatives were limited by class situation. More frequently men lived out their lives within the coercive boundaries of class possibilities. Within these boundaries, however, a greater or lesser degree of variation was still possible, and in *Search for a Method*, Sartre criticized orthodox Marxism for its insensitivity to individual differences. Nonetheless, if Sartre preserved a role for individual psychology, it was only as a mediating discipline concerned with detailing how the individual lived his objective class situation in his own unique manner. Psychoanalysis, previously dismissed as illegitimately determinist, was now seen as the method that made it possible to understand why for the most part class prejudices, ideas, and beliefs could not be transcended; they had first been experienced in childhood when reason was too weak to be exercised independently.[25] But psychoanalysis had no special content of its own; what was

[25] J.-P. Sartre, *Critique de la raison dialectique. Précédée de question de méthode.* Paris, 1960.

321

ingrained into the child through parental authority and identification was discoverable only by Marxist, i.e., class,
analysis.

Between *Being and Nothingness* and *Critique of Dialectical
Reason*, then, Sartre's anthropology, and his conceptualization of the problem of freedom, had completely changed. The
promising middle position, which presaged a comprehensive,
balanced theory synthesizing biological, socio-historical, and
individual-idealist factors, was shattered, the balance tilted
almost completely in the direction of a very crude biology and
sociology. In this long movement from ontological to social
analysis, it remained only to relativize, by the kind of explanation called for in *Search for a Method*, his own early intellectual enterprise, the analysis of man's ontological quest.
This was one of the main purposes of the first volume of Sar-
tres' autobiography, *The Words*.

The Words was an odd book in many ways, a movingly
eloquent confession of despair and futility by a famous and
important writer who, at the age when he ought to have been
able to review his career with satisfaction, found instead that
writing was meaningless and ineffectual and that he continued
to write only because he did not know what else to do with
his life. Writing was, as he put it, his habit, his profession, and
his character; one could get rid of a neurosis, but one could
not be cured of oneself. Yet the impression could not be
escaped that though the sense of failure and fatalism were
sincere, they were nonetheless theoretically convenient to
Sartre's later intellectual position. His account of himself in
The Words was a further extension of the kind of interpretation of bourgeois society advanced in *Reflections on the Jewish Question*, which had enabled him to shift at least part of
the ontological problem from a metaphysical to a highly specific social level. Now, however, he argued in effect that the
supposedly universal ontological problem itself was an individual biographical accident. *The Words* purported to show
that the state of mind that a book like *Being and Nothingness*

322

reflected and from which it emerged was the product of peculiar family circumstances—the absence of a father to identify with—within the larger framework of a bourgeois existence cut off from material need and collective experience.

In one important sense, Sartre's interpretation did preserve an unbroken thematic line from his earliest work. His early fiction had shown his ironic but bitter contempt for the smug self-righteousness of the bourgeoisie. In *Nausea,* for example, he had characterized the town fathers of Bouville as complacently arrogant men who felt that they existed and governed by transcendent right. At this stage in his work, such descriptions had neither philosophical nor political implications; they were intended primarily as a foil for Roquentin, exemplars of the kind of inauthenticity against which he experienced the radical contingency of his own existence, his own feeling of not existing by right. In Sartre's transitional period, however, the hated self-importance of the bourgeoisie was no longer extraneous to the main theme but assumed positive theoretical significance. The bourgeois did not suffer from a consciously felt sense of contingency. As he put it in the early Marxist essay "Materialism and Revolution,"

"Any member of the ruling class is a man of divine right. Born into a class of leaders he is convinced from childhood that he is born to command, and in a certain sense, this is true, since his parents, who do command, have brought him into the world to carry on after them. A certain social function, into which he will slip as soon as he is of age, the metaphysical reality, as it were, of his person, awaits him. Thus, in his own eyes, he is a person, an *a priori* synthesis of legal right and of fact. Awaited by his peers, destined to relieve them at the appointed time, he exists because he has the right to exist."[26]

The bourgeois was the alter-ego of the proletariat and colonial native, the firm rock in comparison with which they

[26] J.-P. Sartre, "Materialism and Revolution," in *Literary and Philosophical Essays,* New York, 1962, p. 229.

323

experienced their own insubstantiality of being. For those whose existence consisted of exploitation by the bourgeoisie "each single event in his life repeats to him that he has no right to exist. His parents have not brought him into the world for any particular purpose, but rather by chance, *for no reason.*"[27] The traditional family thus played the central role in transmitting to the individual the sense of his selfhood as determined by his social situation.

By his own theory, Sartre was an anomaly of bourgeois development, since he did not, despite his comfortable bourgeois birth, participate in the bourgeois sense of divine right. Not only did this circumstance not embarrass him, however; it was precisely the point he wanted to make. For, if his own development was anomalous, his ideas, insofar as they reflected and did not transcend that development, were of no general significance. His development was anomalous precisely because he did not grow up in a traditionally structured bourgeois family.

Sartre's father had died when Jean-Paul was an infant; he was brought up by a docile mother in the household of an imposing-looking but doting grandfather who demanded no obedience. Sartre attributed the absence of a sense of mission to this set of circumstances, and to his own consequent lack of a superego. If by the latter he meant that he did not suffer from a sense of guilt or that he did not have ambivalent feelings about authority figures, he was surely mistaken; but his attention was on something else. Sartre understood the superego both in the psychoanalytic sense, which made it the heir of the Oedipus complex, the incarnation of objective ego-ideals and prohibitions derived from identification with the father, and in the existentialist sense, in which it figured as the formulation of the sense of permanent identity. From both of these points of view, Sartre was left deficient because of his unique family situation: "If my father had lived, I would know my rights and my duties; he died and I do not

[27] *Ibid.*, p. 230.

know them. I have no right because love overwhelms me; I have no duties since I give out of love. Just one mandate: to please; everything in order to show it."[28]

In his chameleon-like existence, in which he reflected back whatever he thought was expected of him or whatever he could invent to please, no permanent core of self that felt genuine could develop. And despite the feeling of dependence on his grandfather for his very sense of being—which, contrary to Sartre's claim that he lacked aggressiveness, had generated in him strong feelings of hostility[29]—he could also have the feeling of being potentially everything and actually nothing. "I was," he wrote, "the very incarnation of indeterminacy."[30] The writing vocation that developed later was simply the last in a series of roles played by the child actor, the one that he tried to become to fill his emptiness, but that remained forever external, like an ill-fitting suit of clothes.

In this way Sartre argued that the basic themes of *Being and Nothingness* were merely disguised pieces of an autobiography. *The Words* brought to a climax the dissolution of Sartre's early existentialism. On the one hand, the "pure" metaphysical anxiety Sartre still talked about in *Reflections* no longer existed; Sartre's own self-conscious concern with the problem of being was the result of an anomaly of bourgeois development without universal significance. On the other hand, the anxiety and bad faith of individuals and groups in society was the consequence of victimization by *les justes*. Sartre had attributed the practice of scapegoating to the Manichean attitude of *les justes*, who could not face their own potential negativity. His own sociology, however, displayed a Manicheism of its own, a mythology of a totally self-

[28] J.-P. Sartre, *Les Mots*, Paris, 1964, p. 22.

[29] *Ibid.*, p. 29. Sartre's attacks on the sentimental humanism of the bourgeois intellectual were certainly derived in part from this hostility to his grandfather, a retired professor and devotee of literature. Cf. H. S. Hughes, *The Obstructed Path, French Social Thought in the Years of Desperation, 1930-1960*, New York, 1967, p. 172.

[30] Sartre, *Les Mots*, p. 29.

contained, metaphysically and psychologically impervious bourgeoisie, who, with or without malevolent intent, were wholly responsible for the identity anxiety of victim groups. The net result was that the scope of the original existential insight into the nature of motivation was severely limited without any corresponding enrichment in the understanding of its general context. Heidegger, Binswanger, and Boss had ended in the idealist horn of the old dilemma, leveling concrete social and historical differences and subsuming them all under the rubric of finitude, while contradictorily blaming alienation on such vague demons as "modernization" and technology. Sartre, for all the complexity and sophisticated nuancing of his psychological insight, ended in Marxist environmentalism.

The inadequacy of the socio-historical context to which Sartre had reduced the conditions of the existential problem was even more obvious when the question was raised about the reasons for the historical emergence of existentialism as a European phenomenon in the twentieth century. The simultaneous over-generality and over-particularity of his explanations became clear in a number of ways. The social conditions to which Sartre implicitly ascribed the origins of existential anxiety and bad faith were in their broader form the general features of Western European social structure for well over a century, and in their narrower form the result of the peculiar development of French society, with its relatively slow industrial evolution, its continuing heavy emphasis on landed wealth, and its strongly rooted peasant culture. Neither was sufficient to account for an intellectual movement that, despite its obvious nineteenth-century origins, was a specifically twentieth-century phenomenon affecting both Western and Central Europe. Furthermore, it was obvious that the details of Sartre's biography could hardly exhaust the causes of the widespread concern with problems of meaninglessness and purposelessness. It is to this general issue that we must then turn before closing this study.

326

THIS BOOK has been primarily concerned with analyzing the relationship of existentialism to psychoanalysis from within, as the clarification and deepening of certain of the insights and dilemmas that constituted the substance of the modernist revolution in thought and art at the turn of the twentieth century. No real attempt has been made to relate these developments to social and historical change, though some mention has been made of certain crucial events—the turning point of the First World War is perhaps the most obvious and important one. It is evident that profound changes were taking place in the social and political basis of belief and identity throughout this period. The collapse of liberal rationalist values, beliefs, and self-confidence under the impact of conservative and populist assaults from the Right and Marxist attacks from the Left, as well as the impact from internal changes within the middle class itself, is being ever more precisely documented in its relationship to cultural change.[31] Nonetheless, a good deal more work in social history must be done, especially for the period after the First World War, before any reasonable account can be given for the emergence of existentialist concerns in self-conscious form and for the changed structure of the self they manifest as compared to that of Freudian psychoanalysis. Any remarks made here can be only suggestive and speculative.

At the outset, it is necessary to be clear about what one is trying to explain, for there are at least two separate, if interrelated, issues involved; existential philosophy as a body of thought, including the fictional and psychological examples employed by existentialists for illustrative purposes, and the clinical case studies that suggested to practicing psychiatrists

[31] See above all Ringer's book on the *German Mandarins* and the articles by Carl Schorske on the birth of modernism in fin-de-siècle Vienna, "Politics and the Psyche in *fin-de-siècle* Vienna," *American Historical Review*, 66 (1960-1961), pp. 930-946; "The Transformation of the Garden: Ideal and Society in Austrian Literature," *AHR*, 72 (1966-1967), pp. 1283-1320.

the need for new approaches and categories of description and explanation. So far as the second is concerned, much rigorous investigation, including conceptual and statistical analysis, is necessary to test the impression, widespread in psychoanalytic and other circles, that the types of neurotic disorders have indeed changed over the past sixty or so years from a preponderance of hysteria, obsessional neurosis, and phobias to a predominance of problems about meaninglessness, anxiety, and identity. While there is broad agreement that the presenting complaints of patients are different, there is little consensus about the significance of this fact, about whether, for example, the neurotic population has actually changed or whether it is a matter of new questions being asked in the light of new concepts developed from advancing research. An investigation to resolve this issue, should it yield the former conclusion, would have to be followed by an intensive analysis of the familial and social backgrounds of the cases in order to see if general structures and changing patterns can be discovered. These tasks lie in the domain of psychology and sociology and so outside the scope of the present work.

So far as existentialist philosophy and fiction are concerned, a historical sociology of knowledge presents its own serious difficulties. Existentialism was a cross-national European phenomenon. Despite the personal, social, and national differences among the existentialists, despite their mutual refusal to be classified together, there is a central core of common concern that demands an explanation broad enough to cover developments in a number of European countries. Efforts to understand Heidegger's work in terms of defeat and social upheaval in Germany after the First World War, or in terms of the sense of crisis of a "mandarin" class whose traditional position had been thoroughly undermined by the transformation of the conservative Empire; efforts to explain Sartre's ontology as resulting from the French defeat and occupation during World War II, or France's sense of isolation and anxiety in the inter-war years, or the marginal situation of French middle class intellectuals, educated to revolutionary ideals but outflanked on the left by Marxist claimants to the revolutionary heritage in the new politics of the twentieth century—all must fail, apart from other inadequacies, because of their specificity, though they may be parts of a broader explanation. In view of the vast amount of work necessary for an adequate explanation, the following discussion will be limited largely to those indications for a social and historical understanding to be found in the writings of the figures examined in this study. These indications will be compared with the conclusions of an essay by Herbert Marcuse that has addressed itself to an explanation of the very changes in psychic structure discussed in the present work, an essay with the suggestive title of "The Obsolescence of Psychoanalysis."

Despite the generally ahistorical character of Freud's theories, he made one very interesting historical point about the neuroses. He believed that the neurotic forms that were the subject of psychoanalytic theory were in part at least the result of the breakdown of communal religious faith and observance. Dogma and ritual, public belief and public ceremonial, were being replaced by secular ego-ideals, superego prohibitions, and the private rituals of the neuroses. Freud stressed the difference between the public and the private nature of the rituals, but the corollaries of these differences were differences in agencies of control that had shifted from public, external, and institutional to personal, internal, and categorical.[32] Ego-ideal and superego thus represented not only the form that control took but the form of individuation as well.

The socio-historical underpinnings of this character structure were not pointed out as such by Freud, though they were directly part of psychoanalytic theory itself. The superego was the internalized representative of a father who was the ruler

[32] For an interesting discussion of this whole issue in historical perspective see M. Walzer, *The Revolution of the Saints*, Cambridge, Mass., 1965, p. 303.

of the family, a genuine embodiment of authority and autonomy, and the chief intermediary between the child and social norms. This family structure was characteristic of a relatively stable middle class existence in the countries of Western and Central Europe in the middle of the nineteenth century, where private and family businesses and professions predominated and son followed in father's occupation or pursued one of a number of traditional middle class possibilities. The assimilation by the European bourgeoisie of elements of the aristocratic life-style reinforced patriarchal authority and the strength of tradition. If, as later psychoanalysts were to argue, Freud underemphasized the role of the mother and the enormous significance for development of the child's pre-oedipal ties to her, it was in part just because of the centrality of the father's authority in socialization in the nineteenth-century bourgeois family. It may even be ventured as a hypothesis that this had something to do with the discovery of psychoanalytic theory itself. The character structure at the heart of Freud's discovery was one of ambivalence and conflict— categorical obedience to the father alongside rebellion and competition. The familial root of this structure lay in the conflicting demands made upon sons by a traditional paternal authority for both unconditional respect and obedience, on the one hand, and the critical autonomy necessary for effective competition in the economic and political markets, on the other.

These contradictory demands were embodied in ego-ideal and superego. While found throughout Western and Central Europe, they were particularly characteristic of the traditional family in Germany and Austria; historically, this represented the more extensive carryover of pre-modern social and political institutions in Central as compared to Western Europe. If to these factors are added the increasing political exclusion and decreasing prestige of the liberal bourgeoisie in the Austro-Hungarian Empire, and the particular situation of the Jewish father, who demanded respect at home but had none in the streets, one has a set of conditions in which it was

possible to distance oneself sufficiently from paternal authority to examine it consciously while yet realizing its effective
importance.

The structure of the self manifested in existentialism included a weakened ego without strongly internalized definitions or goals, desirous of identification with and assimilation
to social roles and wider collectivities, and at the mercy of a
host of external forces tending to drain it of its residual individuality. Scattered throughout the existentialists' writings
were suggestions of the social context of this personality
structure. Some have already been touched upon. Thinly
veiled behind the abstractions of Heidegger's description of
inauthenticity in *Being and Time* was a picture of urban mass
society in which the origins of authority and the arbiters of
culture appeared so diffused within society as to be unlocat-
able yet everywhere. Standards of behavior were not internal
and determinate but external and relative.

"In one's concern with what one has taken hold of, whether with, for or against the Others, there is a constant care as
to the way one differs from them, whether that difference is
merely one that is to be evened out, whether one's own
Dasein has lagged behind the Others and wants to catch up
in relationship to them, or whether one's Dasein already has
some priority over them and sets out to keep them
suppressed."[33]

Heidegger's and Boss's critiques of technology also pointed
toward concrete social change. It was suggested in the contrast between the two sources that Heidegger drew upon for
his illustrations: peasant and small town artisan life, on the
one hand, urban life, on the other; but it emerged most clearly in Boss's observations about India. He wrote explicitly
about the breakup of traditional Indian society, with its
rigidly authoritarian, hierarchical family and caste system, in
the face of industrial modernization and its demands for extreme geographical and social mobility, for flexibility in occu-

[33] Heidegger, *Being and Time*, pp. 163-164.

pation choice and for rapid adaptability to new conditions. The role of family elders in choosing wives and occupations for the younger members was giving way under the impact of these changes, and with it all the established guidelines. In his analysis of Indian developments, however, Boss's constant pole of comparison was Europe. He saw India evolving in the direction that the West had already traversed, and it is clear that for him those were developments that had occurred since Freud's early discoveries.

These admittedly fragmentary points make an interesting comparison with the general picture of economic and social change drawn by Marcuse. He argued that at the very point of its maturation, psychoanalytic theory already belonged more to the past than to its own time.[34] Under the conditions of advanced industrial society the role of the father in socialization was diminishing, as the individual and family enterprise declined in economic importance. Despite the increased freedom of choice and occupation and geographical location, however, this change did not result in a real increase in personal autonomy. The father's role was being taken over by anonymous social institutions—schools, the mass media, public entertainment and above all by the new productive and consumptive imperatives of large-scale economic organizations. "We seem," wrote Marcuse, "to be facing a reality which psychoanalysis only glimpsed—*the fatherless society*."[35] The result of this decline in the father's real authority was the absence of an object to identify with and the consequent failure of a strongly individuated autonomous ego to develop. Instead of being internalized, the ego-ideal was divorced from the ego and "transferred onto a collective ideal."[36] This meant regression to a more primitive level of development.

Marcuse's sociological conclusions were not really new; they were in the main restatement of ideas worked out thirty

[34] H. Marcuse, "Das Veralten der Psychoanalyse," *Kultur und Gesellschaft*, 2, Suhrkampf, 1963, p. 86.

[35] *Ibid.*, p. 96.   [36] *Ibid.*, p. 104.

years before by Max Horkheimer and Erich Fromm in *Studies on Authority and Family*. The same year that Marcuse's paper was first delivered, there appeared a book by the German psychiatrist Alexander Mitscherlich called *Society Without the Father*, which bore the clear influence of the Frankfurt School work on social change. The novelty of Marcuse's essay was the application of this work to the American scene and particularly to the recently publicized syndrome of the "identity crisis." The striking thing, however, was not the contemporary linking of social change and identity anxiety but the fact that the original work of the existentialists appeared or was being written at the same time as Fromm and Horkheimer were reaching their conclusions about the transformation of classical liberal bourgeois society —the inter-war period.

Existentialism and the theory of mass society were born at the same time. This coincidence raises the question of whether the developments described in the latter can in any way account for the former. Once again, there can be no attempt in the present work to make a full-scale evaluation of the theories of *Studies on Authority and Family*. I will offer only a number of suggestions that perhaps bear further investigation.

Fromm and Horkheimer were primarily concerned with the failure of the "European" (i.e., German) bourgeoisie and proletariat to withstand Fascism, and their ready surrender of individual autonomy to an authoritarian regime. Their work, however, bore directly on the more general issue of the fate of group and individual self-esteem in European society in relation to social structure after World War I. The assigning of value to merit, defined in terms of productive achievement and accumulation, was historically connected with the bourgeoisie's struggle against the aristocracy and the latter's value standard of birth. Individual achievement was thus the basis of positive identity; personal worth was never given or guaranteed but had to be earned, and in a competitive, accumulative framework of goals, achievement and success

333

were not absolute but measurable only relative to others. These developments, however, were neither universal nor uniform throughout Western and Central Europe; they were overlaid with a host of factors of varying importance in different European countries: slow rates of capitalist and/or industrial development, persistence of more traditional economic sectors side by side with the new, assimilation by the middle classes themselves of certain traditionally aristocratic values and attitudes, which gave bourgeois life a far greater degree of traditional formalism in Europe than it had in America. "Modernization" was a complex, uneven process and European society was never so fluid, mobile, or anti-traditionally progressive as abstract liberal social theory suggested. The economic transition from individual entrepreneurial capitalism to large-scale finance and corporate capitalism gravely endangered the sources of self-value in late nineteenth-century Continental bourgeois society as achievement became increasingly de-individualized and collectivized. But it did more than this; it put great pressure on the more traditional sources of identity as well by further undermining the status and economic position of the more economically conservative and/or dependent sectors of the bourgeoisie. Nor were these developments caused solely by economic changes; accompanying social and political changes, or threats of change, further eroded the position, security, and self-esteem of these sectors of the middle class, as proletariat and socialist organizations threatened to overthrow or alter the political structures with which they had identified themselves. The First World War accelerated or crystallized trends in these directions that were underway earlier.

Indications of these pressures on the relatively stagnant or declining and in any case threatened sectors of European society can be found throughout the work of the existentialists. Boss spoke of the breakup of the Swiss *Gemeinde*, the closed, parochial community with its tightly organized civic and business elites, its traditional forms, and the central role played within it by religion. Heidegger expressed his distress at the encroachment of large-scale industrial technology on his own native culture of rural southwest Germany, a distress that sharpened his sensitivity to the situation and the feats of the lower middle-class masses in the cities. Sartre's work gave evidence of the pressures of urban financial wealth on the mores and security of provincial France. It is significant that the existentialist thinkers discussed in this study were either born in or spent at least part of their childhood in the provinces or in small towns. Sartre, who was born in Paris, was brought up by a transplanted Alsatian, and he described the environment as one whose culture and mores belonged more to the bourgeois monarchy of Louis-Phillipe than to his own time.

It may well be, then, that the shock of the war and the post-war social and political dislocations and conflicts, by completing the assault on the more traditional and conservative aspects of nineteenth-century bourgeois civilization and the undermining of classical individualism itself, acted as the "instance of dereification"[37] that brought the individualist and libertarian ethic of modernity home to large sectors of the population, not as a promise but as a curse. Men were no longer free but condemned to be free. The existentialists embraced this freedom, unlike so many who tried to escape it, but with a despairing spirit far different from the hopeful expectation of the announcement of man's freedom in the eighteenth century.

[37] Berger and Pullberg, "Reification," *History and Theory*, Vol. IV, No. 2, 1965, p. 209.

Bibliography

The range of issues covered in this book makes a comprehensive bibliography impossible. Only those works are listed which are cited or indirectly referred to in the text or notes.

I. PRIMARY SOURCES

This listing includes the writings of the main figures in the study.

A. SIGMUND FREUD

On Aphasia, trans. E. Stengell, London, 1953.

The Origins of Psychoanalysis. Letters to Wilhelm Fliess, Drafts and Notes: 1887-1902, ed. M. Bonaparte et al., trans. E. Mosbacher and E. Kris, New York, 1954.

The Standard Edition of the Complete Psychological Works of Sigmund Freud, general editor and translator James Strachey, Vols. I-XXIII, London, 1953-1966.

The Letters of Sigmund Freud, selected and ed. Ernst L. Freud, trans. Tania and James Stern, New York, 1960.

B. LUDWIG BINSWANGER

"Bemerkungen zu der Arbeit Jaspers' 'Kausale und "verständliche" Zusammenhänge zwischen Schicksal und Psychose bei der Dementia praecox,'" *Internationale Zeitschrift für Ärztliche Psychoanalyse*, 1913, I.

"Psychologische Tagesfragen innerhalb der klinischen Psychiatrie," *Zeitschrift für die gesamte Neurologie und Psychiatrie*, Bd. 26, 1914.

Einführung in die Probleme der allgemeinen Psychologie, Berlin, 1922.

"Verstehen und Erklären in der Psychologie," *Zeitschrift für die gesamte Neurologie und Psychiatrie*, Bd. 107, H.5, 1927.

Über Ideenflucht, Zurich, 1933.

Grundformen und Erkenntnis menschlichen Daseins, Zurich, 1942.

Ausgewählte Vorträge und Aufsätze, Bd. I, Bern, 1947.

Henrik Ibsen und das Problem der Selbstrealisation in der Kunst, Heidelberg, 1949.

Erinnerungen an Sigmund Freud, Bern, 1956. English translation, *Sigmund Freud, Reminiscences of a Friendship*, trans. N. Guterman, New York, 1957.

Ausgewählte Vorträge und Aufsätze, Bd. II, Bern, 1955.

Drei Formen missglückten Daseins, Tübingen, 1956.

Schizophrenie, Pfullingen, 1957.

Der Mensch in der Psychiatrie, Pfullingen, 1957.

"Daseinsanalyse und Psychotherapie," in *Acta Psychotherapeutica et Psychosomatica*, Vol. 8, No. 4, 1960.

Melancholie und Manie, Pfullingen, 1960.

Being-in-the-World, ed. with a critical introduction by J. Needleman, New York, 1963.

Wahn, Pfullingen, 1965.

C. MEDARD BOSS

Körperliches Kranksein als Folge seelischer Gleichgewichtsstörungen, Bern und Stuttgart, 1940.

Sinn und Gehalt der sexuellen Perversionen: Ein daseinsanalytischer Beitrag zur Psychopathologie des Phänomens der Liebe, Bern und Stuttgart, 1947, revised English edition published as *Meaning and Content of Sexual Perversions*, trans. L. L. Abell, New York, 1949.

"Vom Weg und Ziel der tiefenpsychologischen Therapie," *Psyche*, Bd. II, 1948.

"Beitrag zur daseinsanalytischen Fundierung des psychiatrischen Denkens," *Schweizer Archiv für Neurologie und Psychologie*, Bd. LXVII, H.1, 1951.

"Die Bedeutung der Daseinsanalyse für die Psychologie und die Psychiatrie," *Psyche*, Bd. VI, H.3, 1952.

Der Traum und seine Auslegung, Bern und Stuttgart, 1953, trans. as *The Analysis of Dreams*, by A. J. Pomerans, New York, 1958.

Einführung in die psychosomatische Medizin, Bern und Stuttgart, 1954.

Psychoanalyse und Daseinsanalytik, Bern und Stuttgart, 1957.

Indienfahrt eines Psychiaters, Pfullingen, 1959.

"Martin Heidegger und die Ärzte," in *Martin Heidegger Festschrift,* ed. G. Neske, Pfullingen, 1959.

"The Ego? Human Motivation?" *Acta Psychologica,* Vol. XIX, 1961.

"Anxiety, Guilt and Psychotherapeutic Liberation," *Review of Existential Psychology and Psychiatry,* Vol. 2, No. 3, 1962.

Psychoanalysis and Daseinsanalysis, New York, 1963 (revised and enlarged edition of *Psychoanalyse und Daseinsanalytik*), trans. L. B. Lefebvre.

"Warum verhält sich der Mensch überhaupt sozial?" *Proceedings of the Third World Congress of Psychiatry,* Toronto, 1964, pp. 228-233.

Gespräche mit Prof. Martin Heidegger in Taormina, Sizilien, vom 24 April-6 Mai 1963 (private notes).

Private Conversations, Oct.-Dec. 1965.

D. MARTIN HEIDEGGER

Being and Time, trans. John Macquarrie and Edward Robinson, London, 1962.

Kant and the Problem of Metaphysics, trans. James S. Churchill, Bloomington, 1962.

Über den Humanismus, Frankfurt a.M., 1949.

An Introduction to Metaphysics, trans. R. Manheim, New Haven, 1959.

Die Technik und die Kehre, Pfullingen, 1962.

E. JEAN-PAUL SARTRE

Le Mur, Paris, 1954.

Nausea, trans. Lloyd Alexander, Norfolk, 1949.

The Transcendence of the Ego, trans. F. Williams and R. Kirkpatrick, New York, 1957.

The Emotions, Outline of a Theory, trans. B. Frechtman, New York, 1948.

The Psychology of Imagination, trans. B. Frechtman, New York, 1948.

Being and Nothingness, trans. Hazel E. Barnes, New York, 1956.

No Exit and Three Other Plays, trans. S. Gilbert and L. Abel, New York, 1959.

Baudelaire, trans. M. Turnell, London, 1949.

Anti-Semite and Jew, trans. George J. Becker, New York, 1948.

Literary and Philosophical Essays, trans. A. Michelson, London, 1955.

Saint Genet, Actor and Martyr, trans. B. Frechtman, New York, 1963.

Situations, trans. Benita Eisler, New York, 1965.

Critique de la raison dialectique. Précédé de Question de méthode, Paris, 1960.

Les Mots, Paris, 1964.

II. SECONDARY SOURCES ON MAIN FIGURES

A. SIGMUND FREUD

Amacher, P., *Freud's Neurological Education and Its Influence on Psychoanalytic Theory, Psychological Issues*, Vol. 14, No. 4, Monograph 16, New York, 1965.

Andersson, O., *Studies in the Prehistory of Psychoanalysis*, Stockholm, 1962.

Barclay, James R., "Franz Brentano and Sigmund Freud," *Journal of Existentialism*, Vol. v, No. 17, Summer 1964, pp. 1-36.

Bernfeld, Siegfried, "Freud's Earliest Theories and the School of Helmholtz," *The Psychoanalytic Quarterly*, July 1944, Vol. XIII, pp. 341-362.

———, "Freud's Scientific Beginnings," *The American Imago*, Vol. VI, Sept. 1949, pp. 162-196.

———, "Sigmund Freud, M.D. 1882-1885," *International Journal of Psychoanalysis*, July 1951, Vol. XXXII, pp. 204-217.

Coltrera, J. T. and Ross, N., "Freud's Psychoanalytic Technique—From the Beginnings to 1923," *Psychoanalytic Techniques*, ed. B. B. Wolman, New York, 1967.

Dorer, Maria, *Historische Grundlagen der Psychoanalyse*, Leipzig, 1932.

Ellenberger, H. F., "Fechner and Freud," *Bulletin of the Menninger Clinic*, Vol. 20, No. 4, 1956, pp. 20ff.

Galdston, I., "Freud and Romantic Medicine," *Bulletin of the History of Medicine*, Vol. 30, pp. 489-507.

Holt, Robert R., "Two Influences upon Freud's Scientific Thought: A Fragment of Intellectual Biography," in *The Study of Lives*, ed. Robert W. White, New York, 1963.

Jones, E., *The Life and Work of Sigmund Freud*, Vols. I-III, New York, 1953-57.

Kronfeld, A., "Über die psychologischen Theorien Freuds und verwandte Anschauungen," *Archiv für die gesamte Psychologie*, Dec. 1911, Vol. xxv, pp. 130-248.

MacIntyre, A. C., *The Unconscious*, London, 1958.

Marcuse, H., *Eros and Civilization*, Boston, 1955.

"Das Veralten der Psychoanalyse," *Kultur und Gesellschaft*, 2, Frankfurt a.M., 1965.

Merlan, P., "Brentano and Freud," *Journal of the History of Ideas*, 6, 1945, pp. 375-377.

———, "Brentano and Freud—A Sequel," *Journal of the History of Ideas*, 10, 1949, p. 451.

Ricoeur, P., *De l'interprétation. Essai sur Freud*, Paris, 1965.

Rieff, P., *Freud, The Mind of the Moralist*, New York, 1959.

———, Introduction to *The History of the Psychoanalytic Movement*, Collier Books, New York, 1963.

Shakow, D., and Rapaport, D., *The Influence of Freud on American Psychology, Psychological Issues*, Vol. IV, No. 1, Monograph 13, New York, 1964.

Shope, R. K., "The Psychoanalytic Theories of Wish-Fulfillment and Meaning," *Inquiry*, Vol. x, 1967, pp. 421-438.

B. Ludwig Binswanger

Keller, W., "Psychiatrie und Phänomenologie," Abschrift aus der Sonntagausgabe der *Neuen Zürcher Zeitung* vom 29. October 1961.

de Man, P., "Ludwig Binswanger et le problème du moi poétique," unpublished article.

Needleman, J., book-length introduction to *Being-in-the-World*, New York, 1963.

Szilasi, W., "Die Erfahrungsgrundlagen der Daseinsanalyse Binswangers," *Schweizer Archiv für Neurologie und Psychologie*, Bd. 67, H.1, pp. 74-82.

C. Medard Boss

Condrau, Gion, *Die Daseinsanalyse von Medard Boss und ihre Bedeutung für die Psychiatrie*, Bern, 1965.

D. Martin Heidegger

Astrade, C., *Martin Heideggers Einfluss auf die Wissenschaften*, Bern, 1949.

"Deux Documents sur Heidegger," *Les Temps Modernes*, Nos. 4-6, 1946, pp. 713-724.

Fédier, F., "Trois attaques contre Heidegger," *Critique*, Nov. 1966, pp. 883-904.

———, "À propos de Heidegger: une lecture dénoncée," *Critique*, July 1967, pp. 672-686.

King, Magda, *Heidegger's Philosophy: A Guide to his Basic Thought*, New York, 1964.

Löwith, Karl, *Heidegger: Denker in dürftiger Zeit*, Frankfurt a.M., 1953.

Minder, R., Faye, J. P., Patri, A., "À propos de Heidegger," *Critique*, Nov. 1967, pp. 284-297.

Neske, Gunther, ed., *Martin Heidegger zum siebzigsten Geburtstag; Festschrift*, Pfullingen, 1959.

Pöggeler, O., ed., *Heidegger*, Berlin, 1969.

Richardson, William J., *Heidegger: Through Phenomenology to Thought*. Pref. by Martin Heidegger, The Hague, 1963.

Runes, D., *German Existentialism*, New York, 1965.

341

Schneeberger, Guido, *Nachlese zu Heidegger: Dokumente zu seinem Leben und Denken*, Bern, 1962.

Versenyi, Laszlo, *Heidegger: Being and Truth*, New Haven, 1965.

Waelhens, Alphonse de, *La Philosophie de Martin Heidegger*, 3. ed., Louvain, 1948.

E. JEAN-PAUL SARTRE

Barnes, Hazel, *The Literature of Possibility: a Study in Humanistic Existentialism*, Lincoln, 1959.

Desan, W., *The Tragic Finale*, Cambridge, 1954.

Fell, Joseph P., *Emotion in the Thought of Sartre*, New York, 1965.

Jeanson, F., *Le Problème moral et la pensée de Sartre*, Paris, 1947.

Kern, Edith G., *Sartre; A Collection of Critical Essays* (Twentieth Century Views), Englewood Cliffs, 1962.

Laing, R. D. and Cooper, D. G., *Reason and Violence, A Decade of Sartre's Philosophy, 1950-1960*, Tavistock, 1964.

Stern, A., *Sartre, His Philosophy and Existential Psychoanalysis*, New York, 1953.

Yale French Studies, Sartre, No. 30.

III. OTHER WORKS

Ackerknecht, E. H., *A Short History of Medicine*, New York, 1955.

Alexander, Franz G., and Selesnick, Sheldon T., *The History of Psychiatry*, New York, 1966.

Bentham, J., *The Theory of Legislation*, ed. C. K. Ogden, London, 1931.

Brombert, V. H., *The Intellectual Hero, Studies in the French Novel, 1880-1955*, Philadelphia, 1961.

Berger, P., and Pullberg, S., "Reification and The Sociological Critique of Consciousness," *History and Theory*, Vol. IV, No. 2, 1965, pp. 196-211.

Brett, G. S., *History of Psychology*, ed. and abridged by R. S. Peters, London, 1953.

Burrow, J. W., *Evolution and Society*, Cambridge University Press, 1966.

Charlton, D. G., *Positivist Thought in France During the Second Empire*, 1852-1870, Oxford, 1959.

Chisholm, R. M., ed., *Realism and the Background of Phenomenology*, Glencoe, 1960.

Diegpen, P., *Geschichte der Medizin*, Bd. II, 2 Hälfte, Berlin, 1955.

Foucault, F., *Histoire de la Folie*, Paris, 1961.

Gabel, Joseph, *La Fausse Conscience*, Collection Arguments, Paris, 1962.

Goldmann, L., *Mensch, Gemeinschaft und Welt in der Philosophie Immanuel Kants*, Zurich, 1945.

Greenson, R., *The Technique and Practice of Psychoanalysis*, New York, 1967.

Hegel, G. W. F., *The Phenomenology of Mind*, trans. J. B. Baillie, 2nd ed., New York, 1931.

Hesse, H., *Steppenwolf*, trans. B. Creighton, revised J. Mileck, New York, 1963.

Hodges, H. A., *The Philosophy of Wilhelm Dilthey*, London, 1952.

Hughes, H. S., *Consciousness and Society*, New York, 1958.

————, *The Obstructed Path: French Social Thought in The Years of Desperation, 1930-1960*, New York, 1968.

Husserl, E., *Phenomenology and the Crisis of Philosophy*, trans. Q. Lauer, New York, 1965.

————, *Ideas; General Introduction to Pure Phenomenology*, trans. W. R. Boyce Gibson, London, 1931.

————, *Ideen zu einer reinen Phänomenologie und phänomenologischen Philosophie*, Zweites Buch (Husserliana Bd. IV), The Hague, 1952.

————, *Cartesianische Meditationen und Pariser Vorträge* (Husserliana Bd. I), The Hague, 1963.

————, *Die Krisis der europäischen Wissenschaften und die transzendentale Phänomenologie* (Husserliana Bd. IV), The Hague, 1954.

Jaspers, K., "Kausale und 'verständliche' Zussamenhänge zwischen Schicksal und Psychose bei der Dementia Praecox," *Zeitschrift für die gesamte Neurologie und Psychiatrie*, Vol. 14, 1912.

———, *Allgemeine Psychopathologie*, Berlin, 1913.

———, *General Psychopathology*, 7th ed., trans. J. Hoenig and M. W. Hamilton, Manchester, 1963.

Jung, C. G., *Collected Works*, Vol. 7, 2nd ed. rev. and ed. by Sir Herbert Read et al., New York, 1966.

Kaufmann, W., *Hegel*, New York, 1965.

Laing, R. D., *The Divided Self*, Chicago, 1960.

———, *The Self and Others*, London, 1961.

———, and Esterson, A., *Sanity, Madness and the Family*, New York, 1964.

Lanteri-Laura, G., *La Psychiatrie phénoménologique*, Paris, 1963.

Lichtheim, G., "The Concept of Ideology," *History and Theory*, Vol. IV, No. 2, 1965, pp. 164-195.

Löwith, K., *From Hegel to Nietzsche*, trans. D. E. Green, New York, 1964.

Lukács, G., *Histoire et conscience de classe*, trans. K. Axelos, Collection Arguments, Paris, 1960.

MacIntyre, A., *Against the Self-Images of the Age*, New York, 1971.

Marx, K., *The German Ideology*, parts I and III, ed. R. Pascal, New York, 1939.

Masur, G., *Prophets of Yesterday*, New York, 1961.

May, Rollo, et al., *Existence, A New Dimension in Psychiatry and Psychology*, New York, 1958.

Merleau-Ponty, M., *The Structure of Behavior*, trans. A. L. Fisher, Boston, 1963.

———, *Phenomenology of Perception*, trans. C. Smith, London, 1962.

———, *The Primacy of Perception*, ed. J. M. Edie, Evanston, 1958.

Mitzman, A., *The Iron Cage*, New York, 1970.

Nietzsche, F. W., *The Use and Abuse of History*, trans. A. Collins, New York, 1957.

Nolte, E., *Three Faces of Fascism*, trans. L. Vennewitz, New York, 1966.

Nordenskiold, E., *The History of Biology*, 2nd ed., Vols. I and II, New York, 1928.

Novalis, *Hymns to the Night and Other Selected Writings*, trans. C. E. Passage, New York, 1957.

Parsons, T., *The Structure of Social Action*, 2nd ed., Vols. I and II, Glencoe, 1949.

Peters, R. S., *The Concept of Motivation*, London, 1958.

Politzer, G., *Critique des fondements de la psychologie*, Vol. I, *La Psychologie et la psychoanalyse*, Paris, 1928.

Reich, W., *Character Analysis*, trans. T. P. Wolde, 3rd ed., New York, 1949.

Ringer, F. K., *The Decline of the German Mandarins: The German Academic Community, 1890-1930*, Cambridge, Mass., 1969.

Roth, J. J. ed., *World War I: A Turning Point in Modern History*, New York, 1967.

Rousseau, J-J., *The Social Contract and Discourses*, trans. G.D.H. Cole, London, 1947.

Scheler, M., *Zur Phänomenologie und Theorie der Sympathiegefühle und von Liebe und Hass. Mit einem Anhang über den Grund zur Annahme der Existenz des fremden Ich*, Halle, 1913.

Schorske, C., "Politics and the Psyche in Fin-de-Siècle Vienna," *American Historical Review*, 66 (1960-1961), pp. 930-946.

————, "The Transformation of the Garden: Ideal and Society in Austrian Literature," *American Historical Review*, 72 (1966-1967), pp. 1283-1320.

Sokolowski, R., *The Formation of Husserl's Concept of Constitution*, The Hague, 1964.

Spiegelberg, H., *The Phenomenological Movement*, 2nd ed., Vols. I and II, The Hague, 1965.

345

Staude, J. R., *Max Scheler: An Intellectual Portrait*, New York, 1967.

Stern, F., *The Politics of Cultural Despair*, Berkeley, 1961.

Szasz, T., *The Myth of Mental Illness*, New York, 1961.

Taylor, C., *The Explanation of Behavior*, New York, 1964.

Thévénaz, Pierre, *What Is Phenomenology?*, ed. and trans. J. M. Edie, Chicago, 1962.

Weber, M., *The Protestant Ethic and the Spirit of Capitalism*, trans. T. Parsons, London, 1948.

Weinstein, F., and Platt, G. M., *The Wish To Be Free*, Berkeley, 1969.

White, R. W., *Ego and Reality in Psychoanalytic Theory*, *Psychological Issues*, Vol. III, No. 3, New York, 1963.

Wyss, D., *Depth Psychology, A Critical History*, trans. G. Onn, New York, 1961.

Yankelovitch, D. and Barret, W., *Ego and Instinct*, New York, 1971.

Zetzel, E., "Current Concepts of Transference," *International Journal of Psychoanalysis*, 37, pp. 369-376.

Index

abreaction, 32, 33, 34, 155, 156
absolute values, 19, 21, 141, 163,
    168, 170, 287
aesthetic philosophy, 278–281
aggression, 203, 204, 232
Alexander, F., 122
alienation, 290, 296; alienated
    behavior, 27; self-alienation,
    8, 152, 191–192, 199, 203, 205,
    210, 247, 292
Allgemeine Psychopathologie, 72
anality, 136, 137, 140
Analysis of Dreams, The, 130
Andreas-Salomé, Lou, 203
Anna O., case of, 26
anti-Semitism, 314–317
anxiety, 25, 100, 103, 104, 149, 163,
    205, 208–210, 237, 287, 292, 296,
    297, 298, 328; anxiety neuroses,
    25
aphasia 62
association psychology, 5, 39, 91
Augustine, St., 228
authenticity, 4, 9, 10, 21, 103,
    105, 108, 161, 165, 176; and
    Freud, 190–192, 223, 224, 250;
    and Heidegger, 252–265; and
    Sartre, 266–274, 275, 295
authority, 11; of analyst, 157, 163,
    165; in psychoanalytic theory,
    193, 196, 285, 289, 293, 297,
    301, 330
autonomy, 3, 4, 8, 9, 21, 64,
    161, 164, 169 170, 176–185, 198,
    208, 213, 233, 247, 275, 290

Baader, F. von, 228

Bacon, F., 302
bad faith, 242, 272, 312, 326
*Basic Forms and Knowledge of
    Human Existence*, 220, 223–229
Baudelaire, 243–247, 312, 318
Bauhaus, 213
behaviorism, 82
Being, 96, 101, 102, 261, 262, 264,
    265, 286, 287, 288, 295, 300, 303
Being and Nothingness, 117, 236–
    243, 266, 267, 268, 270, 272,
    273, 275, 312, 313, 314, 316,
    317, 318, 320, 321, 322, 324, 325
Being and Time, 6, 90–107, 108,
    110, 111, 173, 211, 213, 215,
    224, 233, 252, 255, 256, 260, 261,
    262, 264, 286, 294, 300, 301,
    305, 331
being-in-the-world, 7, 92, 108, 124,
    128, 133, 134, 152, 301, 325
Bentham, J., 177
Bergson, H., 14, 76, 90, 91
Bernheim, S., 30
Beyond the Pleasure Principle,
    203, 205
Binswanger, Ludwig, 5, 6, 7, 11,
    15, 20; early work in philo-
    sophical psychology, 70–84;
    first critique of Freud, 84–90,
    108, 109, 110, 111, 112, 115,
    117; mind-body problem, 118–
    122; symbols, symptoms and
    dreams, 124–129; the
    unconscious, 131–132, 134;
    infantile sexuality, 135–139;
    instinct theory, 142–149, 151,
    154; therapy, 158–159, 162, 172,

347

Library of Congress Cataloging in Publication Data

Izenberg, Gerald N   1939-
  The existentialist critique of Freud

  Based on the author's thesis, Harvard.
  Bibliography: p.
  Includes index.
    1. Freud, Sigmund, 1856-1939. 2. Psychoanalysis.
  3. Existential psychology. I. Title.
  BF173.F85I93   150'.19'52   76-3263
  ISBN 0-691-07214-0